A PATH
WELL TRAVELLED

By Cathie O'Dea

A Path Well Travelled

ISBN 9798708965455

Acknowledgments

Cover Design – Martin O'Dea

Advice, proofreading and editing - Nick Keith and Anna Brett

Disclaimer

This memoir is written to the best of my recollection. I have been unable to remember or verify some of the exact timelines, spellings of names or facts. None of the names have been changed but some have been intentionally omitted. I have done my best to contact the people mentioned in this book or their closest relatives to gain permission for their inclusion. Where this has specifically not been granted, I have removed them. Some of the venues and hotels have been changed or intentionally omitted. Some of the stories were told by tour guides and may not be strictly accurate. Many of the people featured within the anecdotes are included to add interest and humour and any offence caused as a result is unintentional.

About the Author

Cathie lives in Notting Hill in West London. She lived and breathed the travel industry for 48 years and has seen many changes from using chunky manuals to embracing the latest technology. She has travelled far and wide and she has seen the best and worst of the travel industry. She was self employed for the last 14 years until she retired in September 2020 during the Covid-19 pandemic. Since her retirement she has reignited her interests in art and crafts, photography and writing.

A "Path Well Travelled" is Cathie's first book where she shares an overview of an ever changing travel industry, the people, her career and her memories of travelling the world.

Dedications

I dedicate this book to those who helped to lay my path but are no longer here to read my story.

My dad, John "Jock" Skerret, Martin. Patrick and James O'Dea from Lisseycasey, Maggie Mackenzie, John "Cozzer" McEvoy, Adrian Bell, "Old Jack" Wallace, Mary Pugsley, Jeanette "Jean" Joynson, Jo Wallace, Maureen Hill, Louise Heasman, Vivien Longley McKnight and Brenda Seel.

Gone but never forgotten.

Contents

Foreword

I have very few regrets about my life in travel. The past 48 years were truly a path well travelled. I am so lucky to have seen around 75 countries, most of which are contained within these pages. I have stayed in some of the world's top hotels, seeing some of the most incredible sights on earth and reliving some of the world's oldest history. I have taken many thousands of photographs, including some of the world's iconic sights, Taj Mahal, The Pyramids of Giza, Machu Picchu or just having fun over a drink or three with my family and friends.

I can't remember all the exact timelines, nearly all of this book is from memory and references from old diaries and blogs. Some of the facts that were told to me by various tour guides have turned out to be not quite accurate, embellished, or out of date, but nevertheless, the stories sparked my interest and made me wonder and appreciate the world around me. Turning a lake into a legend or a mountain into a monster has definitely helped to me to remember little things I would have otherwise long since forgotten. I have tried to verify a few of the facts but surprisingly little is documented about this era of the travel industry. So many of the tour operators and airlines that I remember are consigned to history, hotels have changed hands, shops have closed down and most of the people I worked with are no longer working in the travel industry. This is mostly why I have written the book, in order to revive and relive those memories as I remember them.

I loved most of the places I have visited. I missed out on a few that I always wanted to visit. South Africa, Japan, Bali, Chile and Iceland were all on my list but I never got the opportunity to visit them. I wanted to visit every country in Europe but I haven't quite managed that either, at least not yet.

My first visit overseas was to Paris when I was a very small child and my last was to Lanzarote in January 2020. This book is very much about the in between.

Thank you to all those who shared my path and helped me in so many different directions.

Glossary

ABC – Printed rail and airline timetable manuals. There is another reference to ABC where it is an abbreviation of Aerated Bread Company, a former UK bakery chain.

APD – Air Passenger Duty, Government tax on air tickets.

BA – British Airways.

BABS- British Airways booking system in the seventies and eighties.

BEA – British European Airways later merged with BOAC to become British Airways.

BOAC – British Overseas Airways Corporation later merged with BEA to become British Airways.

Boots – A large UK Pharmacy chain.

Carbon Paper – paper impregnated with a layer of ink on one side used between two sheets of paper to make a copy when typed or written on.

CBD – Central Business District, the centre of town, Downtown.

Chedi – a Buddhist Commemorative monument.

DFDS – A Danish ferry and freight company.

DIA - Detroit Institute of Arts.

ESTA – Electronic System for Travel Authorization. Permission to enter the USA.

Fam trip/educational – travel agents familiarisation trip,

Fax – an abbreviation of facsimile, sending documents over a phone line.

Finnair – the national airline of Finland.

O'Dea – A Path Well Travelled

Freesale – an allocation of spaces or hotel rooms on a sale or return basis.

Galileo – a GDS reservation system used by British Airways and others,

Gardaí – Irish Police

Gazetteers – Brief information on hotels, contact details and tour operators.

GBP – Great British Pounds/Pound Sterling.

GDS – Global Distribution System a blanket term for live airline reservation systems.

Great Friday – The Greek equivalent of Good Friday.

IATA- International Air Transport Association a licence to legally issue air tickets. Each agency has its own unique number.

jmc – John Mason Cook, Thomas Cook's son and the name of the airline and budget brand 2000-2003 (lower case is intentional)

LEB – London Electricity Board.

LED – Light emitting diode, the earliest calculators had red numbers and were more difficult to read. The next generation usually took 2 x AA batteries.

Liming – enjoying a night out in the Caribbean.

Megafam – a large group or several groups of travel agents on a familiarisation trip.

MTR – Asian Metro systems. Mass Transit Railway in Hong Kong. In Singapore it is known as MRT.

OAG – Official Airline Guide.

OCL – Overseas Containers Ltd. These were taken over by P&O.

O-Levels – predecessor to GCSE's.

PATA – Pacific Asia Travel Association.

O'Dea – A Path Well Travelled

RIO – Retail in one, Thomas Cook's in store booking and filing system.

RSA – Returned and Services Association Inc. in New Zealand. Similar to Royal British Legion clubs.

RSL - Returned and Services League in Australia.

Phenix – Travel Counsellors booking and filing system.

Prestel – a computer system that operated through dial-up.

Sabbath/Shabbat – Friday night/Saturday, The Jewish day of rest when shops and businesses close.

Sabre – GDS reservation system used by American Airlines and others.

Soca – Caribbean dance music

Telex – a post war method of sending messages. Phased out by fax machines.

The Green Line – an imaginary line dividing Turkish Occupied Cyprus from the rest of Cyprus

Travelcat – a DOS based filing system used by travel agents.

UAE – The United Arab Emirates includes Dubai and Abu Dhabi.

Viewdata – a DOS based search and book system,

Wat – Thai or Cambodian temple.

WLAT – West London Air Terminal formerly located in Gloucester Road, London.

Worldspan – GDS reservation system used by Delta and others.

WTM – World Travel Market. The yearly travel showcase at Excel.

Part One: The people who laid my path

There are many people who have made a big contribution to this book and have made all this possible.

My Family

My story begins with my dad who was a pioneer, a traveller, never a tourist. My dad loved to travel and he inspired me and my family to do the same. I doubt there was a corner of Europe, Russia, North Africa or the "stans", that he didn't visit at some time or the other. He talked about doing the Silk Road and visiting China but he ran out of time. His only long haul trip was Cuba. I never managed to travel to Europe as extensively as he did.

My mum, as a single parent, saved hard to visit her mother in her Paris apartment. When I was older, she sent me to stay with my aunt and uncle in Brittany and the South of France for the summer holidays. My mum took me to Ibiza after my O-Levels. That holiday sparked my interest in travelling abroad and embracing different cultures.

When I first met Jim, my husband, he wasn't interested in travelling abroad. As time went on, he eventually became more open and adventurous to the many golden opportunities that were presented to us and eventually he loved travelling too.

My children all followed different paths and went their own way but all of them shared my love of travelling.

My daughter Sharon was never afraid to try new experiences, including living and working abroad in three different countries in three different continents, Bolivia, Singapore and Amsterdam. If anything, she is even more adventurous than we are and she particularly loves South America and Asia.

O'Dea – A Path Well Travelled

My daughters Carol and Sharon, my son Martin and his girlfriend Eve have all travelled with me to Asia.

James O'Dea organised our triennial gatherings in Ennis until Shane O'Dea took over from him as chairman of the O'Dea Clan.

My dad, a self portrait

My Friends

Janet Forbes and I have been friends since Secondary School. Janet was already working at Kennings and I wasn't happy at Boots so she got me the job at Kenning Travel and that was the beginning of my travel path. We went to Spain together a couple of times before I met Jim. Our travel paths crossed again when she joined me at Thomas Cook Fulham. We are still friends and we still meet up now and then.

O'Dea – A Path Well Travelled

I first met Mary Pugsley at Kenning Travel where we worked together. We met up regularly when the children were small. Mary came to work with me at Thomas Cook Hammersmith later on.

Maggie Mackenzie moved down to London in the early seventies with her brother. When I worked in the Castle pub in Holland Park, they were customers. Maggie worked for Virgin Records off Portobello Road where the Virgin empire began. Many of her friends and contacts were in the music industry. She eventually persuaded Jim that America wasn't full of gun wielding murderers on every street corner, after all, she had already managed to survive several business trips. Our first long haul trip as a family was thanks to Maggie.

Best friends, John "Cozzer" McEvoy and Adrian Bell whom we also met in The Castle were our travelling companions many times to Corfu, Spain and the USA. Our Florida trip in 1986 inspired them to explore the whole of the USA. Adrian was a serious sun worshipper and Cozzer definitely wasn't. Being a redhead, Cozzer burnt very easily but Adrian had skin like leather and relished every single ray of sunshine. They especially loved exploring small town America and cowboy country. Our last trip together was our revisit to St. Pete Beach in 2013.

I first met Ann Barber in 1996 on our Eilat fam trip when we shared a room. We had both worked for Thomas Cook for a long time. We laughed at the same things and found we had a great deal in common so we vowed to keep in touch. My daughter, Carol, went to Manchester University the following year so I arranged to meet up with Ann again. She came down to London at least once a year to World Travel Market, and occasionally for trips. I once sent her a mock email reservation for a garden view in my house headed The Hilnot based on me living in Notting Hill and my house not exactly being the Hilton. It has been christened the Hilnot ever since. My Notting Hill base is convenient for Central London, Heathrow, Gatwick and the World Travel Market and more so, when it was at nearby Earls Court.

Carol Warburton, is a friend of Ann's and a retired Travel Counsellor like myself. We have met up in Manchester, Cyprus and Tenerife. Jim

O'Dea – A Path Well Travelled
and Carol get on brilliantly and have shared a few vodka and
cranberries together.

We first met Anna Brett in The Prince of Wales and we got much closer
over the years. I fancied a pre-Christmas cheapie to Spain but Jim
didn't want to go so that was my first holiday with Anna. We went on
three little pre-Christmas breaks to Spain, Tenerife and Sharm-el-
Sheikh. After that we often travelled as a trio, first of all to Crete in
2013 and then to many other places. Anna has many hilarious mishaps,
broken chairs and a young man album. Wherever she goes, she is
absolutely guaranteed to make us laugh. She leaves a lasting impression
everywhere she goes.

Lil, who has travelled with us a couple of times to Fuerteventura, is
great fun to be with. She often gets her words mixed up with hilarious
results.

We have met many friends in our favourite Cretan home, Elounda.
These include Manos at the Hiona apartments, Pat and John from
Newcastle, David O'Neill from Manchester, Popi at the Akti Olous,
Elena at the Garden of Eden, Costas at the Malibu and Dave at The
Peacock.

Ann Barber first introduced me to Gabi Birbeck at World Travel Market
and then I met her at many events with her friend Anna Davies. Gabi
has invited me on several occasions to weekends in Cyprus at Stademos
Hotels. She now lives in Santorini and owns her own company, Santo
Dreams.

My Colleagues

Ali at Kennings taught me everything I needed to know about air
ticketing. My boss Mr. Bonser and my colleagues, Janet Forbes, Janet
Blair, Mary Pugsley and Jo Bracken (now Ewins).

At Pickfords my boss was Mr Stokes and my colleagues were Shiela,
Gary and Marian.

O'Dea – A Path Well Travelled

At Thomas Cook, I am grateful to all my bosses especially Sue Heyes, Claire Greener, Gary Maher and Gary Stevens and my colleagues, far too many to mention.

I owe the past 14 years at Travel Counsellors to the founder David Speakman, the current CEO, Steve Byrne, the directors and staff at head office, too many to mention, my colleagues and friends especially Gillian Davis, Lesley Clements, Gail O'Donohue, Dennis Jackson, Marie Rayner, Karen Hobbs, Barbara O'Neil, Daryl Glean, Frazzy Reeve-Lewis, Aida Furmston-Evans, Trevor Smith, Michael Martinez, Ann Mitchell, Sophia Sheth, Catherine Haynes and Madeline Rose who have all helped and supported me.

Also thanks to….

Roomies on my fam trips at different times, Leith Taylor, Pauline Doherty, Gill Nicholls and Alison Ryder.

All my clients, without them I wouldn't have had a business for 14 years and a career for nearly half a century.

Event organisers, hotel representatives and tourist boards, with special mention to Angela Hamilton-Jones , Sarah Hammond, Carol Hay, Stephen Hurp, Michelle Roberts, Nicoletta Pilardi, Colin and Liz Sanderson, Debbie Walker, Jane West, Adam Wetherby and Charles Wilson.

People who have taken me on fam trips or have welcomed us warmly and hosted us at their hotels including Karen Black, Janine (Namibia), Debbie Melchior (Saint Lucia), Gillian Sodah (Grenada), Gillian Young (Cayman Islands), Lisa Gilbert (Cairo), Christine Lloyd (Tenerife), Sonja Rogers, Lorraine Grant, Jackie Bookal. Andrew Hillier (Saint Lucia, Trinidad and Tobago), Sharon Earls (Avalon river cruise), Kyriakos Pirillos (Cyprus), Caroline Golding (Cyprus), Aristos Diomedous, Mark Richardson, Ellis Burns (Cyprus), Sandra Perich, Jo Preocanin (Costa Brava), Richard Greenaway, Julie Eze (North Cyprus), Patrick Even (Luxembourg), Matej Knific, Mattej Valencic

O'Dea – A Path Well Travelled
(Slovenia), Seema Sood (USA), Gemma Lazenby (Tuscany), Julie Franklin, Sasha Darling (Norway), Antonella Maiellaro (Sardinia).

Part Two: The Travel History Path

World events that affected the travel industry

The first major event I remember was early in my travel career. The Turks invaded the north eastern part of Cyprus in 1974 putting "The Green Line" straight through Nicosia airport, leaving families separated and their land taken from them. Cyprus was left without an airport so out of necessity, Larnaca airport was hastily built in just 6 weeks.

In 1989, exciting things were happening in Europe. The Berlin Wall came down, Eastern Europe was free and relatives who had been separated for years in East and West Berlin were able to reunite again.

The Balkan wars began in 1991 and divided the once popular Yugoslavia which now consists of Croatia, Serbia, Slovenia, Montenegro, Bosnia and Macedonia. It took the divided Yugoslavia ten years to recover but they never regained their seventies popularity in the British market.

The Gulf War in 1990-1991 saw a sharp decline in business and redundancies followed.

Nobody knew what would happen on New Year's Day 2000. Would all the computers default to 1979 or would everything completely self destruct? Nobody knew the answer to this but everybody all over the world backed up every single bit of data just in case. What actually happened on 1st January 2000 was ….

Nothing. Life went on as normal and everyone breathed a sigh of relief.

We had a television in our shop and on 11th September 2001, we watched the news unfolding. We watched and we cried. New York stopped, King Street stopped, Hammersmith stopped, the world stopped. Travel was never the same again. Security was stepped up at every airport and the maximum 100mls of liquids and gels limit for hand luggage was introduced .

The Iraq War followed in 2003 and travel suffered a further blow leading to further redundancies.

In 2010 there was an ash cloud coming from an unpronounceable volcano in Iceland. Everything stopped for 6 whole days. There were no flights in Europe and people were stranded. It was absolute chaos but that was just a dress rehearsal. Little did we know that 10 years later flights would be grounded for many months and would be even more devastating to the industry than all the rest of these events put together.

On 23rd June 2016 the UK voted to break away from Europe and finally Covid-19 changed everything from March 2020.

The Tools of the Trade

Our shelves were full of manuals, telephone directories, the rail ABC containing timetables, the book of rail fares, the ABC World Airline Guides, blue A-R and red S-Z. Some editions contained a Finnair list of airline phone numbers which was incredibly useful. The ABC's contained all the world's flights, flight numbers, the date range and days of the week they operated on, 1 being Monday, 2 Tuesday and so on. They were really chunky with all the possible connecting flights in there as well as all the direct flights and the writing was miniscule. The OAG contained mileages and rules. The two have since merged and are now online. We had a fares manual which was issued by British Airways. The ABC Rail Guide is still published in print version. Thomas Cook rail guides for Europe and Worldwide were issued for summer and winter each year. They went online in 2016 and are no longer printed. Although we normally used Rail Europe (later Voyages SNCF) online to work out fares and routes, I still found even the out of date printed manuals useful to work out complicated routes right up until I retired. Gazetteers was another useful manual with telephone numbers for tour operators and hotel chains. It had information about hotels and which tour operators sold them. This went digital and finally it was wound down altogether. Many agents really miss Gazetteers.

Picture the scene, manual typewriters, an old chunky telephone, early LED calculators, and a drawer full of threadbare carbon paper for our letters and invoices. The phone rang constantly. We all smoked at our desks so our office was a smoky haze. On a typical day in the seventies, first thing, a secretary would bark orders at us to have the tickets delivered that afternoon. She would ask for a flight for her boss so I would go to the shelf, pick up the ABC, check the flight closest to the time she wanted. I would then use my Finnair card to phone the airline and book the flights.

Issuing air tickets required a good supply of blank tickets from each individual airline, 2-coupon for straightforward one ways and returns, 4-coupon for everything else and a big heavy contraption called a ticket validator that embossed each ticket with the individual agency name and IATA number. We had to use the end of a biro to move the wheels to the correct date each day before using it. The air ticket was hand written showing any manual fare construction, currency code, usually GBP and currency conversion if necessary. The opened ticket was then inserted upside down, there were two clips that held it on and then we had to give it a good thump to emboss the self carbonised tickets all the way through. If I made a mistake I had to put two diagonal lines across the ticket write VOID and start again. These required much concentration especially if there was more than one ticket "in conjunction". I had to tear off the top agency coupon with any coupons that were surplus to requirements, and staple them together to put on the returns which were sent in at the end of each month.

Fare construction, if necessary, was done manually. If the flight was indirect, I would have to check if it was within the maximum permitted mileage using our fare construction bible, the OAG. If it wasn't, I then had to work out how much it was over the direct route with the help of the manual.

Later, instead of having tickets for each airline, we had blank IATA tickets and plates for each airline which were stored in a business card holder for every single airline that we swiped through, rather like an old credit card swiping machine, but bigger.

Rail tickets needed carbon paper between the copies, top for the client, a copy for the weekly returns and the last copy was left in the book. Later on these were self carbonised. We had to call through for reservations and write them out by hand on a reservation label and keep the carbon copy.

The client needed an invoice so more carbon paper was needed, either to handwrite or type it. By this time the phone had rung many times and we were all on deadlines to get all the urgent tickets ready for our delivery driver.

That was all quite straightforward, but what happened if the client needed a hotel? Firstly we needed the phone number. If it wasn't in a manual or written in an address book, we would have to ring directory enquiries. Many hotels were sold on freesale. The room allocations went back to the hotels usually within a month of travel. Sometimes this would go wrong and they overbooked.

If it wasn't on freesale, we would have to telex. A telex was an extremely noisy and cumbersome piece of equipment. I reckon even in 1972, ours was a museum piece. It was probably Britain's oldest and noisiest telex. The way it worked, was by first typing a message. After some delay going through the telephone exchange, it was typed out at the other end. Most hotels only processed telexes at the end of the day. Even large hotels would look at the diary to check availability and then type a message back to confirm. The whole process would take 2-3 days and up to a week if it was in another time zone. Telexes were eventually replaced by faxes and later by email.

By the eighties, fax machines had been invented. Fax machines were innovative in their time, but the early ones had special waxy paper which faded within months. Later on they were more like a photocopier using ordinary A4 paper. A document would get fed into the machine at one end and it would come out at the other end across a phone line. Almost every commercial property had both a phone number and a fax number. This had many advantages over telex. The machines were smaller and we could send documents instantly. This speeded up hotel reservations and cancellations considerably.

What about payment? In the seventies and early eighties it was nearly all cash or cheques. In the early days of credit cards we had to phone for authorisation and write a manual slip. We would then put the hand written slip onto a plate and swipe it to imprint our shop details.

Brochures were vital in the Seventies and Eighties as they were our only guide to the hotels. We hung onto our file copies for dear life. No matter what we did, no matter how big the File Copy stickers were, they would still disappear into thin air. We would go into one of the other local travel shops to see if they had a spare copy. Later on when faxes were invented, we could get one of our other shops to photocopy and fax the relevant page.

The first system we used in the shop was Prestel. It was a square box and it used a dial up system so it was ugly, slow, noisy and expensive. The system we used to book holidays was called Viewdata which worked on the old Prestel sets and also the brand new computers which eventually replaced the old Prestel sets.

Viewdata wasn't pretty, but it was a very efficient way of booking package holiday and charter flights. The advantage it had over web based systems in the early days was the ability to do a quick search of several airports over a range of dates. Most web based systems can do this, but they don't show everything on one page as viewdata did. For us travel agents it was very simple and in most cases we could find the client the bargain that they wanted. Many agents still miss viewdata. I was very sad when it disappeared altogether.

We sat at the desk most days frustratingly on hold to tour operators and even our own departments for hours, sometimes even days which meant that it was almost impossible to get through to us, as all our extensions were either ringing in or ringing out. Even in the early 2000's we still only had telephone or fax as our only means of communication.

During my time at Thomas Cook we went from a manual system, to installing laser printers and a DOS based system called Platform. This was during the late nineties and this served as a database as well as a booking system. It had an index so we could access the database, viewdata to book holidays or Sabre and later Worldspan GDS to book flights.

Platform was fairly quickly replaced by RIO which was an access based system that could be used both in travel and foreign exchange. Platform and RIO gave us access to databases within our own shop. RIO also included the capability to book flights using Worldspan within the system in a separate window. It could capture flight or holiday details straight into the system. It also meant that for the first time we could recall previous client's details by name, address or last date of travel to put in a new enquiry and then upgrade to a confirmed booking. RIO was a nice, easy system to use and quite stable.

Eventually, the practice of handwriting tickets was phased out. We had a ticket machine installed with feeder holes on the sides on a dot matrix printer. I would love to say this was an improvement on manual ticketing, but in reality it was a pain in the neck. I would load a batch of tickets into the feeders, and command it to print. I had to check that the ticket number on RIO matched the one that was printed on the ticket machine. Sometimes it worked perfectly and we would tear the perforations, take the void coupons out and tear the perforations off the sides. All too often, the numbers were out of sync, it would catch on one side and tear and the ticket would have to be voided and reset. At the end of each month we still had to do the airline returns manually. There was usually a pile of spoilt tickets which were either out of sync or had got mangled in the machine.

Airlines

I have been in travel long enough to remember when BEA and BOAC were two different airlines. The two airlines merged in 1974.

Concorde came into commercial service in 1974. The first route from London was to Bahrain which was quickly dropped when they acquired the London to New York route. In all my years in travel I never ticketed Concorde, although I did book a few when I worked for British Airways.

It was soon after we came back from California in 1988 that a Pan Am plane carrying 243 passengers and 16 crew exploded mid-air over the Scottish town of Lockerbie also killing 11 on the ground. It was the end of an era for Pan Am, an airline which was once the leader in smart uniforms and real service with a smile.

I remember when Ryanair started off as a small Irish airline in the nineties. They were the first of many European low cost airlines. Initially, we used to book them on GDS and print our own tickets. It seems such a long time ago. As soon as Ryanair became web based, they couldn't ditch us fast enough as they didn't need us anymore.

Many other low cost airlines followed, most of which were very short lived. These included Go, British Airways low cost arm. Easyjet has proved to be the strongest over the years with many popular leisure and business routes. Recently many legacy airlines are operating on a two tier system with the cheaper option being priced on a low cost model basis. This enables them to advertise lower lead in fares.

Airline alliances began to emerge in the nineties. The idea of these was for airlines to have greater access to other airlines' hubs and routes and to increase customer loyalty. The benefits to the customer are rewards such as lounge access and even free tickets. KLM and Northwest joined forces in 1989 giving KLM more access within the USA and for Northwest to have greater access to Europe. Star Alliance and One World soon followed.

Package Holidays

In the seventies, Spain, Italy and Yugoslavia were the most popular destinations. They totally dominated the brochures. During that era, there were very few brochures, Clarksons, Cosmos, Global, Thomson and Yugotours are the ones I remember. Brochures were much less stylish and sophisticated than they are today, most had yellow and red gaudy messages on the cover with prices from £29. In the early seventies, many people who had only ever gone to Clacton or Bournemouth, suddenly wanted to go to Spain. Hotels were quickly built to meet demand with little thought to style or design.

In those days we picked up the phone and called the tour operator to book the holiday. The price in the brochure was exactly what was paid and things were simple. Coach holidays to UK and Europe were much more in the forefront than they are now. Cosmos were famous for their cheap marathon coach tours visiting 16 countries in 14 days, staying miles out of town and barely remembering each place.

Clarksons was a huge tour operator but by 1972 they were in financial difficulty. Court Line took them over and then they went bust in 1974 taking Clarksons with them. Yugotours was the fourth largest tour operator and Yugoslavia was once the second biggest destination. As the name suggests, Yugotours specialised in Yugoslavia. Most of the coastline is in what we now know as Croatia but the most popular resort in those days was Budva which is now in Montenegro. Yugotours was famous for its nudist section towards the back of the brochure. Yugotours demise began when the Balkan war happened. By 1992 they disappeared.

The eighties was the time of bargain holidays. With Viewdata, we could find holidays with Sunmed, Grecian, Argo, Kosmar or Blue Sky for as little as £59 in May or June. It usually meant a midweek night flight and unnamed accommodation with no pool, just very basic, no frills accommodation on a Greek island. You can imagine the commission we made on those! Volume was everything, pile 'em high, sell 'em cheap. The only one of the cheap and cheerful Greek specialists of that era that survived was Olympic but they have expanded and now specialise in Mediterranean islands rather than just Greece.

Sunmed specialised in Greece. We used to play their videos of the Greek Islands in the shop over and over again which were enticing to watch but "Zorba the Greek" did get irritating all day, every day throughout the summer season. They started offering Turkey as well as Greece but they disappeared soon after that.

Thomson introduced the Square Deal. They may not have been the first, but it is certainly the one that springs to mind. All the customer knew was the airport they flew from, where they were flying to and the grade of the hotel and then where you would end up was a complete mystery. I once heard of a client who was expecting a ski holiday in the Sierra Nevada and flew to Malaga at night only to wake up in the morning to a beach on his doorstep. We laughed about it for years but the customer wasn't amused.

I loved Intasun. They took us to Florida and then they introduced Thailand. I went to their offices once in Bromley where they discussed whether introducing Turkey was a good idea. We were intrigued. Nowadays, it is a very popular and cheap destination but in the mid-eighties it was completely unknown to the British market. Intasun grew too quickly. ILG stood for International Leisure Group but I always thought of them as Intasun, Lancaster and Global as they acquired both. I was really sad when they collapsed in 1991, a victim of the Gulf War and by then, as the largest tour operator it left a monumental mess in every high street travel agency up and down the country. We worked all over the weekend to contact all our customers and to try and rebook them.

British Airways had several brands: Sovereign were the luxury brand, Enterprise were the family brand, Flair were the budget brand, Speedbird were the flight only and fly-drive brand. Only Sovereign survived as a brand. British Airways Holidays ditched the charter market altogether and eventually they cut out the travel agent and became direct sale.

There was a new tour operator called First Choice who offered all-inclusive. This was a completely new concept in Europe. At first, Thomas Cook had a partnership with First Choice. It didn't last long and First Choice have been part of the Thomson/TUI group since 2007. Thomson/TUI swallowed up many of the tour operators we knew and loved including Martyn, Horizon and Wings who all disappeared. Hayes and Jarvis, Crystal, Sovereign and Crystal still exist as part of TUI and they have kept their own separate brands.

A small northern company called Airtours was based in Rossendale. They were founded in 1972 but it was years before they operated from London Stansted. They introduced charter flights as far afield as Hawaii, Acapulco, Phuket and even Sydney but although very cheap, there is a limit to the level of discomfort customers will suffer. I don't think many people did these journeys twice. They also made cruises affordable and, although basic, branded as Sun Cruises, they were fantastic value for money. Airtours took over Panorama who specialised in Tunisia and ski. When the Airtours group became part of Thomas Cook, they ditched Sun cruises. Thomas Cook was another tour operator that swallowed up smaller fish including Airtours. They also swallowed up Club 18-30 and Cresta, the short break operator.

In the late eighties and early nineties, I would have sat at my desk with a Travelscene, Paris Travel or Time Off brochure and organised the traditional yearly spring break as late as possible in March on a 3 nights for the price of 2 deal. Requests for city breaks were usually predictable, Paris, Amsterdam, Rome, Venice and Bruges.

Time Off's brochure was actually an A4 card folded into thirds so they were easy to pick up. The tear off bit at the back acted as a booking form. The concept was simple, no pictures, no named hotels, just the grade of hotel. There was one for each destination. Travelscene and Paris Travel sold on a similar basis but they did have brochured hotels as well and both had a very thin A4 brochure. Both of them had some additional options such as excursions and shows.

Since the advent of Eurostar and low cost airlines, it was cheap and easy to hop over for a weekend to a whole range of new destinations just waiting to be discovered. Spring and autumn are still the most popular times when cities are neither too hot and sticky, nor covered in ice.

Long haul travel became more accessible and affordable in the nineties. During that era, Virgin Holidays totally dominated the market for Florida and the Caribbean with very competitive prices. Eventually just like BA, they went direct sale.

Kuoni did most of the long haul destinations and they had many good exclusive contracts. They had a very handy weather guide for their destinations which was a simple idea and pre-Google it was an extremely useful guide.

Part Three: My Travel Career Path

My career path into the travel industry began in 1972 at Kenning Travel. It wasn't my first job as I had worked in the ABC Bakery in Portobello Road and as a trainee pharmacist in Boots the chemist in Acton High Street.

The travel business was my life and passion for 48 years. I lived and breathed the travel industry. My job and my hobby were inseparable. It was often hard and frustrating work but travel was a fun industry which made people happy. I met thousands of lovely people over the years. None of the shops I ever worked in exist now but my memories do.

Kenning Travel

My first travel wage was £11 a week. It wasn't a fortune even in 1972. My friend Janet already worked at Kenning Travel and she got me the job. The shop in Holland Park Avenue, now Perkins Dry Cleaners, is so tiny, Googlemaps hides it behind a tree! We were attached to Kenning garage and car hire company which is now a Tesco Express. My job, along with four or five others, was to arrange corporate travel for tyre companies including Firestone, Michelin and Brown Brothers.

Our facilities were very basic. They would never be allowed nowadays. We had an outside toilet which was absolutely freezing in the winter, so we used to hold on as long as possible or dive into The Castle pub and use their toilet.

Our manager was Mr. Bonser. He was very typical of travel managers of that era, male, balding and late fifties. Managers were rarely addressed by their first names. First of all I worked with Janet and Jenny. Jenny left shortly after I joined.

Ali taught me about mileages and how to use the huge manuals that were on the shelves, the ABC, the OAG and the British Airways fares manual. He was so patient and when it wasn't too busy, he would reflect on his life in Tripoli in better times. I will never forget him but we lost touch long ago.

Two more girls joined, both originally from Ireland, first Mary Pugsley and then Jo Bracken. Mary and Jo became the best of friends and ended up living on the same housing estate in Ealing. Our adult children are all of similar ages so they grew up together.

 Our retail counter in the front of the shop was a high one with very high chairs like bar stools. Every time I got down to fetch a brochure, I literally used to disappear behind the counter leaving the customer wondering where I had gone!

Everyone has heard of Freddie Laker. He made air travel affordable, not just for businessmen and people visiting family and friends. He revolutionised air travel for the leisure market. We were invited to Stansted airport by Laker Airways. It was a chance to experience the aircraft and on board services.

Roy, in Kenning Car Hire agreed to give up his Sunday and drive us to Stansted. We turned up on time so what could possibly go wrong? The M11 and Stansted Express didn't exist. After several hours driving around Essex, completely lost, we eventually spotted a signpost to Stansted airport which was nothing more than a shed, so we missed the 11am flight. We were given the option of the 3pm flight but with no café at the airport and nothing within miles, 4 hours at the airport was at least 3½ hours too long and Roy wanted to get back so we never got to experience Laker Airways.

Jyoti, my new colleague, was so sweet. I was a bit of a prankster and a customer wanted some information on Barbados. At that time the single "Barbados" was a current hit by Typically Tropical so I sent Jyoti looking for Coconut Airways. The poor girl started looking for it while we all started singing. I rescued her for the sake of the client.

I stayed at Kenning Travel for 4 years and left in 1976. I worked in The Castle pub next door in the evenings to supplement my pitifully low wage. That turned out to be one of my best decisions as it was there that I met Jim who I later married. Andrew Kenning was furious that one of his staff was working in the pub so I knew it was time to move on.

After I left, Kennings introduced a hideous red and blue uniform. I was so glad I didn't have to wear one at my new job at Pickfords.

Pickfords

I joined Pickfords, a tiny old fashioned shop a few doors down from what is now Shepherds Bush Market station. It was my first experience in retail travel and at least the toilet was indoors!

There were five of us in the shop, our boss, Mr Stokes, Shiela, an older Irish lady who had worked there for years when it was still Howship Travel, Gary, who had a Rod Stewart style mop of red hair and Marian. Gary left to join British Airways and I followed him about a year later. Marian once came to work in a t-shirt with a 4-letter word emblazened across the front of her t-shirt. It was the age of punk but it was still pretty shocking.

We had mostly 3 types of client, Irish, Caribbean and elderly ladies on day trips to the coast. Venture coaches from Shepherds Bush were very popular and we were one of the top agents in the country for BWIA, the Caribbean airline affectionately known as BeWe. We got to know every Caribbean and Irish accent, so most of the time we knew exactly what the customer wanted before they even told us.

We sold many Sealink and B&I ferries to Ireland. Tickets were manually written using carbon paper and we had to cross our sales off on a form and post it to the ferry companies each week. I'm not sure how many of those got lost or how reliable this system was but in the seventies, who cared if a ferry was overcrowded? Sealink is still operating but B&I finished in 1992. We had to complete the British Rail returns each month, registering each ticket sold. You can imagine us fighting over that job!

One thing I did learn in Pickfords which proved useful when I went to Thomas Cook was a course on Continental Rail tickets. Continental Rail in those days was very complicated. People travelled by train much more than they do now. Rail journeys from the UK before Eurostar involved a ferry crossing. We had a manual, of course, but issuing these tickets required a great deal of concentration. We had to call to book the reservations. Each ticket had to be calculated from border to border, so if the ticket was from London to Rome this would be from London to Dover, Dover to Calais, Calais to French/Swiss border to Swiss/Italian border, both sides of each border had to be written on the tickets, and all added together to calculate the fare.

I always remember an advertising campaign that Pickfords once did. They sent us a huge display with a life size man with a pot belly in a knotted hanky sitting in a deck chair. I've never forgotten that, it was hideous, but so funny.

O'Dea – A Path Well Travelled

Working for Pickfords had its advantages. My mum moved house in 1977 and they moved her entire contents for just £27, a steal even back then. The new landlord thought my mum was rich when the Pickfords lorry pulled up outside. He was soon to be very disappointed!

I can't remember exactly when Pickfords in Shepherds Bush disappeared but it was probably 1992 the year Hogg Robinson and Pickfords merged. The duo were renamed Going Places under the Airtours umbrella. The shop in the W12 shopping centre was the larger and more modern of the two.

Temping at OCL and American Express

After leaving Pickfords in 1977, I wanted to join an airline just like Gary had, but I wasn't looking at British Airways at that time. I applied for Lufthansa and a few others. In the meantime, I went to an agency for temp jobs while I was looking around.

My first temp job was as an implant at OCL in the City. The travel implant's role was to act as a contact between the travellers within the company and their appointed travel agency, Carlson Wagonlit. I loved working near Liverpool Street. I used to go to Houndsditch and Petticoat Lane at lunchtime. As travel jobs go, however, it was the most boring job I ever had. I was used to being busy. OCL was enormous but I only got a couple of enquiries a week. I was being paid ridiculously well for reading books all day. Looking back, I wonder why they needed a travel implant.

By contrast, my next job was American Express in Knightsbridge. I loved working in Knightsbridge as it meant I could go to Harrods and Harvey Nicholls in my lunch hour, just browsing, rarely buying. Unlike OCL, it was the first job I had where I really felt under pressure. As they had so many temps it was impossible to follow up on old bookings that had been handled by numerous people. The clients were nearly all tourists who often didn't speak much English. One gentleman came in asking for "Loma". It took me ages to realise he wanted Rome!

The other problem was that the USA clientele didn't really understand that travelling across Europe was very different from travelling across the USA. Different countries worked in very different ways, standards differed from place to place, there were border crossings, different languages, different currencies and often visas were needed too. At that time confirmation in writing meant waiting at least 48 hours for a telex reply so travelling to more than one country at short notice presented many hurdles.

My temp jobs involved going to Holborn once a week to pick up my wages so by that time I decided that temping wasn't for me and I applied for British Airways.

British Airways West London Air Terminal

British Airways was the first time in my life that I had to have a proper interview and a test. Even though I had never used a computer before, I found the speed test really easy. I already knew my airport codes and fare construction, so I passed all my exams with flying colours. Each small starting group had six weeks intense training but it wasn't all hard work. During our training we did fun things like aircraft inspections, these included Concorde and a Boeing-747 Jumbo jet. We went on the aircraft simulator and watched the pilots in training. We went to Zurich for the day to test out the new Gatwick route. The people I remember in my group were Ken, Bill, Rosemary and Karen. Ken and Rosemary both worked for British Airways for years.

For the first time in my life, I joined the union and they fought hard for us so that we always had regular breaks, the best working conditions, excellent promotion prospects and a good wage. We had a subsidised canteen and bar and special staff fares. There was no APD in those days but air fares were comparatively more expensive and didn't fluctuate like they do now. We only paid 10% of the air fare. Auckland, the most expensive fare, was £72 for us in 1978.

O'Dea – A Path Well Travelled

After the six week training we all sat in the same section on the sixth floor of WLAT under three supervisors, two guys, both called Andy and a lady called Val. We used a headset and a voice would tell us where the call was coming from Birmingham, Southampton, Glasgow etc. A massive board on one wall with flashing lights told us how many calls were waiting. Things were pretty easy going. We used a green screen monitor on the BABS system. I bought my first Amstrad home computer in 1988 so that gives you an idea of how advanced airline technology was in the seventies. The reservations that we made only stayed in the system for a limited amount of time, then they were archived to a microfiche. I only had to use this a couple of times. Microfiche is still used by libraries and museums to store data long term.

We were offered a free ticket each. It had to be a day trip but we were allowed to go out or back overnight. I used mine to go to Boston for the day in April 1978 which I really enjoyed. I chose Boston because it is a walking city and I had never been to the USA before.

I loved my time with British Airways but this time I left for very different reasons. Jim and I got married in 1978 at Kensington Registry Office. A few of my British Airways colleagues came to our wedding reception which consisted of a few drinks in our local pub, The Portland Arms, and our cake stood on the pool table. The Portland Arms has long since disappeared.

As I was pregnant, I didn't change to shift work like the rest of the group, but I did weekend overtime and I often worked on queues. Queues were Waitlists, cancelled flights and schedule changes. I had to try and phone the customer or the agent to advise them of any changes and if I couldn't reach them, the booking would stay on queue.

Because of my previous travel and ticketing experience, I was offered a maternity leave cover position in staff travel at Terminal 3, with free travel to the airport every day from Cromwell Road. I loved the vibe of working at the airport. My job was to arrange travel for existing and retired staff. The Heathrow travelator had just been built so I could get to the staff canteen in Terminal 1. That was a novelty in 1978.

Once the Piccadilly line was extended to Heathrow, there was no longer a need for an air terminal in central London so the building was sold to Sainsburys and the reservations team moved to Hatton Cross. Many of my friends at WLAT were made redundant. Eventually many agencies had their own flight systems and over time, systems became web based. The reservations department became virtually redundant, having shrunk from hundreds of agents on two floors to a handful of agents answering the odd query.

Shortly before I left to give birth to my first daughter, Carol. I used my concession to go to Ireland to see my sister-in-law and our nephews. Our return fare to Cork was just £7.80 each!

Thomas Cook

By 1985 I had two girls, Carol and Sharon who had started school. Mothers were not expected to go back to work but without my girls for company all day, I wanted to work, and the extra wage would be useful.

I was willing to do any job in retail, reception or administration so I went to the job centre. A part time travel job caught my eye so I went in and enquired about it. My interview at Thomas Cook Hammersmith was pretty informal. I remember it being an absolutely freezing day in January so I wasn't looking my best with boots, gloves, scarf and a red nose but I must have done something right as I got the job starting the following week. I couldn't believe my luck, getting a part time travel job after half an hour of looking for any job. That's how things worked in the eighties.

 I started off working 3 days a week part time and then when the children were older, I worked 5 days a week. I usually worked on Saturdays but I loved being back in travel. I joined in January so it was a baptism of fire. I had to stop and think how to write flight tickets but my hesitation only took a few seconds. I was soon back in the swing of things. I am still in touch with Filomena and Jackie who worked with me. At that time we had a corporate division in the back of the shop. Colin and Lisa was the first travel romance I encountered and I was invited to their wedding. They are still married and I am still in touch with Colin who still works in corporate travel. He joined Travel Counsellors briefly but unfortunately it didn't work out for him.

I remember once when I was at Thomas Cook Hammersmith in the eighties, a gay couple came in wanting a short break. Everything was booked over the phone so we would fill out the booking form and then call them with the information. I gave Time Off the names and requested a double. A shocked reservation consultant said are you absolutely sure they want a double! I said yes and did my very best to stay composed while the client sat in front of me. Attitudes were very different then.

During my time in Hammersmith working under Gary Maher, our assistant manager was Brenda who I really liked. She went back to Zimbabwe and remarried, but we lost touch. Another assistant manager was Jo who later joined Travel Counsellors. I recommended my friend Mary, who had worked with me at Kennings and Gary employed her. We worked together for a few years before I moved to Fulham and Mary went to Ealing. We were a great bunch. As well as working with one of my best friends there was Brenda, John and Diane in travel. Mark and Lawrence both worked in foreign exchange. Mark is a QPR supporter so I meet him occasionally at football matches.

I thought I had lost touch with Diane but she reconnected with me recently on Facebook and put me back in touch with John. Diane always made us laugh. I remember once she spotted a bargain with Club 18-30 and booked it for her and her mum! Thomas Cook later acquired Club 18-30. We often said that Thomas Cook would have turned in his grave. I wonder what he would be thinking right now.

In the mid-eighties, Thomas Cook ran a series of incentive competitions. They consisted of a shop quiz with regional, then national challenges to complete. The first one was a trip to the Seychelles. I got through the first couple of rounds. In the next incentive the top prize was a Royal Caribbean cruise. One of the rounds involved canoeing on the River Trent. I am terrified of deep water and capsizing into it and the Weil's disease warnings didn't help, but the lure of a cruise at the end was enough motivation and to my delight, I won a place on the cruise.

Sharron Wallace was only 16 when she came to us on work experience. She was very promising and was taken on initially as a Saturday girl and then full time. She progressed well and went to Fulham as a Customer Service Manager where I worked with her and Amanda, the manager. Sharron and I have kept in touch.

In the eighties when we used to have airline and holiday reps coming in, we often ended up with freebies, usually chocolates or biscuits but occasionally they gave us flight tickets. I was given a free ticket on British Caledonian to Edinburgh. Those were in the days the cabin crew wore a smart tartan uniform, and served a proper full breakfast with a smile. Flying was a pleasure, not just a means of getting from A to B. I was gutted when British Caledonian was swallowed up by British Airways.

A new airline was launched, British Midland. The rep gave the whole shop a free ticket to Paris. We had a lovely day out and we found ourselves a nice little bar in Montmartre.

School holidays were always a problem and my girls usually went to the Fun Factory, but sometimes they came to work with me and helped to sticker the brochures and stack the shelves. The reward of a McDonalds was well below minimum wage, but it was perfectly acceptable to have children in the office. Jim did a few little odd jobs in the office. In those days it was cash in hand. He was fixing the lock on one of the drawers in foreign exchange. This set the alarm off and the police came in and asked him to put his hands in the air.

O'Dea – A Path Well Travelled

A few holiday companies were based in Hammersmith. One of them was Magic of Italy and their airline, Pilgrim Air. One day I saw a flight for £59. I booked it for my mum so she could see her sister in Italy. That was the last time my mum ever travelled outside the UK and the last time she saw her sister. They are both still alive but they are now too old and frail to travel.

My friend Janet worked for British Airways holidays in Hammersmith. Sometimes we met up in the Salutation after work. When BA moved to Victoria, Hayes & Jarvis occupied the building for several years.

We got another free ticket for six of us in the shop, this time to Amsterdam with an overnight stay. Julian, our manager, took us to a gay club in Amsterdam. There were 3 of us girls sitting with 3 gay men. We had a really good night and the men in that club were gorgeous but of course they weren't interested in us!

We had some interesting characters in Hammersmith. We had a betting shop next door and people came in regularly with betting slips, and also trying to pay electricity bills as the LEB was across the road and both shops were orange. Another, very much the worse for wear, mistook our counter for a public toilet. Fortunately that only happened once.

In the late eighties, we had a new manager, Ray. He was always very smartly dressed with a suit and tie. I will never forget his face when I told him we were adding to our family. That was totally unexpected as Sharon was 11 by then. In 1991 the Gulf War happened and Ray had to make some of us redundant. He called me in first to tell me that I could stay, even though I was pregnant. The next two or three people had to walk out of the back door and say nothing. That was awful. Business was dead for months.

During my time at Thomas Cook our uniforms changed roughly every 3 or 4 years. I went through five of them in total. I started off with the Navy Blue tight skirt and Jacket with a white blouse and a cravat, then came the "coco the clown" uniform, with a huge red bow, then the teardrop uniform which was my favourite and after that was the palm tree uniform but I quite liked the polo shirt that came with it, and lastly the turquoise and yellow striped uniform.

I decided I needed a change from Hammersmith and I went to Fulham in 1993. On reflection, that was a strange move with a baby but I was happy there and stayed for eight years. One of the reasons I went to Fulham was that we did considerably more long haul travel than I had at Hammersmith and that would add to my experience.

The clientele at Fulham were a strange mixture of the well-heeled traveller from Chelsea and the market traders in North End Road with wads of cash. In the winter, Paul, on the card stall outside the shop, used to come in all the time to keep himself warm.

I had been at Fulham for a couple of years when I won one of my best ever competitions. There was still no internet but it was a fantastic prize so it was well worth doing some detective work for it. The competition was run by Ritz Carlton and British Airways. I had to name all the Ritz Carlton hotels worldwide. As far as I remember there were only eight. I knew about the ones in Marina del Rey and Hong Kong and somehow I found the other six.

The prize included 3 nights in the Ritz Carlton in Hong Kong, a limousine transfer, up to four flights on any British Airways route and £500 spending money. Apparently, only a handful of people had entered. Our choice was Australia but we had a two year old. We had to leave him behind for 3 weeks. My heart was torn. I felt awful leaving my baby behind but it was an opportunity I felt I would never get again and he was in good hands with my mum and his two sisters.

After moving to Fulham I worked with Amanda and then Mike, who was a really nice guy. The Customer Service Managers were Kevin and then Paul. Dina, our admin lady, still works in travel.

Sharon Frame was enthusiastic and, being from Cape Town, her knowledge of Africa is really useful. After Cooks she joined Kuoni and stayed there. We often met at events over the years. Sharon is a really passionate and knowledgeable travel professional. Jenny Hall became close friends with Sharon: they even flat-shared for a while. Jenny is no longer in the travel industry.

Sara was a real asset to us, very keen and quick to learn. After Cooks, she worked for airlines for many years, Qatar, Virgin and finally Etihad. She is now firmly on the ground in her Sardinia home and we have kept in touch.

Karla had a bubbly, larger than life personality We all loved Karla. After leaving Thomas Cook, she became a Club 18-30 rep in Tenerife for a while. My daughter Carol worked with her briefly at Thomas Cook in Ancoats, Manchester. She surprised us all by becoming a sensible wife and mother and she set up her own highly successful recruitment agency.

Janet faced redundancy from British Airways Holidays in Hammersmith as the office closed so I asked Mike to take her on at Fulham.

After Mike left, Sue Heyes replaced him. Everyone got on with Sue. She was great at organising and had much respect from other managers in the region. Sue looked after us well and we had many social nights out.

Our shop was very close to Chelsea Football Ground. Sue is a passionate Chelsea fan so we arranged supporters' flights to Europe. I used to design a few window posters using MS Publisher and Word Art extensively, an example is "Get a Pizza the action in Milan from £169" and a *terrible* cartoon picture of a slice of pizza! I cringe when I think about it now but it was cool in the nineties.

Sue had good contacts and organised an awards night at Chelsea FC. She gave me the job of designing the drinks vouchers and Steve, the job of photocopying them. The plan was that we were allowed 3 vouchers each. Steve and I might have had a few extra… just maybe. Anyway it wasn't difficult to identify those who might have had more than 3 Kronenbourgs by the end of the night! We learned the next day that Claire Greener went to the loo and fell asleep and woke up freezing and locked in. We didn't know Claire then but I got to know her really well later on when she became our boss at Hammersmith.

I was lucky with competitions and entered as many as I could. It was all done by post. Sue would roll her eyes as I opened yet another envelope saying, "you have won"…

In around 2000, Thomas Cook introduced a window card template to use in Comic Sans. It did look better than the old handwritten ones, providing of course, that the spelling was correct. Writing window cards was a very time consuming exercise and they had to be updated at least daily and often several times a day. They had to be accurate, enticing and relevant. This wasted hours every single day and few people took much notice of them except the regional manager who always seemed to find the out of date one in the corner that none of us had spotted.

Another thing that drove me absolutely insane for many months, perhaps even years, was a poster sent by head office to every shop in the country inviting customers to "Get your Euro's here, the rate today is ---". I point blank refused to put it in the window and designed my own at home inviting customers instead to buy their Euros here.

Sharron's mum, Jo, was our very efficient admin lady and we had Eric, Melanie and Michelle in Foreign Exchange. I have kept in touch with most of my colleagues from my Fulham days. Dina, Kelly, Sara, Karla, Steve, Leona, Zoe, Rose, Sharron, Michelle and Nick are all on Facebook.

 Sue, Kelly, Steve, Leona, Zoe, Janet and myself had a reunion a couple of years ago at The Hammersmith Ram. It was lovely to catch up with them again. Circumstances make this much more difficult now. I did meet Sue recently and we vowed we would soon meet up for a coffee. I have also met up with Michelle a few times.

I couldn't possibly write about Thomas Cook without mentioning the launch of jmc. Every single office in the country took all their staff to a central location. All the Manchester shops went to a location in Leeds and all the London shops went to a dark and dingy nightclub in Bromley for the unveiling of the mystery new product. After a couple of glasses of undrinkable wine and some nibbles and a long drum roll, came the grand unveiling of a larger than life lime green logo with jmc on it in white lowercase letters.

The look of bemusement on hundreds of confused faces is something I will never forget as long as I live. The room went silent and then the question why? It was hilarious! It was only at that stage that they explained what it was all about. jmc stood for John Mason Cook, Thomas Cook's son. We were all given a t-shirt with a lime green ice-lolly on it which we wore home on the coach and once or twice in the shop.

jmc was the family holiday brand and the aircraft. You couldn't miss the lime green logo. However, it didn't represent us in the best light, as the logo looked cheap and nasty and it didn't really mean anything. It was affectionately known by everyone in the travel trade as "just more crap". We had to remember never to say that to our customers!

jmc was probably the beginning of the end for Thomas Cook, a short lived and very expensive exercise. The ill-fated jmc only lasted 3 years and afterwards the aircraft were repainted to a much smarter blue and yellow logo with Thomas Cook on the tailfin. Finally that was replaced by the gold heart which was very simple but it conveyed a more meaningful message "at the heart of everything we do"

Fulham was always awkward to get to. Sometimes I was stuck in North End Road for half an hour in traffic jams. One day I covered at Hammersmith. Gary Stevens was the boss at that time. I liked the young team that worked there and it was only a ten minute walk from my son Martin's school in Brook Green so it made sense to transfer back to Hammersmith.

Sam lived next door to me so we used to go to work together. Liz was a young and hard working trainee who was still doing her travel and tourism course. Liz worked her way up to being a cluster manager and now works for Barrhead Travel. Lisa used to work across the road in Going Places but spent all her breaks with her friends in our shop so Gary suggested she may as well work in our shop as she spent so much time in it. Lisa has shiny dark hair and stunning blue eyes and could charm all the young lads into buying a holiday. One flick of the hair and a flutter of the eyelashes and they were happy to part with their money. Kath also made her way up from trainee to manager. We were an amazing team. Carol worked in Foreign Exchange with Kim and then there was Alison, our admin lady, who always made us laugh.

We were sad when Gary left and in walked Claire Greener. She had business cards with lots of letters after her name. We were terrified but it didn't take us long to get through the tough exterior to really know and love Claire. She had a heart of gold and really looked after us all.

Our shop was constantly busy and we were always looking for deals by hook or by crook. One family came in, a very young gran with her teenage daughter and her baby. Airtours offered child places up to 19, so I managed to get the mum a free child place and the baby was free.

Claire took on several trainees, Marisa, with whom I reconnected at Holborn, Coco from France, Alessandro from Italy, Abi and Nicola. Claire also took on Claire Chambers who had previously worked at the call centre in Falkirk. She quickly progressed to becoming the manager at the Old Brompton Road shop.

Claire Greener kept in touch with all of us. She even invited us to her wedding. I have kept in touch with all my colleagues from that era except Nicola. I often wonder how she is.

We were Claire's London family and we all used to end up in Wetherspoons and The Hop Poles on a Friday night. One Friday night we were in such a rush to get to Wetherspoon, we locked Coco in the shop. Thank goodness we had mobile phones by then. One Friday night, Claire persuaded me to go to the nightclub which was once Hammersmith Palais. It was very different to the dance hall I once knew dancing to the Ray McVay band with my mates.

O'Dea – A Path Well Travelled

We also had a couple of lovely Customer Service Managers, Marika is a lovely Italian lady and she was very efficient. We have kept in touch regularly and have met up a couple of times. Tina, a ringer for Britney Spears, was another.

Thomas Cook had a big push on car hire and Abi with great enthusiasm did her best to sell car hire to every single customer. She went a little too far one day with a couple who were going to Venice! Claire had to stop her in her tracks and explain that Venice is a car free city full of canals.

It was during this era that a client came in clutching a bargain quote she had been given on a BA flight direct to Goa for £169. I had to break the news to her gently that the quote was actually for Genoa in Italy. The airport code is GOA and Goa in India was nearer £700! I can't remember who quoted this but even if I did I wouldn't tell you!

One day it was my turn to do the window cards so I knew what was in the window. I was baffled when a lady came in and asked about Grenada and Carriacou. I took her outside to show me. It was a card for Gran Canaria!

We used to get various window displays to put in the window, depending on the current advertising campaigns. I will always remember one of them. It was a massive grey picture of rain, just rain and puddles, so simple but it was the most effective campaign they ever did. People just wanted to get away from the rain and get some sunshine.

When the Iraq War happened, I was tempted by a generous voluntary redundancy. By then I was getting bored and I was itching to do something different but still in the travel industry. Claire said it was a bad idea and she was right. I was always hopeless at interviews and nobody was recruiting.

After a short spell at First Choice, I went back to Thomas Cook Hammersmith on a full time basis. Martin was getting older and his school was local so my friends used to walk him down to the shop. He

47

was quite happy quietly doing his homework in the shop until 5.30. After so many years as a travel consultant and now full time, I still felt I wasn't really going anywhere and I wanted to go for Customer Service Manager.

I was offered Thomas Cook in Marble Arch. I had often covered in other shops but I had never worked at Marble Arch. In hindsight I should have checked what the job entailed. It turned out to be the most stressful job I have ever had in my long travel career.

The way it was described to me was a job share on a 3-day week, 12 hours a day, 36 hours a week so in theory, it was fewer hours and more money.

 One thing I learnt quite quickly at Marble Arch is that however brilliant I was as a travel consultant, it didn't give me the right skills to be a good Customer Service Manager. It wasn't all my fault though. It was a much bigger and busier shop than I had ever worked in before and there simply wasn't enough staff to cover the long shifts. Our shop manager had never worked in travel before and the job share didn't work out, so all too often I had to work more than double the hours I was contracted to do, in a role I had neither any support nor experience in. I was totally sleep deprived and I never felt I belonged there.

I worked downstairs with Balku, Ruth, Hollie, Anne and Teresa. Upstairs was the biggest and busiest foreign exchange I had ever seen or worked in with Liz, Peter, Michelle and Eugene. I was shocked when the shop closed down. Ruth and Theresa went to shops more local to their home and Hollie went to Trailfinders.

After a few months, for the sake of my mental health, I went back to being a travel consultant again so I went to Thomas Cook in Holborn. It was Monday to Friday. At least I would get my weekends off to spend time with Jim and Martin and watch football on Saturdays.

At first I liked Holborn. It was a smaller, friendlier shop and still on the Central Line. I liked the manager and my colleagues. I had already worked with Marisa at Hammersmith. Marisa worked for Thomas Cook until the bitter end. She was a shop manager for Hays before recently being made redundant.

I celebrated my 50th birthday at Holborn, My colleagues Lee, Marisa, Claire, Fleur, Helen, Emma and Maureen surprised me with balloons, cake and presents, a lovely touch and the highlight of my time at Holborn.

Holborn wasn't very busy but we had some lovely clients and in particular Sylvia. She is such a lovely lady and we would sit and chat about her family over coffee. When Holborn closed after 125 years of trading, she followed me to Travel Counsellors.

Our Woolwich shop closed down so they sent 3 members of staff to us, Jayne and sisters Lisa and Hollie. As we had those extra members of staff, it gave me the chance to learn more foreign exchange.

We learned that our shop was going to be filmed in an episode of "Who do you think you are?" featuring Sheila Hancock. Her grandfather had been the original manager of our shop. Sheila was really lovely and took the time to speak to us all.

We tried to have a 4½-day week at Holborn as all the offices around us did. Friday afternoon was party time. We had a bottle of wine behind the desk which we passed along. We never did much on a Friday afternoon. One Friday afternoon my most awkward customer walked in just as I had poured myself a wine so I carried on serving her but unfortunately knocked the wine over. The thought that was in my head could not be uttered. I just had to carry on as if nothing happened and hope the smell of alcohol didn't waft over the desk.

Maureen in Foreign Exchange liked spicy sauce in her sandwiches and asked me to get her some from Antigua so I picked out the one with Hot in big red letters, a devil's head and flames on it. It made my eyes water as she opened it but it still wasn't strong enough.

O'Dea – A Path Well Travelled

I was asked to be cruise coordinator for the region as I sold quite a few cruises. It was a role I loved as it gave me a new challenge and it meant I was offered an unforgettable transatlantic trip on Queen Mary II.

On 7th July 2005, we all went to work as normal then Maureen rang to say she couldn't get in because of a hold up at Edgware Road. We soon learnt that there had been a terrorist explosion on two tube trains and a bus at Russell Square killing 52 people simply going to work and going about their business.

London fell into an eerie silence that day. Everything stopped, there were no trains, no buses and no taxis. No phones were working. Nobody could contact anybody. It was London's darkest day. We all walked home silently.

My good friend Sue Sevenoaks whom I didn't know then, was working at Edgware Road. The things she witnessed that day changed her life forever and she was given a bravery medal by London Underground. This was only the second time these were ever awarded and not since World War II.

First Choice

When I took the redundancy from Thomas Cook Hammersmith, I found a part time job in First Choice in Hounslow. My manager was Kevin who had briefly been my assistant manager at Fulham. Since he knew me, the interview was a form filling formality. It was only 15 hours a week but it was a job that kept me in travel.

The training was at their office in Reading. I was born in Reading but my dad had the sense to leave it behind when I was a toddler and head back to London. I had never been back to Reading until then. I walked in and two members of staff were chewing gum, shoes off, feet on the chair and chatting away, ignoring me as I walked in. The training room was even worse. There was an empty fridge with a bottle of sour milk and a very mouldy cake. They were obviously expecting us. Welcome to Reading!

The Travelcat system was easy to learn and I was ready to work in the shop. I was pleased to get away from my birthplace as quickly as possible on the fast train back to Paddington. I loved working in Hounslow. It had some really good shops and I loved seeing the low flying aircraft landing just a few miles away at Heathrow, but it was an hour journey each way to work those few hours.

Apart from OCL, it was the most boring job I ever had. My seat was at the back of the shop and we had about six customers a day on average so I only ever got to serve a customer if three walked in at once. I probably fell asleep a few times as there was literally nothing to do apart from stacking brochures and admin. The music was on one short loop which never changed. That music has stuck in my head to this day!

The uniform was green and I'll always remember my friend Maria calling me the Jolly Green Giant when I picked Martin up from school. I popped into my old office in Hammersmith, having not served a single customer all week and did an air ticket for them. That's when I decided that Thomas Cook wasn't all bad after all, and I missed working with the team. I was much happier when I was busy.

Travel Counsellors

My good friend Ann Barber suggested I should join her at Travel Counsellors, the original homeworking travel franchise. She had suggested it before but the time wasn't right. I had to have the right mindset to leave a safe and regular salary. Making the move from high street to homeworking meant giving up working in an office environment to being isolated in my own home. I was ready to make that move.

I couldn't ask for a day off for the interview so I had to throw a sickie and make my way to Bolton. My friend Ann met me and showed me the way to Churchgate House. She introduced me to some of the head office staff. Cathy immediately put me at my ease, it was more of a chat than a formal interview and she made me feel like part of the family straightaway. She showed me the intranet and explained how Travel Counsellors worked and then she showed me round the building. Ann and I had fish and chips and a well-deserved pint afterwards.

I had a DVD to watch on my return which I showed to Jim and Martin. Martin spotted Ann in the audience even before I did and then he said "Mum, they are all just like you". Jim and Martin knew what Thomas Cook was doing to my mental health and they approved of my gamble to go it alone.

It was literally only a day or two before I was told I was accepted as a Travel Counsellor. That was it, one door closed and my final chapter in travel opened as a Travel Counsellor and being my own boss. There were many reasons that I went into the uncertain world of self-employment with Travel Counsellors, but ironically one of them was that it would give me the freedom to use technology to service my clients. At last in 2006, for the first time I was able to access websites and web-based systems but the system that we used as a database was a

DOS based system called Travelcat. I had used this before when I briefly worked in the First Choice shop in Hounslow. It was a simple system but the paperwork it produced left a lot to be desired.

Although I had to give a month's notice at Thomas Cook, they decided to put me on gardening leave so I didn't have to work there much longer. Just before I joined, I was invited to an event so I went as a Travel Counsellor. I met up with Lesley Clements at that event. She noticed my badge and asked me how long I had been a Travel Counsellor. I told her I would be joining officially the following week. She immediately took me under her wing and we have remained friends since.

My first day was on 4th April 2006 and there were four of us on my course. On my 3-day course I got to meet David Speakman, the founder of Travel Counsellors, and I learned of his aversion to oranges. If he was in the office nobody was allowed to eat oranges but if he wasn't, the illicit oranges surfaced. The other three on my course left very soon afterwards. I stayed for fourteen and a half years.

The concept of having a personal Travel Counsellor was still fairly new and the internet wasn't that widely used. Having someone who was prepared to meet over a coffee and chat about their holidays and everything else for as long as it took, whether that was half an hour or two hours or even all day, it didn't matter, their time was my time. If that was after work or at weekends that was fine too. I was enjoying this way of working

Travel Counsellors always gave me the best opportunities for events and educational trips, so those were my most prolific years of travelling with all the valuable contacts I met and all the competitions I won.

As I didn't meet up with my colleagues every day, we didn't have to cope with office politics or each other's irritating habits so I formed some great friendships and we often phoned each other for help and support. We met up socially occasionally as well as for work purposes.

O'Dea – A Path Well Travelled

I met Barbara at an event in my early days. Barbara is currently the oldest Travel Counsellor, now in her eighties. Barbara became my first cover buddy. I never had to worry because I knew that Barbara would look after my business and my clients when I was on holiday. I didn't have the means to look at my bookings in the early days. We had to rely on our buddies. Having one who was as knowledgeable as Barbara was a real bonus.

When I joined, there were about 600 of us. Travel Counsellors was still a family company and we really did feel like part of one big family. As we were still a fairly small company, fam trips and overnight ship visits were plentiful but towards the end it was much more difficult to get places as we had doubled in size in the UK alone by the time I retired.

I loved dealing with the little specialist companies. I knew exactly who I was speaking to and they knew their product inside out. We didn't deal with these specialist companies when I worked for Thomas Cook. All this was a novelty.

As an independent agent, I got invited to so many more roadshows and events than I had as a high street agent so I ended up with many more friends and contacts.

A couple of years later my friend Gillian Davis whom I had met in Grenada was made redundant so I introduced her to Travel Counsellors. We remained friends and met regularly at events, sometimes socially and we travelled to Cyprus together a few times.

In 2014 Travel Counsellors won its second Queen's Award, this time for International Travel. I was proud to be part of that. In that same year, David sold the maximum shareholding so it was no longer family owned. A huge investment was made into technology and as we got bigger, we became more competitive. We became much more of a tour operator creating our own holidays rather than phoning tour operators. I enjoyed the development of the new technology and the challenge of creating our own ATOL holidays. I had never worked for a tour operator so this was a new experience. Phenix was our new system and slowly the paperwork began to look much more consistent and professional as we phased out Travelcat.

By the time I retired in September 2020, there were almost 2000 Travel Counsellors worldwide, over three times as many as when I joined.

Part Four: My Round the Word Path

Travelling over the decades

In the sixties we always travelled to Paris on BEA. My mum found it convenient to use West London Air Terminal to get to Heathrow. We didn't go every year as my mum was a single parent and had to work very hard to save up. I was destined to work At WLAT years later. In the late fifties and early sixties, we travelled on the Vickers Vanguard and later the Vickers Viscount. I recently got on these aircraft at Brooklands Museum in Surrey which I really enjoyed. There are retired pilots on the aircraft and I got the chance to chat to them about my days at British Airways and how I remembered flying on those aircraft. It was really interesting to see how much aircraft have changed and to see how antiquated the old Vickers aircraft look now.

I was one of the few kids who went abroad in the sixties. At that time most of my mates went to Walton-on-the-Naze, Leysdown or Hayling Island. I never did that until I had children of my own. I was curious about these places because my mates loved them and maybe I was a little jealous as they often talked about friends they had met and the fun they had. All I did was visit my family whom I couldn't understand half the time. Occasionally I had the opportunity to go on day trips to places like Clacton, Southend and Brighton with the Playcentre or the playscheme in the local park and I really enjoyed those.

By the early seventies, tourism was growing but it was still very limited. UK coaching was still very popular. Holiday brochures featured Spain, Italy and Yugoslavia by plane or coach. Even when I worked in travel, in the early days I didn't travel that much.

By the eighties we were a family of four so we tried Devon, Norfolk and Kent and stayed in B&B's. When the girls were a little older we went to Ireland to stay with Jim's sister, Mary. When I went back to working in travel in 1986, we became more adventurous. We explored the world as a family as well as on my own with work colleagues. This was the decade of discovery when travel was very cheap and in high demand. Jim wasn't keen on travelling except to his home in Ireland.

For most of the nineties we were a family of five, so with two of our children over 12, holidaying became expensive again so holidays meant caravans and chalets using our generous discounts with Pontins and Haven. During the nineties customers were beginning to travel further afield including to the Middle East and Asia. By the mid-nineties high street agencies were already in decline.

By the Noughties, Carol was at university and Sharon had no interest in travelling with us so for most of our trips, we travelled as a family of three or I travelled on my own on work trips. The internet and low cost airlines were already beginning to have an impact on travel agencies.

The decade from 2010-2019 was my most amazing decade of travelling to 35 countries in five continents. The world had never been so accessible. This was the decade during which I travelled the furthest south and east to New Zealand, the furthest north to Ålesund in Norway and the furthest west to Skagway in Alaska. I went to the Indian Ocean, India and Latin America for the first time. I saw much more of Asia and I saw many more UNESCO World Heritage sites. We went on our first river cruise and we have been on several more since.

I only managed one trip in 2020 and that was to Lanzarote. I think the pandemic will change the face of travel forever as people are scared by the pandemic; they are becoming aware of climate change and the effect tourism has on the environment. However, many countries depend heavily on tourism and need us to come back. Thousands of hotels, bars and restaurants all over the world will never reopen so it might be years before tourism fully recovers. I sincerely hope I am wrong and everything will be back to normal sooner rather than later.

Many of my trips were work educationals or prizes I had won in competitions. I would never know in advance where my next adventure would take me. I won numerous prizes because I entered many competitions either in trade papers or at events including World Travel Market and Destinations. I have heard many colleagues complaining that I win everything. I have been fairly lucky but many of those I did win had surprisingly few entrants. Sometimes, when I asked my colleagues if they had actually entered the competition that I had won, they admitted they hadn't.

You really do have to be in it to win it!

UK AND IRELAND

Northern Ireland

In the Eighties, I probably would have chosen to go almost anywhere else but by 2016 Belfast was a city that had been thoughtfully modernised while preserving its cultures and architecture. It has learnt to shake hands, move forward and perhaps agree to disagree over politics and religion but instead of fighting over it, they reflect on the futility and loss of life on both sides and concentrate their energies on being a great city, embracing their own cultures whilst quietly accepting the other as part of their history. There will always be an element of bitterness and anger but none of this is evident in the modern city centre nor the pubs where everybody just wants to enjoy the craic.

"The craic" means something like, relax, have fun and enjoy the music, soak up the atmosphere, chat with a stranger who isn't a stranger for long or perhaps this could turn into a few jokes, their life story and the history of Ireland over Guinness or two.

Two things I loved most about Belfast were real pubs full of character and the street art. Street art is a reflection of Belfast's famous icons, singers, sportsmen, shipbuilding and Guinness in Donegal Square and on the sides of buildings all over the city. The famous murals and the Peace Wall are a symbol of a troubled past.

The new Titanic exhibition is more than just a museum. The building itself is unique, a fabulous piece of modern architecture over four floors. The exhibition has been well designed and it is very impressive. The ticket includes the SS Nomadic, the last surviving White Star Line ship. It may look small, but there is enough to keep all the family amused. Crumlin Road Gaol tour is an hour long. The guide was excellent and told us about the 150-year history of the jail from Victorian times until it closed on 31st March 1996.

There is more to Northern Ireland than just Belfast and as the weather was gorgeous, we saw the scenic Antrim coast with its lovely beaches and little villages at its best. Mull of Kintyre, just 12 miles away was clearly visible. We stopped at Carrickfergus, a lovely fishing port and castle.

Anna bravely crossed the Carrick-a-Rede bridge, a rope bridge above the treacherous Atlantic but when we got to Giants Causeway she looked at the many thousands of hexagonal columns found the smallest, lowest one possible to sit on for the photo and fell off!

Ireland

We went to Ireland a few times to stay with Jim's sister, Mary. The first time we went was in 1977. Jim's dad, Martin, was still alive. Martin worked on the railways and was quite happy to travel by rail and ferry, in fact he never got on a flight in his entire life. It was a terrible way to travel, all that driving and 8 hours on the ferry across the Irish Sea on Sealink or B&I, sitting on our suitcases as we never booked cabins. We were wrecked for days. I wouldn't even contemplate doing that now. An hour on the plane and car hire suits us fine.

O'Dea – A Path Well Travelled

On one occasion, we took our beautiful Wolseley with a mahogany dashboard over to Ireland. Our destination should have been just a couple of hours drive, but we got lost and ended up driving round in circles. Whichever road we chose, we kept ending up in Tullamore. We tried to ask for directions from the only car we had spotted for many miles, the Gardaí, but we couldn't get any sense out of them as they were drinking whiskey in the back of the car. Remember, times were very different in the seventies. In the end the engine blew up so we had to sell the car for a £100 note, the only one we've ever had or even seen in our lives.

When in Ireland, find a bar with some session music, some places have more than others but every town and village is sure to have session musicians at least once a week.

The O'Dea clan gathering is held every 3 years in the town of Ennis in Ireland. The first one we went to was in 2002 and we have been to five of them altogether. Jim's uncle Patrick went to all the clan gatherings from its very beginning in 1990, even into his nineties. His last clan gathering was in 2014 and his uncle Jim travelled all the way from Australia to be there as often as he could.

Uncle Patrick was a cross country runner when he was young, the fastest in Ireland. There is an annual cross country race named in his honour. He used to love telling everyone how he won the race against all the odds. Patrick O'Dea was just a little country boy who cycled 20 miles to enter. The crowd sneered and laughed at him but he persevered and beat the favourite, an army champion. After winning the race, he cycled all the way back proudly carrying the lamp he had won for winning the race. His mother couldn't even use the lamp as they didn't have electricity . We all loved listening to him every time he told that story with such pride and passion.

We crown our new chieftain at Dysert O'Dea castle in Corofin, Co. Clare every three years. In the afternoon we have food and drinks at O'Dea's bar in Ennis. The outside looks innocuous, a dull grey, with a sign O'Dea Bros. Inside, there is a bar at the back and a huge garden.

O'Dea – A Path Well Travelled

This gives us the opportunity to meet and interact with our distant cousins from all over the world.

In 2002, we had a minor accident involving our coach and a car. We had to wait for the Gardaí to arrive. They got on the coach, by the time they realised all the witnesses were called O'Dea, O'Day, Day or Dee, they gave up and we were on our way.

In 2005 Mieczyslaw Odya from Poland told us of the story of how the O'Dea's ended up in Poland. Two O'Dea brothers sailed East in the 17th-century. They were shipwrecked in the waters off Pomerania, which is now Poland. As they took one of the brothers ashore, they asked him his name. Spelling wasn't important then, so his name was registered as Odya rather than O'Dea. The Odya's now have around 600 descendants in the Gdańsk area of Poland. They have their own clan gathering in Poland. The weird thing is that Mieczyslaw's features even diluted over 400 years still have a strong resemblance to our Irish families.

We met up with Jim's cousins Eileen and Mary. They drove us to the memorial of Ellen Hanley (1803-1819), a 16 year old girl who had been washed ashore on the coast of Limerick. She was tricked into marrying and very badly treated and then she was murdered. The culprits were found and hanged. During her short life she had a benefactor, Peter O'Connell who is a direct ascendant of Jim's paternal grandmother nee Bridget O'Connell. Peter wrote the first Gaelic to English dictionary which is in The British Museum. Ellen's story was written as a play, The Colleen Bawn by Dion Boucicault in 1860.

In 2008, we took the bus to Galway, a pretty and very colourful city alive with music and dancing and it is full of character and history.

In 2011, we chose the Inisheer excursion. We hadn't visited the Aran Islands previously so this appealed. We had tried to do this from Galway in 2008 but the weather was against us. Inis Oírr is the Gaelic name for the smallest of the three Aran Islands and it translates as little island. Bill O'Brien operates trips from Doolin according to tides and weather. Knowing this was a very small boat, we feared a rough ride. In fact, we couldn't have wished for a better day. The sun shone and the Atlantic was like a millpond.

We arrived at Inis Oírr to be greeted by a pony and trap offering us a tour of the island. The ponies looked really unhappy and the carts seemed overloaded so we all declined and walked instead. Inis Oírr has a beautiful beach which was crowded because of the unusually gorgeous weather. It has such a quaint and wild feel to it. There are fishing boats by the sea and ruins up on the hills.

We only had a couple of hours there because timings are determined by the tides so we had to go back early so as not to be stranded. The little boat went right up close to the base of the Cliffs of Moher where thousands of seagulls and guillemots sat on the rocks. I have been to the Cliffs of Moher before, but to see them from underneath is truly amazing. It was one of my most memorable experiences.

Craggaunowen near Limerick is a reconstruction of different eras of ancient Ireland. The guide who took us round was excellent and told us all about the 16th-century castle, the Ringforts of 5th-12th centuries and the Crannogs, built on artificial islands on lakes to protect them from their enemies. We walked through the woodland to see Tim Severin's replica of St. Brendan's boat made of leather which may have got to America centuries before Columbus. In 1976, Tim Severin proved it was possible by sailing across the Atlantic. The boat that he used for his experiment is the one on display.

We visited Limerick and started off in the Hunt Museum where we saw Bishop Cornelius's bejewelled mitre and crozier. The Hunt Museum is very close to his tomb in St Mary's Cathedral which is now a Protestant cathedral, the oldest building in Limerick dated 1168.

King John's Castle is a great day out for all the family. There are views of Limerick city from the top. It was reopened after refurbishment and modernisation. I enjoyed my visit last time but since then, they have done a wonderful job in improving the castle and museum to bring it to life. There are interactive displays, soldiers describing what life was like in Medieval Ireland with some humour to keep it entertaining and memorable.

Bandon, Jim's home town in Ireland is a small town in West Cork. It was also the home of Graham Norton. The Riverwalk has been renamed after him. Bandon has a few interesting features, a ruined castle, a river, two massive churches, one Catholic and one Protestant.

Jim's sister Mary took us to visit the holy woman, Mrs. Eileen O'Driscoll, who attracts people from all over the world. We were invited to visit her amazing back garden shrine which has statues, icons and effigies from all over the world, thousands of them.

Another thing we discovered completely by accident was an exhibition of the history of the West Cork Railway which once ran through Bandon. Jim's dad worked at Bandon Station until he came to England in 1958 and transferred to Paddington. It was interesting to see those memories but we couldn't identify any photos of him. The line closed permanently in 1961 and the rails were sold to Nigeria.

Bandon isn't on the tourist trail but it is a good base for the beautiful raw Atlantic beaches like Inchydoney, a surfers' paradise. Luckily, the sun shone so we could appreciate the sea air and the coastal beauty of West Cork. Kinsale is a short drive away. This was made famous by the Spanish Armada and the town is heavily influenced by this with bars like The Spaniard and the Armada Tavern. At the top of the hill is Charles Fort which has a fabulous view of the yacht harbour and the whole of Kinsale below.

Ballinascarthy, the original home of Henry Ford isn't far from Bandon. There is a memorial to him, a life sized silver model of an early Ford, a plaque in his honour and the Henry Ford Tavern.

EUROPE

Before joining the Common Market, we needed visas to get to Czechoslovakia, Hungary and Poland. The Baltic countries Estonia, Latvia and Lithuania were still ruled by USSR and East Germany was still in the other side of The Berlin Wall. Not so long ago, before the Euro, every country in Europe had its own currency and in the seventies, every time we bought currency it was registered on a page stuck inside the back of the passport.

France

I often went to France as a child, firstly to Paris where my grandmother lived. Later on, she bought a country house in Velennes, about an hour from Paris, so we holidayed there a couple of times. She died when I was quite young and the house was sold.

I once flew to Bordeaux as an unaccompanied minor. I remembered this in later years when I added on the service for my clients. The summer holidays I loved most were those that I spent in Perros-Guirrec in Brittany and Les Landes near Bordeaux.

Carcassonne

Carcassonne was one of Ryanair's routes waiting to be discovered and we did just that in 2007. It is a walled city full of character. Inside the walls was a fascinating maze of narrow cobbled streets and a mixture of quaint artisan shops as well as souvenir shops, wooden swords and reminders of a bygone era of knights in shining armour.

We decided that a nice leisurely cruise down the Canal du Midi would be a good idea. It turned out to be eventful rather than leisurely. There were two boats to choose from, one wooden and the other metal. Martin decided the metal one would be more likely to sink. The leisurely cruise started well, enjoying the peace and observing the flora and fauna on the river banks and as we got to just about the furthest point, some ominous looking smoke rose from the back of the boat. It didn't sink but it did catch fire! One of the crew went to investigate, stuck his head down the hole and came back up resembling Dick Van Dyke's chimney scene in Mary Poppins! We headed back through the lock. It seemed to take forever as we were choking on the fumes. In the end evacuation was the only sensible answer so we had to use the emergency ladders to get out of the lock.

Disneyland Paris

We were offered an agent's megafam in 2008 to learn about Disneyland Paris. There were hundreds of agents from all over Europe and five Travel Counsellors amongst them, Marie, Debbie, Suzanne, Jo and me. I was interested in visiting my fourth Disney Park after Florida, California and Hong Kong and this visit would definitely help me sell it to clients. We stayed in the New York Hotel which is within easy walking distance of the two parks, Disneyland Paris and Walt Disney Studios. Disneyland Paris is much smaller than Florida and California. I really enjoyed Walt Disney Studios which was a new experience, but I wasn't brave enough to try the new Twilight Zone Tower of Terror.

It was a lovely weekend in great company. I got to know some of my new colleagues better and it made me more knowledgeable about selling the various hotels, attractions, meals, shows and extras, thus it proved really useful, especially as I had a large family group to book shortly afterwards.

Marie Rayner, Debbie Lees, Suzanne Knowles, Jo Osmond and me

Lyon

In 2017, I was offered a tourist board educational to Lyon including flights on Air France, which meant changing in Paris. We were split into four groups. Our group was allocated Hotel Fourvière, a quirky hotel, previously a convent, oozing with character. We had amazingly good weather for mid October. The sun shone with hardly a cloud in the sky.

Lyon is on two rivers, the Rhône and the Saône and we had the chance to see the sights from both rivers on our dinner boat. The food on board was of very high quality and beautifully presented.

The Basilica of Notre-Dame de Fourvière is absolutely stunning especially the mosaic tiles. The Gallo-Roman museum and the remains of the well-preserved amphitheatre are both within walking distance.

We meandered round the quaint narrow streets of Vieux Lyon, the old medieval city. Many of the medieval buildings including the Rose Tower are pink with traboules which are a unique feature of this region.

Traboules are secret passageways which go from house to house. A good example of these is inside the puppet museum which looks an interesting possibility for next time. Another thing which caught my eye was the beautiful stained glass shop signs.

Our evening dinner was in a traditional and very ambient Bouchon, a traditional French café, with handwritten chalk boards, decorative mirrors and signs.

Lyon also has ultra-modern architecture, the bright green Euronews building, the Orange Cube and the impressive Musée des Confluences where the Rhône and the Saône meet. The latter is an interesting example of modern architecture, a well designed science and anthropology museum based on four themes, origins, species, societies and death and eternal life. The almost complete mammoth skeleton is a notable exhibit. During our visit there were temporary exhibitions on lumière and early cinematography.

 Les Halles de Lyon Paul Bocuse looked uninspiring on the outside, but once inside, there was the most beautifully presented and delicious feast of food with cakes, chocolates, hams, cheeses, sausages, huge mussels and Oysters on offer. We had lunch in the Radisson which occupies floors 32-37 of the city's tallest building. The views were stunning and the food was excellent.

The shopping mall has everything from Primark to top designer shops. I managed to find a few unusual Christmas presents in Pylones, an affordable French design chain store. A couple of the others visited the park with the lake and the zoo, all good reasons to return.

The pâté I bought my mum was confiscated. I should have put it in the suitcase. Our flight with an already very short connection was 20 minutes late, leaving just 25 minutes to catch the last flight back from Paris to London. I ran as fast as I possibly could to catch the plane and almost collapsed by the time I got to the gate as I couldn't stop to find my inhaler. I wasn't the last on, so I needn't have nearly killed myself running. The luggage didn't catch up with me but to Air France's credit they sent me a text message straightaway and the luggage was delivered to my door the next day. Maybe it was just as well I didn't pack the pâté after all!

Our group in Lyon

Spain and Gibraltar

Thomson Holidays launched in 1970. My first holiday with them was to Benidorm with my mum on a 3-night package. I won a horrible fluffy donkey full of pins which I bought home. Luggage wasn't a problem then. Our flat was tiny and we lived in just one room. Goodness knows why my mum let me bring it home. She took me to Ibiza the following year and that was the turning point, the week which inspired me to travel far and wide.

Majorca

My first ever grown up holiday was with Janet to Palma Nova in the early seventies. Most of that holiday was a blur as we danced all night and slept all day. Janet met Manolo so we spent much of our time in his bar over free drinks but three's a crowd. Manolo did his best to pair me off with his mate whom I really didn't fancy at all. One night on the way home from the nightclub his mate thought it would be fun to throw me in the dustbin. I laughed about it after picking orange peel out of my hair but I couldn't get the smell out of my coat and I had to wear it home as the temperature in London was sub-zero.

Joan, a friend of ours, had her big birthday celebration in Majorca in 2015. Anna was sharing a room with her. Jim and I decided to go out just for the weekend to surprise Joan. Anna knew we were coming but Joan didn't. Joan had her suspicions that something was afoot but couldn't quite work out what it was. It was my first time back to Magaluf since that week in Palma Nova with Janet.

The thing I loved about this little break was that we were introduced to Joan's circle of friends, Christine, Beryl, Sheila, Barbara, Marion, Maggie and Iris. We have met up regularly in London since then, usually for lunch in Wetherspoons They are a great crowd. I really enjoy meeting up with them and I hope we can meet again soon.

I won 2 nights at the Hilton Sa Torre in Llucmayor in 2018 at a Hilton event. We planned our visit when Anna's friends from Scotland were going to be in Puerto Pollensa. We had never stayed in Puerto Pollensa before, so it seemed like a good idea to combine a few days there with the 2 nights in Llucmayor.

We enjoyed the meet up with Moira and Cameron in the town and market in Pollensa town and then we they took us to a lovely little bar in the afternoon. It transpired that Anna knew the manager's brother from a chance meeting in a bar in Magaluf on a previous visit.

Sa Torre was a hidden gem, so picturesque with beautiful scented gardens, butterflies everywhere and the service was fantastic.

Mojacar

Janet had a friend with a villa in Mojacar. This would have been 1973 or thereabouts. Mojacar was very different to Palma Nova, very Spanish and oozing with character. To get to and from the beach, we had to hitch hike which was easier than it sounds. We thought it was a sleepy little place until we were woken up one morning by crashing and banging. It was the local baker driving down the stairs at 6.30am! He happened to be a friend of Margaret, our host.

Mojacar has a local legend and a distinctive symbol of a man carrying a rainbow bringing much needed rain and prosperity to the region. The Indalo can be seen on many of the houses and on jewellery sold in the region.

Torremolinos

 Janet and I booked another holiday to Torremolinos, this time for two weeks in the summer but by the time we went in 1976, I had just started dating Jim, so I couldn't wait to get back. I hoped he would still be waiting for me.

We got on a donkey on a mountain somewhere and ended up getting lost on a coach trip and ended up on the German coach instead of ours. We had no idea where we were going as neither of us spoke German. We somehow managed to get back to the hotel to enjoy the rest of our holiday.

Jim did wait for me. The rest is history.

It would be a long time before we went back to Andalucia. We were curious about the new all-inclusive concept with First Choice. We tested it with Martin, who was still a toddler and our friends, Cozzer and Adrian. We stayed at Cortijo Blanco near Puerto Banus and Marbella. This would have been the summer of 1994.

We used the local bus to Puerto Banus and Marbella. We also went up the winding mountain road to the ancient hilltop city of Ronda. We took the day trip to Gibraltar from Puerto Banus in 1995. One of the barbary apes took a fancy to Adrian's bag and tried to snatch it. He just about managed to hang onto it. Apparently a few do get stolen by the apes, they are surprisingly big beasts and very fast too.

O'Dea – A Path Well Travelled

We explored St Michael's caves and went shopping down Main Street. It was a lovely day out but very much geared to cruise day trippers buying duty-free cigarettes and booze. Our only other visit to Gibraltar was even briefer, on a short cruise stop with Ocean Village.

Anna and I fancied a short break to the Costa del Sol. We chose a very cheap 4T Thomson Square Deal. This was my first holiday with Anna which was in December 2004. We arrived there at night and got on the coach, and of course, we had no idea where we were going. The first place we arrived at was the Holiday Club which used to be Pontinental. We breathed a sigh of relief that we had booked the 4T rather than the 3T package. We were dropped off at Pez Espada, between Torremolinos and Benalmadena, the oldest hotel on the Costa del Sol.

Pez Espada oozed character from the strange giraffe style tiles to the signed photos of many celebrities of the sixties who had stayed there, including royalty, actors including Sean Connery, Ava Gardner, Ingrid Bergman and Sophia Loren and Frank Sinatra who had the biggest influence on the hotel. Frankie's Bar is named after him and his gold discs adorn the corridors.

Our hotel overlooked a gorgeous sandy beach. Many of the bars and shops were closed for the winter but there were more than enough still open. It was a little chilly, but definitely much warmer and sunnier than London. Benalmadena was a very easy walk, as was Carihuela. It was on one of our walks that Anna spotted a John Smith sign and, besides, we needed the loo. We were sitting at the bar and there was one of those tacky signs that looks like Japanese writing and then as you turn your head sideways it reads something rude. Once I realised this, I said to Anna.

"Aha, I get it now".

"What?" says Anna.

. "That sign" says I "Turn your head sideways".

"But I'm looking at you" says Anna.

"No not that way!" says I.

By the time she looked at the ceiling, on the floor, out of the window, in fact every possible angle and direction except the right one we were both in absolute hysterics. By this time we had attracted the attention of all the expats who wondered what we were laughing at and wanted one of whatever we were drinking. This broke the ice as they decided we were fun people and they wanted to talk to us so we ended up staying for hours and we had a great night.

On another of our walks, Anna was looking for a "young man" a "Pedro" with whom to have a photo taken in order to tease Geoff, her partner, on our return. Eventually we found a Pedro but he happened to be a toothless old fisherman! Anna decided to pose for the photo anyway. Anna's "young man" album has since become a bit of a standing joke with a pose for every destination.

We decided to go to Seville for the day. Anna had a cold and I couldn't get the safe open, so I ended up having to go out with no money. Anna had dressed inappropriately in a smart suit. Firstly she was freezing and had to buy a jumper on the way and then we ended up going to Maria Luisa Park. Anna bought some bird food. As soon as she opened the packet, a thousand doves flew down and pecked her new jacket to bits. What annoyed her even more is that I had the cheek to wander off to a peaceful bird free environment to take photographs but by the time I got back, I missed the shot of her getting pecked to bits.

Menorca

It was a long time until we went to Spain again, this time to Cala'n Forcat in Menorca in 1992. It was our first time abroad as a family of five. We travelled with Cozzer and Adrian.

Martin started walking on that holiday so I was really nervous about the tiled floor in case he fell. Luckily he didn't. 12-year old Sharon was technically still young enough to join the Airtours kids club and she was presented with an Archie t-shirt. The more she refused point blank to join in with the groovy gang, the more we wound her up about it.

Madrid

I won a couple of British Airways tickets to Madrid at a Latin Routes event a few years ago and Anna fancied coming with us.

Both Anna and I can read a little Spanish. On arrival in Madrid Barajas, a huge airport, the signs in Spanish read Equipaje y Salida, the English underneath read, Baggage and Exit. Somehow, instead of reading either language, Spanish or English, Anna read it aloud, very loudly in her very best French/Hyacinth Bucket (Keeping up Appearances) as:-

"Look, There's the "Baggarge".

Of course we nearly wet ourselves laughing and thereafter Anna's luggage has been christened "The Baggarge"

Anna suggested that we take the train to Toledo which is only an hour away. As we waited for our train, we watched a bale of turtles in the station, so much more interesting than Kings Cross. We arrived in Toledo, a beautiful and historic station. As Toledo is very hilly, we took the tourist train up to the top. We went to lunch in a bar which Anna had liked on her last visit two years previously. The owner came out and shouted:

"Anna". He remembered her!

We had a meal and a couple of beers before going back to Madrid. Toledo was definitely worth a visit. It is a walled city with a beautiful view as far as the eye can see.

On our second visit to Madrid in 2017 we had lovely autumn weather. We stayed very near Puerta del Sol. On that occasion there were demonstrations for and against Catalan independence but these had very little impact on our stay.

Rastro Market is a good quality one, but very crowded. There is also a covered food market across the road. We wandered around the narrow streets full of old traditional buildings and quickly found a tapas bar, then we visited the beautiful cupola inside the Basilica de San Francisco. El Rio Manzanares is a lovely place to walk or just to sit and relax. This opened in 2011 as an urban green space for all the family with manicured gardens and play areas.

We wanted to revisit Retiro Park. In early October it was almost 30 degrees. It felt like a summer day with people still rowing on the boating lake but the trees told a different story as they were already showing their autumn colours. There are a few cafés in the park in which to sit and watch the world go by. A unique feature of Retiro Park are the distinctive marshmallow trees as well as a huge boating lake and a beautiful rose garden.

Costa Brava

I went to a Selling Travel Costa Brava evening. They were giving away 10 educational places but only 13 of us actually bothered to turn up so we all got a place. The 13 included my good friend and colleague Gillian, also Alfredo, Peter, Chrissie and Polly all of whom I used to meet regularly at events.

We were blessed with really gorgeous weather during our stay in March 2012, although it was misty in the early mornings. Our first 2 nights were in the city of Girona. In the evening we explored Girona on foot. We wandered past the narrow alleyways of the Jewish Quarter, a small but fascinating area of the city.

Kissing the bottom of the lion opposite the cathedral upon entering the city will extend your life by ten years according to legend. The trouble is that the lion is at the top of a pole so for those of us who are vertically challenged, this is not the easiest of tasks. The top three figures at the top of the cathedral are original. The rest of the façade is only around 60 years old but it does blend in well.

We had the opportunity to visit the Cava factory in Mont-Ferrant which is only open to the public for 2 months of the year. We learnt about the manufacturing process, bottling and storage of Cava and we sampled some afterwards. Still on the theme of alcohol, the Costa Brava region is famous for Gin and Tonic served in a large bowl glass and each bar has its own techniques but watching it Indigo style is a work of art, the way they twist the lemons and then pour the tonic round the swizzle stick.

On Thursday morning a thick mist hovered over Girona. We were assured by Jesus, our driver, that it would lift within the hour. The scenic route to Garrotxa is only about 15-20 mins longer than the motorway and definitely worth the diversion. By the time we arrived at Lake Banyoles, used for the Barcelona Olympics in 1992, the mist lifted right on cue, to reveal a beautiful crystal clear lake.

Once we reached Garrotxa, we went on a gentle hike round Croscat. the highest volcano in the Iberian peninsula. Mike told us about the geology, weather patterns and the flora and fauna around the volcano. We learned that this is one of the few places in the world where cork oaks grow and he told us how they protect the trees from forest fires. The trees are stripped every 9 years for cork, then they take another 9 years to regrow. Mike told us that he had lived in the region for 28 years and that he currently lives in Besalú. We recognised this name as being our lunch stop.

Besalú is a beautiful walled city 20kms from the French border. We fully appreciated the extra half hour we were allowed to browse round the shops and buy handicrafts before stopping at La Cúria Reial, a restaurant with a beautiful view of the river.

Once we reached Figueres we went straight to the Salvador Dalí Theatre Museum. This was built on the site of the old burnt out theatre and Salvador Dalí thought it was appropriate for him to have his own theatre of surrealism as well as his own burial on site. As it was almost closing time we rushed round the Dalí Jewels museum first. The pieces were commissioned by Dalí himself and were absolutely fascinating, then we went back to Dalí's Theatre museum. Even though most of the well-known paintings are in the Florida museum or in private collections, I loved the works that remained including his own favourite painting of a simple piece of bread in a basket, and the building itself is much more interesting than its Florida equivalent.

Dinner that evening was in the Hotel Duran, owned by the Duran family since 1910. What makes this hotel so special is the restaurant and its associations with Salvador Dalí. Our dinner was in an ante room off the main restaurant. We discovered that we were eating at the very table at which Salvador and his Russian wife Gala entertained their guests.

They always used this restaurant because he was a personal friend of the Duran family. He went to school with the current owner's father. He sometimes sketched in the restaurant on the tablecloth or on paper. These sketches can be seen around the hotel. The Durans have made notes on their hotel blogspot which is in Catalan. They are very proud of their associations with Salvador Dalí and are keen to preserve their special and unique heritage.

On our last day we did a short hike along the coastal path from Calella de Palafrugell to Llafranc. This is one of many designated and signposted trails. It is a short and easy walk although there are some steps en route. The scenery along the route is stunning and there are wild flowers and a lovely smell of pine. There are millionaires' homes along the way. We ended up in Llafranc which is a pleasant, small resort. We were at the tail end of the short sea urchin season so we got the chance to sample these as a special starter before our tasty and well-presented lunch in the Hotel Llevant.

Our group in Palafrugell

Valencia

On May 2017 we chose Valencia, which is a city with a beautiful sandy beach, plenty of green space, museums, gastronomy, shopping and history.

There are some beautiful examples of architecture throughout the city, old and new, impressive doorways, wrought iron balconies, shining rooftops, examples of Art Deco, mosaic tiles, stonework and bridges.

The City of Arts and Sciences is an impressive cluster of futuristic museums originally built for the Expo in 2008. These are Palau de les Arts (opera house), Museu de Ciències (Science Museum) Oceanogràfic (Oceanarium) and L'Hemisfèric.

Valencia was the original home of paella. There are plenty of tapas bars in which to sample a bewildering choice of paellas washed down with local red wine which is both cheap and excellent. The Central Market is the biggest indoor food market in Europe where the Serrano ham is freshly sliced, spring onions are the size of tennis balls and there is an array of colourful misshapen vegetables all in a beautiful old building with stained glass windows.

We were looking for the nearest Zara so Anna stopped a couple of girls to ask directions in her best Spanish. They answered in Spanish.

Anna shouted over, "Oi, Cath, Its just around the corner".

The girls laughed. They were English.

In the old part of the city there is the bullring and next to it is Estació del Norte the station which is a beautiful building inside and out. The cathedral and Silk building are also worth visiting.

Jardin del Turia is a 9kms long strip of parkland which runs right through the entire city on the dry Turia riverbed. It runs from the City of Arts and Sciences all the way to the Marina. All along this stretch of parkland are ornamental bridges. There are many seafood restaurants along the front overlooking the beautiful long sandy beach.

The Canaries

Gran Canaria

On our first visit to The Canaries in the late eighties, we stayed in Playa del Inglés. We went on a round the island trip and took our big hefty video camera. I forgot to bring the film so I was lumbered with the camera all day and couldn't take any film of the banana plantation inside a crater, the fishing village of Puerto de Mogán nor the hillsides of Puerto Rico, but I do have a film of a gappy-toothed 7-year old singing her own version of Madonna's "La Isla Bonita".

"Young girls with eyes like potatoes"

Tenerife

We were invited to the Paradise Park hotel in Los Cristianos in Tenerife in November 2011 on an Agents Select Week. We were able to bring a partner or friend with us. Our host Christine Lloyd represented the hotel in the UK until she retired a few years ago. She has an amazing memory. Having just met 18 of us she remembered all our names and where we worked whereas 3 days later I could still only remember a few.

We had two trips included, Loro Parque and Siam Park. We thoroughly enjoyed Loro Parque. The German owner planned a Thai theme. The Thai village was imported from Thailand with woodcarvings and roofs encrusted with 24-carat gold plate. From its humble beginnings as a parrot park, it is now 10 times its original size with killer whales, dolphins, gorillas, meerkats and the largest penguinarium in the world. We had a substantial 3-course lunch included in our behind the scenes tour. Our last day was at Siam Park, the newest theme park in Tenerife. It is a water park with the same owner as Loro Parque, also with the Thai village theme.

The following year Anna and I booked a pre-Christmas break in Tenerife. We took the opportunity to visit the very diverse landscapes of La Gomera. It would have been difficult to do this on our own using the ferry. Our guide explained the unique whistling language over lunch. This is taught in schools and can be heard up to 3 kms away. This is useful for communication in this mountainous outpost.

We spent most of the afternoon in Garajonay National Park which is a natural rainforest. We were told of the tragic legend of Princess Gara and the poor farmer Jonay from Tenerife, hence the name Garajonay.

Our tour ended in the capital San Sebastián. This is a very pretty little town with pastel coloured houses and a small church. Columbus set sail on his epic journey from La Gomera after getting his water from the well. I would have liked a little more time in San Sebastián, but the last ferry back was at 16.30 so we couldn't hang around.

O'Dea – A Path Well Travelled

We took the trip to Mount Teide, which was freezing so we definitely needed a jacket. After a short stop at Vilaflor, the highest Spanish community, we wound our way up to 2000 metres. The cable car to the summit was cancelled that day. To compensate, we made extra stops at Rocas Gomez, The Queen's shoe and Pico Viejo so there were still some good photo opportunities.

We wandered round Los Cristianos Sunday market to buy a few Christmas presents. We walked along the promenade until we came across a guy selling whale trips. We saw a few small Pilot Whales and some dolphins. It was a lovely afternoon out.

In July 2015, we got another invitation to Paradise Park's bright new look as a lifestyle hotel. This time our friends, Ann and Carol Warburton came on the same trip so Jim got to meet Carol properly at last, only having previously met her briefly at conference. They got on like a house on fire and shared a few vodka and cranberries. We have met up a few times since then, in Tenerife, Cyprus and Manchester.

In 2018, Iberostar Sábila in Tenerife was newly opened so there was a special opening deal for agents. The timing of the offer was perfect because it coincided with Carol's big birthday just one week before our Ruby wedding anniversary.

Ann and Carol went a few days before us to celebrate her birthday so we overlapped by about 5 days. The hotel left us a welcome bottle of Cava and a further bottle for Carol's birthday so we had plenty for our pre-dinner balcony parties.

My clients Victoria and Aiden sent us a beautiful anniversary cake. They took the trouble to track us down by the photos I had posted on Facebook which was so sweet of them, It was a decadent cake full of chocolate and strawberries.

Our group in Tenerife in 2011

Fuerteventura

At a Fuerteventura evening at Gatwick airport in 2017, I won 3 nights in Barceló Corralejo Bay which is adult only. Having previously visited five of the seven Canary Islands, Fuerteventura was long overdue a visit. I have yet to visit the least developed of all, El Hierro. On that occasion, I booked Anna and another of our friends into nearby apartments.

Corralejo is flat and mostly pedestrianised. Away from the high street and shops, there are some lovely walks, and plenty of opportunities to breath in the sea air, to stop and admire the wild scenic beaches contrasting against the dark volcanic rocks with the Atlantic waves crashing up against them and to watch the windmills in the distance. There are plenty of benches along the way and cafés in which to stop for a coffee or a glass of wine and some tapas.

O'Dea – A Path Well Travelled

Fuerteventura is well known for being windy but in temperatures of 20 degrees plus, it is more of a refreshing breeze than a howling gale. Corralejo has many decent bars and restaurants which are cheaper than at home. Corralejo has mostly expats running the bars although the hotels, restaurants and shops tend to employ locals.

Corralejo has a couple of commercial centres. With a favourable rate on the euro, there were bargains on popular brands such as Zara, Springfield, Benetton and Berksha. There is also a Tuesday and Friday market selling mostly fake handbags and jewellery. There are plenty of souvenir shops and tobacconists along the Main Street.

On our second trip to Fuerteventura a few months later, we decided we wanted to see a little more of the island. We found there was much more open in April even though the weather had actually been better in December.

Anna had too many "Linda measures" in Murphy's and had to negotiate the hill so Linda came out from behind the bar and helped to push her up the hill. Anna got back to the apartment, kept her friend awake most of the night, lost her way to the loo and locked herself out wearing just her knickers so she was banging on the door until her friend answered. She also managed to lose her teeth which Jim retrieved from under her bed the next morning.

We booked a coach trip to Jandia at the very south of Fuerteventura. This is a very different type of resort. It has a beautiful long sandy beach and it is very quiet and relaxed. Jandia is hotel based, mostly on an all-inclusive basis so it doesn't have the selection of bars and restaurants that Corralejo has.

We used the local bus to get to El Cotillo which is a lovely traditional fishing village and we discovered one of a selection of lovely traditional tapas bars. We stopped at one of them for lunch.

We also took the bus to La Oliva. What a gem this proved to be! There is a board showing plenty of things to do in this small town. There is an 18th-century church Iglesia de Nuestra Señora de la Candelaria. The

Colonel's House didn't look appealing from the outside but it was bigger than it looked with history and a fabulous view of the volcano and the surrounding countryside. We also found Centro De Arte Casa Mané which was well worth seeing. The Art Gallery was very interesting with exhibits by local artists including César Manrique who is responsible for many art installations in Lanzarote. There is a cactus garden outside which was very interesting.

On our third visit in a year, we took Lil with us and introduced her to our usual haunts, An Caisteal, the Scottish daytime bar and our favourite home, Murphy's bar. We missed Linda as she had gone back to Ireland to see her folks and Wes no longer sings at Murphy's but we did see him walking about. Des still has a regular spot there and we ended up there on most nights but we made sure we tried a few other places as well, including a couple of bars that had recently opened

Lil is always guaranteed to entertain us and this time we went into our usual daytime haunt near the harbour, the " one euro" bar. Lil sat back in the wicker chair and the bottom fell through and we just saw a pair of legs sticking up into the air. Before that she was busy doing the crossword. Baby duck, 4 letters? The only thing either Anna or I could think of was duckling but that has 8 letters. "Got it" says Lil "it's chick". But that has 5 letters, we protested "Not the way I spell it" said Lil. I don't think she finished the crossword somehow!

This time we did something we never do normally, we ate in an Indian restaurant. There are two of them virtually next door to each other. The first one hassled us so we chose Jaipur, the second one, which is more established. It was excellent, run by Indians and furnished like an old-fashioned curry house so it was easy to forget the surroundings and enjoy the meal. Even Lil, who is a very fussy eater, enjoyed her meal. We'll be back!

Lanzarote

We visited "Breezy Teguise" in the late nineties. We liked Lanzarote and we did a couple of trips to the fascinating man made Cueva de los

Verdes, Los Hervideros, the vines at La Geria and the lunar-like
landscapes in Los Volcanes Natural Park.

For our only trip in 2020 we took advantage of a BA seat sale and went
back to Lanzarote. I liked Costa Teguise so we booked the first 3 nights
there and 2 nights in Puerto del Carmen. I had always sold Puerto del
Carmen as a party resort and it was featured in Club 18-30 so it always
put me off. Our local publican in The Pig & Whistle also owned a bar in
Puerto del Carmen so we thought we would try a couple of nights there
regardless of my preconceptions.

Costa Teguise had become a little neglected from what I remembered.
We walked into the main town square about 15 minutes away on foot
and that was better. There were some nice bars, restaurants and a good
ambience. We found a nice little bar with an Irish female trio playing.

On the other hand, Puerto del Carmen has changed so much. It looks
really smart now, the beach has a walkway and new palm trees have
been planted. We loved the apartments, which were spacious and in a
good location.

There are still a few loud discos and clubs on the seafront but we found
a few nice ones and we enjoyed Noel's bar, Maguire's. The night we
arrived was the best night as there was a singer who sang Ratpack,
country and western, and ska. A drunk woman fell on the stage and
knocked the microphone into his eye. It obviously hurt but he carried
on. I bet he had a shiner in the morning!

Switzerland

In the four years I worked for Kenning Travel, I only ever managed one
educational. I ended up going to Zurich on Dan Air. Anyone who
remembers Dan Air will also remember how bad they were. Our aircraft
had a hole in the front window. I'm not too sure how we actually
managed to get to Zurich at high altitude but somehow we did.

I enjoyed Zurich and remember going on a boat trip and being
impressed by its cleanliness and how clear the lake was. It wasn't really

much of an educational. We were left to our own devices, but it was a lovely weekend.

Jim, Martin and I took the first of many rail trips to Switzerland. The Golden Pass line runs from Lucerne to Montreux with a change in Zweisimmen. Swiss Railways are slow enough to enjoy the wonderful scenery. The mountains are huge and snow-capped even in summer, and the lakes glisten in the sunshine.

Lucerne is a beautiful city with a swan-filled lake. The unique feature of Lake Lucerne is Chapel Bridge, a wooden bridge with 17th-century paintings under the roof. Some of these were destroyed in a fire. They have been restored perfectly to match the originals.

We stayed a couple of nights at the family run Hotel du Lac in Interlaken. Interlaken literally means between the lakes, Lake Thun and Lake Brienz to be precise. On that first trip we took a few trips up the mountain to Birg, Mürren and Kleine Scheidegg.

We had lunch in Piz Gloria, the revolving restaurant in Schilthorn and watched the paragliders through the window. It is amusing to watch people leaving coats and handbags on the ledge only to realise they are disappearing as the floors and tables move but the ledge is stationary. The James Bond movie "On Her Majesty's Secret Service" was filmed there.

As the train progressed on its journey, Chalets became barn-like buildings, mountains became vineyards and German sounding names became French. We booked the chocolate train from Montreux to the Cailler Chocolate factory in Broc. At the beginning there is a ridiculous film, followed by a factory tour and at the end of the tour we sampled as much chocolate as we could eat. Then the bus took us to the pretty town of Gruyère and the cheese factory.

The next time we visited Switzerland in 2005, we used a 7-night rail pass to go on the famous Glacier Express and also to experience the Bernina Line. We flew into Zurich and started in Lucerne as we had on the previous occasion, but this time we took the William Tell Express

84

from Lucerne. We were handed a souvenir box with a tiny Swiss Army knife and a chocolate. I really wish I'd kept this as they stopped running the service renaming it Gotthard Panoramic Express, the same route, but without the frills. Our trip included a paddle steamer across Lake Lucerne picking up the train again from Ticino to Bellinzano with a connection to Lugano.

Lake Lugano was beautiful. That was our sole visit to the Italian part of Switzerland. There was a funicular up to the top and stunning views over the lake. There are plenty of Italian restaurants so we found eating out considerably cheaper and easier in this part of Switzerland. It was the first time I discovered Chilli oil and I have been using it ever since.

Our trip included a little coach trip round Lake Como which was gorgeous. I have never stayed at the Italian lakes and it is something I would love to do someday. We took the Bernina Express from Tirano to Chur, the oldest town in Switzerland, then the mountain railway up to Arosa which is a stunning alpine village.

We took the Glacier Express, which is said to be the world's slowest express train, from St. Moritz to Zermatt which was to be our next stop. Reservations are compulsory on the Glacier Express so we booked lunch on the train.

We loved Zermatt. It is so pretty with a chalet style high street. Hotel Allalin looked really uninspiring from the outside but the inside was really cosy and designed in hand-painted and hand-carved wood which smelt new. We took the cog railway up to Gornergrat where we got the best view of the Matterhorn. It was amusing to see how many were wearing sandals to step off the train onto the snow.

Zermatt isn't easily accessible but when we went to get breakfast from the buffet, Jim recognised two guys at a corner table. He actually knew them! They live round the corner from us in Notting Hill.

I won a couple of nights in the Gstaad Palace at an event in 2012 and I also managed to get a free night at the Grand Bellevue. We had never been to Gstaad before and we fancied Wengen, so this time we decided to combine the two. Switzerland had an unexpected heatwave which meant it was very hot and humid, much hotter than on any of our previous visits.

We were pleased we upgraded to a Jungfrau view in Wengen. We had an absolutely stunning view of the Jungfrau and the Eiger, covered in thick snow. We took a little evening walk round the pleasant village. There are a few lovely little bars and restaurants and it had a convivial atmosphere.

We took the little mountain railway further up to Kleine Scheidegg and were shocked to discover how much these railways have increased in price since our previous visit. Kleine Scheidegg is very pretty with lovely views of Jungfrau and the towns and villages below, but it is also very touristy. Japanese tourists were having photographs taken with a St. Bernard dog. We didn't venture up to Jungfrau, the highest station in Europe as it was expensive and we would have needed warmer clothes.

Getting from Wengen to Gstaad is relatively easy and the route took us round the beautiful Lake Thun. We missed our connection so we walked round Spiez which was larger than we expected with many shops. That hour that gave us another opportunity rather than being an hour wasted.

We arrived in Gstaad on a mountain railway from Zweisimmen and walked to our hotel at the edge of the town. Gstaad is larger than Wengen, partly pedestrianised with many designer shops. There was a general feeling of excitement as Gstaad was getting ready for a sports festival week and also the Menuhen Festival. Gstaad has more of a working town feel than that of a mountain or tourist village.

The weather took a turn for the worse with heavy rain and thunderstorms, so we decided to make good use of our time and rail passes by going back to the cheese factory in Gruyère and the Cailler chocolate factory in Broc. We had been before but the factory has been upgraded to a fully interactive experience, so consequently it was much more crowded.

Denmark

In the mid-seventies I booked one of the DFDS mini trips from Harwich to Esbjerg and beyond which included the ferry, rail travel within Denmark and overnight accommodation.

The sea was really rough. After all it was the North Sea in March, so I was pleased when we landed in Esbjerg. The onward rail journey was easy and I had a pleasant overnight stay in Odense, the birthplace and childhood home of Hans Christian Andersen, the Danish author of children's fairy tales.

I found to my surprise that everyone spoke good English and they were so friendly. I got to the Hans Christian Andersen museum when it was just about to close but they kept it open just for me so I whizzed through as quickly as possible. When I got back after 2 days a few people commented on my lack of suntan. That's how little people knew about "abroad" in the seventies.

We planned a treat for Sharon's birthday to Legoland in Denmark in the late eighties. We flew from Southend to Billund. Maersk Air provided a cake which we cut up and sent round the plane and some of the passengers sent her some pocket money back. Things have changed so much since then. We enjoyed our weekend trip. This was long before Legoland Windsor opened so it was a real novelty at the time.

Italy

Neapolitan Riviera

On my Cosmos educational in 1977, we got the ferry across from Sicily to Naples. The drive up the Amalfi Coast was scary but absolutely stunning. We visited Pompeii which was really fascinating and Capri which was beautiful but the crossing was very rough. I loved Sorrento but I've never had the chance to return.

Rome

I won a couple of nights in Rome in 2011. Sharon treated me to the flights for my birthday. This was our first mother and daughter trip and my first trip to Rome.

We didn't arrive until late in the evening, but we managed to see a few of the sights by night. The Pantheon is the most complete ancient Roman building and houses the tomb of Raphael the artist. The Trevi Fountain was incredible and there were quite a few nice and fairly inexpensive places to eat in the area. We chose a nice pizzeria nearby where we sampled the local Pinot Grigio.

The next morning began with a short walk to the Forum, Palatino Hill and The Colosseum. The queue to get in was long and slow. We waited a good hour to buy our combined ticket for the Forum and the Colosseum. It was worth the wait and both are definitely worth seeing. We were pleased we visited the Forum first as the queue for the Colosseum was twice as long.

We treated ourselves to delicious gelatos at the world renowned Old Bridge Gelateria across the road from the Vatican City walls and we had enough time to go to the Spanish Steps which were really crowded.

We planned to go to the catacombs of San Callisto. This proved difficult as there was a metro strike. The Archeobus turned out to be the quickest and most convenient way of getting there. Our tour of the catacombs included an English speaking guide.

I only booked hand luggage but tried to get away with a handbag as well. We encountered a jobsworth at the gate charging a lady in front of me 30 euros. It would be a cold day in hell before I would pay that, so the only solution was to stuff the handbag into the case and wear at least half the contents of the case. I then had to hastily repack once we boarded. Sharon didn't know whether to laugh or disown me!

Tuscany

I was invited by Classic Collection in November 2017 to sample three of the Italian Hospitality Collection spa hotels in Tuscany which are featured in their Italy brochure. I had always perceived spa weekends as an expensive luxury but the weekend taught me that there are many health benefits. Many guests are on medical referrals for breathing and joint problems. I suffer from both, so experiencing the natural thermal waters was truly beneficial.

The Italians are famous for food and wine. We had plenty of opportunities to sample some wonderful cheeses, pasta, fish dishes, juicy olives, wine, Prosecco and their own speciality Tiramisu.

Fonteverde is a converted palace with many original features surrounded by beautiful Tuscan countryside and amazing views. It has seven pools including one for dogs. Even in misty late November there was enough heat from the thermal waters to bathe comfortably outdoors. After a couple of hours I could feel the benefit of the hot water and minerals on my arthritic knees.

Grotta Giusti is a 19th-century villa next to a thermal cave. People with severe breathing difficulties can breathe in the minerals that are present in the caves. The grotto has three sections Paradiso, Purgatorio and Inferno. It is restful and surprisingly easy to breathe down there and upon returning to London I noticed how quickly I became breathless when surrounded by diesel fumes.

Some of the rooms at our last hotel, Bagni di Pisa, have a view of the Leaning Tower of Pisa on the horizon. It has a very unique spa with a very high salt content. There are many different treatments available including a warm salt treatment, floating in a hot salt bath and bubbling pools.

Sicily

Pickfords gave me an educational to Sicily and Sorrento in 1977. This was my first ever trip to Italy. On arrival at Catania airport, we had to hunt around for our suitcases on the tarmac outside in the dark. Fortunately we all ended up with the right luggage. I loved Cefalù which was really pretty, Naxos was more of a resort. We spent up to 8 hours a day on the coach on the motorway without seeing much of interest, just miles of endless barren land.

I went back recently and it is very different now. The airport is a typical European international airport, very bright and modern with numerous shops. Nowadays Taormina is extremely crowded with tourists. Taormina itself is very historic and interesting with a Greek amphitheatre. The tiny cathedral has a sculpture of the Last Supper. The entrances at each end are all that remains of the original walls.

There are many interesting tourist souvenir shops and excellent gelaterias. What I loved about Taormina were the picturesque little alleyways with staircases leading to art shops, churches, gardens and restaurants. From Isola Bella, there are spectacular views of the nearby resorts of Giardini Naxos and Letojanni.

We stayed in a family owned apartment in Recanati, a few miles from Giardini Naxos overlooking Mount Etna. It was surrounded by lemon trees with views of Mount Etna from our balcony. We were lucky enough to have some clear views with snow on the top. 2019 was the first time in 50 years that it snowed in May so that was a real treat. Sometimes there is cloud cover and Etna is either invisible or just a black rock.

We booked Alcantara Gorge and Circumetnia. This was a very long day starting at 6.30am. Alcantara Gorge was worth the entrance fee to see the bottom of the gorge and walk round the gardens. It was a difficult walk with many steep steps and stones but it was worthwhile. On our train journey, we saw an array of bright pink and yellow flowers and vineyards on lava rocks as far as the eye could see. It is amazing how many people live on the slopes of one of the most active volcanoes in the world and how much the little stations along the journey are used by the locals.

Mt. Etna at altitude was freezing so we walked for a while and admired the view below but we searched for a bar just to keep warm. We didn't go all the way to top as it is expensive and even colder.

Sardinia

The Calamosca hotel is on the outskirts of Cagliari. It is barely a 2-star and we call it our Fawlty Towers, but it is so peaceful with a gorgeous view and it is at one end of the long and beautiful Poetto Beach. The menu is so badly translated into English, it is actually easier to read the French menu, but we love its quaintness.

On our next visit, I liked the walled city of Alghero, smaller than Cagliari but very interesting. We discovered an award winning gelateria and treated ourselves to the sweetest, gooiest gelato. It was wonderful!

We took a not quite "pleasure" boat out to the nearby caves. We should have checked the weather first. The sea was extremely choppy, thank goodness it was only 15 minutes. To make the crossing even worse, we were choking on diesel fumes. We couldn't wait to get off at the caves, away from the fumes. One elderly gentleman had so much difficulty getting off, the crew literally pushed him down the ramp!

In September 2019, I was invited on an educational trip to the popular north east. My friend Aida was on the same trip and it was a nice, friendly little group. This proved to be my last fam trip.

Su Gologone, a country hotel, was named after the natural spring in the area. We had a warm welcome and a table of local delicacies and drinks. It is one of the quirkiest, charming and most unusual hotels I've stayed in. This hotel is frequented by celebrities, most famously Richard Gere and Madonna who both have their own rooms. This hotel has an art gallery and workshop, a vegetable garden, a bakery and an exhibition of carnival masks. Every single room is individually designed in different colour schemes, with furniture made from juniper trees and local embroidery. Everything is home cooked and it even has its own bakery and a vegetable garden. We sampled their fennel ravioli which was divine, as well as delicious local cheeses and wine.

O'Dea – A Path Well Travelled

The beach is quite gritty at Due Lune in San Teodoro, but the unusual rock formations are a unique feature. We had the beach to ourselves. A short walk away is a yacht marina, surrounded by bars, restaurants and designer shops.

We enjoyed local Sardinian produce from Insula in Porto Cervo with platters of cheeses, rosemary and olive drizzled crackers and artichokes. Porto Cervo is a port and yacht harbour. Across the bay, there is a pretty designer village, with all the familiar designer labels such as Gucci and Bvlgari. There are bars, restaurants and a summer ferry service which runs across the bay.

We had lunch on the 18-hole Pevero golf course on a fabulous setting with the sea on both sides. We had a lovely light fish taster course, which was beautifully presented, then afterwards, we were taken on a quick buggy tour of the golf course.

Gabbiano Azzurro in Golfo Aranci was fabulous. Our host Antonella was lovely and so accommodating. She gave up her time to interact with us. The beach is soft talcum powder-like sand with clear shallow water where fish swam around my feet as I waded in. We had a sunset stop at Baia Sardinia before our final stop in Olbia City just 15 minutes from the airport.

Our group in Sardinia

Greece

Corfu

I took a real gamble on booking Corfu with Intasun in 1985 as Jim still wasn't keen on "abroad", but in October half term, it was affordable. Greece was so new in the holiday market, I wasn't aware that the weather was unpredictable. It took us 8 hours to get to Corfu as a heavy thunderstorm meant we were unable to land at Corfu's short runway so we had to spend a few hours on the tarmac at Athens.

We arrived in Corfu to discover that half of it was shut, but the Messonghi Beach hotel catered well for children and the girls made friends easily. The sea was crystal clear so we took out a pedalo.

One evening we tried a bar/restaurant with an English entertainer who borrowed Carol. He sat her on the table and then picked up the corner with his teeth and did some Greek dancing with her still on the table. We had a lovely week despite the limited food choices, the hotel literally closing around us and sitting for hours on the airport floor for the delayed 3am flight. It was a much needed break and one that persuaded Jim that "abroad" wasn't that bad after all.

In 1987, we went back to Corfu with Adrian and Cozzer . We stayed in Paleokatstritsa, a really pretty resort in a little B&B right on the seafront. Corfu didn't understand vegetarianism in the eighties so our meals were mostly omelette, carrots and shredded cabbage. This did get rather monotonous.

After a week of omelettes we were all flapping our arms about and clucking like chickens. One day they served Jim a chicken leg.

Adrian with his usual dry sense of humour said;

"Well it doesn't have any meat on it".

He was right, it was all skin and bone.

We hired a car to get around the island, often getting hopelessly lost on dirt tracks. There was no satnav and things weren't always very well signposted. That was all part of the fun.

A friend of ours, Ted the Leg, had been bitten by a dog in the Jasmine Bar in Kassiopi a few months prior to our visit. He had to have several rabies jabs on his return which were really nasty. We decided to pay the bar a visit, just for the photo to show him on our return.

Crete

At the Small Luxury Hotels of the World event, I won 3 nights at any one of their hotels. We chose Crete for our 2011 birthday trip. We instantly fell in love with Elounda, a beautiful and peaceful area of Crete.

The Alexandros family suite in the Elounda Gulf Villas overlooked gardens blooming with bougainvillea, hibiscus, flamboyant and jasmine, the huge infinity pool and the sea beyond. The sun shone and it was still pleasantly warm, a lovely day for the pleasant 2km walk along the waterfront into town.

O'Dea – A Path Well Travelled

We stopped at the Hiona pool bar run by Lali and his wife Karen from Oxford where we had a really pleasant afternoon. Lali and Karen sold the bar and went back to England. The bar is now run by Manos, who is now our friend. One year they merged with the Jungle Bar in the Sunshine Apartments next door but it didn't really work so now they are separated again.

In 2013, we returned to Elounda. Anna had been to Crete before but had never been to Elounda. This was the first time we travelled as a trio. Our flight was delayed by 3 hours so it was very late by the time we arrived. Anna delayed it further by picking up the wrong suitcase, we wondered why the coach was waiting for so long. It turned out that a couple had an identical red suitcase with a Travel Counsellors luggage label, an easy mistake to make.

By the time we arrived it was around 2am and we were dumped on the high road. We were told to walk down the steps. Having been to Elounda many times now, we know the procedure and we know it is perfectly safe but we didn't then. We got to the bottom of the alleyway and I thought I remembered we should be turning right but Jim insisted it was left.

At this point we had a stroke of luck. We bumped into Pat and John from Newcastle who were on their way back to the Hiona and they knew exactly where it was. I had remembered correctly, we should have turned right. It was literally just a few minutes walk. The bar was in darkness. Pat and John and found the key that had been left for us. Pat and John took us to all their favourite haunts, We have remained friends ever since. They visited us in London and we have visited them in Newcastle.

The Hiona has a Greek barbeque night once a week which gives everybody a chance to bond. Manos does his fire dance and he brings in a music and dance trio. In 2013 an English guy called John lived locally with his dog, Boo. John played the guitar and sang a song "Afghanistan" dedicated to his son.

Anna got up towards the end of the night and sang "Big Spender". A Norwegian couple arrived in the middle of her rendition looking for directions. They knew immediately that they would enjoy their holiday amongst us bunch of nutters!

The first of Anna's chair wrecking escapades was in the Skybar watching the sun go down. Jim liked the look of the red Perspex hydraulic chairs which, in theory, gently adjust to your weight. I went up to the bar to order drinks and I heard an almighty crack. Anna sat on the chair awkwardly and snapped it in half. I was crying laughing as Anna held up two bits of broken Perspex. In the second chair wrecking episode she was left holding a piece of canvas in Mario's bar.

Anna went walking on her own and bumped into a man with a German Shepherd puppy. Anna can't resist cats and dogs so she asked the man if his puppy was friendly but she didn't quite catch his reply. The puppy took a fancy to Anna and jumped up.

Then the man said "He make peace"

so she thought: "Oh good, he likes me".

Then she felt a trickle down her leg.

 What the owner had actually said was "He make piss"!

She bumped into him the following year with the now fully grown dog and he had remembered their previous encounter.

We walked into town one evening and Anna after admiring herself in the mirror, decided on a sparkly top. She thought it looked amazing until Jim called her Gary Glitter, I thought it looked more like one of those reflective blankets that are worn after the marathon.

At that point, Jim chipped in with

"Oh yeah, like Jimmy Saville"

The following day, on Anna's birthday, we decided to go for a walk to Plaka which looked as though was just around the bay. We walked for what seemed like forever. Eventually we arrived at an hotel bar where we stopped for a small can of beer which cost a ridiculous amount of money, 10 euros I believe, but we were desperate. We finally reached Plaka which is about 5 miles from Elounda, a long way in the hot midday sun. We stopped for lunch then we had a few drinks in the Spinalonga Tavern. Jim, on seeing the local lager "Fix", asked for 3 pints of Jim'll Fix it. Anna gave him a sideways glance.

After walking all that way we got a cab back. It turned out the cab had a fixed rate of 7 euros. If only we had known! I was wearing a pair of sandals with Velcro which stuck to the carpet and as I got out of the cab, the carpet came with me. It was Anna's turn to start laughing. Jim had a face like thunder. He reckons he can't take us anywhere!. Anna got back to the apartment and the first thing she did was find the Gary Glitter/Jimmy Saville top and chucked it straight in the bin.

One thing you have to expect in a hot climate is the odd cockroach. On one occasion there was a huge one in our room so we called down to reception and they sent up a fishing net. Jim was like a madman, trying to catch this cockroach with a fishing net as it kept outrunning him. I forgot about being freaked out by the giant cockroach as I was being entertained by Jim trying to catch it. He did succeed in the end and thankfully we didn't see any more.

Pat and John suggested the Happy Train which was run by an Englishman called Ziggy. We went through Plaka and up into the hills where there is a stunning view of Spinalonga and Elounda below, then to a disused olive oil factory and a small village raki bar.

Anna wanted to visit Knossos which is near the capital, Heraklion. Our guide was excellent. We wouldn't have had the same experience walking round on our own. It was nice to have the background explained to us properly which gave us a much better understanding.

The main shopping area in Heraklion consists of familiar names like Zara and M&S. There was a good market area which was cheaper than Elounda. We stopped for a cold beer and some street food down a little alleyway frequented by locals. The Minoan show lasted about half an hour or so before our journey home. It was a long day but well worth the money.

We booked a trip to a Santorini. Anna had already been so it was just Jim and I. Our pick up was supposed to be at Samaria bar in Elounda which doesn't actually exist. We hedged our bets and stood at the usual high road coach stop, thinking that it wouldn't be too difficult to spot a coach at 6 am. Despite a raging storm all night, the catamaran crossing was very smooth and it took roughly 3 hours.

Santorini is a stunning island, full of classic picture postcard views of white houses and churches, with blue roofs and ornate gates. It stands on top of volcanoes looking down the cliffs into the Aegean Sea. There were literally thousands of tourists by cruise ship and day trippers from Crete and Mykonos. There are lovely little artisan shops down narrow cobbled alleyways . From Oia we took a short coach ride to Thira, walking the last mile along the picturesque sea road. Thira is bustling with many lively tourist bars and tacky t-shirt shops, but there is also a decent market.

We stayed on a few more days in Hersonissos as, at World Travel Market, I had won a couple of nights at the Royal Aldemar. Hersonissos is much hillier and busier than Elounda but we enjoyed a restful break and swimming in the gorgeous pools.

In 2015, we flew direct to Chania to explore West and Central Crete. We stayed in Platanias, a lovely little place full of good restaurants, almost all centred around the main road and the alleyways leading to the sea. The old village up in the hills has a beautiful sunset view over the resort and the sea.

We found some simple apartments opposite a posh hotel so some of their residents came to our bar. On the night we arrived, we got talking to a Norwegian couple. The lady's name was a Norwegian variation on Anna so they spent the next twenty minutes or so trying to pronounce each other's names.

"I am Anna from Scotland and you are Anna from Norway".

"I am Anna from Norway and you are Anna from Scotland".

Anna from Norway was rather the worse for wear. The apartment owner offered us cake left over from her daughter's birthday. We ate ours. Anna from Norway stubbed her cigarette out in the cake first and then ate it afterwards!!

We were in the Jungle Bar, owned by a British/Greek family. We got talking to them and discovered that West Crete, popular in the eighties and nineties, now had few British visitors and was predominantly Scandinavian.

They had a Norwegian Country and Western singer, who was excellent. Anna disappeared for ages but she does have a habit of chatting to people so we thought nothing of it. What actually happened was that she was locked in the loo just as the singer was singing,

" I hear you Knocking".

The manager eventually did hear her knocking came to her rescue and put the key under the door. To make matters worse she had chosen the Gents!

We took one of several Little Fun Train routes on their Grand Canyon route seeing beautiful scenery, an olive oil factory and fresh fruit and wine on the roadside. Chania Town has many Turkish characteristics. There are some lovely little craft shops along the alleyways, souvenir shops on the seafront and inexpensive bars. We also took the bus the other way to the fishing village of Kolymbari where we had a huge, fresh, delicious seafood lunch.

In Platanias, we discovered a Western Crete vegetarian speciality called Boureki pie in the Carpe Diem restaurant which was delicious. We've had these in many restaurants since but none as good as that one. Rethymnon was very quiet in early June with hardly anything open. Beachside cafés were deserted. We saw some lovely sunsets but there was hardly anywhere open to sit and enjoy them.

O'Dea – A Path Well Travelled

In Elounda there are many ways to explore pastures new, lovely country walks around the bay where the sun sparkles into the clear blue sea or venturing up into the hills, where sheep and goats graze and butterflies flutter.

In 2016, we had an overnight stay in Daios Cove, which was stunning. The room was beautiful. We had our own private pool and a view to die for. It was really lovely to spend the night being spoilt in a luxury hotel. It was also nice to get back to Elounda where we felt more at home.

That year Martin and Eve came to join us so we took them to Spinalonga which has had much restoration and signage work done in recent years, enhancing the experience. We took the ferry back to Plaka so we could explore the lovely little craft shops and visit our favourite restaurants.

It was lovely to see all our friends again, Pat and John from Newcastle, Dave and his family from Manchester, Manos at the Hiona, Costas at the Malibu and Elena at the Garden of Eden.

In 2017, it was a lovely day in London so it meant we didn't need a jacket. Anna turned up all in orange. She asked me to take a picture just by the entrance to the Easyjet area at North Terminal. I posted it with the caption: We won't lose Anna in Easyjet orange! She didn't know whether to kill me or laugh but she didn't wear it again.

We found a nice apartment in Stalis not too far from the centre of town. Anna knew Stalis well and took us to a few of her favourite haunts and we visited nearby Sissi which is very quiet, a pleasant way to spend the afternoon.

We were in a bar in Stalis. Anna went out for a cigarette and got chatting to a Norwegian lady. She asked her name, half expecting it to be another Anna. Her name was Urine. That was definitely taking the p*** and Anna had to run away choking with laughter.

Back in Elounda we met up with Pat and John who took us up to the Raki man. It was a long walk up but the view was amazing.

O'Dea – A Path Well Travelled

The morning before we were due to go home, Jim woke up early and turned the television on to BBC News. Straightaway he realised that one of our local tower blocks was on fire. We soon learnt it was the one Jim almost moved into before we met, Grenfell Tower. Jim ran downstairs and woke Anna up to tell her. We live just yards from Grenfell Tower and we dreaded going home. Notting Hill became a circus for weeks afterwards as tourists and entire families as well as the press came from everywhere with cameras to look at all that remained of Grenfell Tower. We are still looking at the now covered building nearly 4 years later every time we leave the house.

In 2019, my friend and colleague Gill Nicholls was staying in the same hotel as us, the Akti Olous with some of her family and friends celebrating her cousin's special birthday, the start of the never ending big birthday that went on for months. Thank goodness that was in 2019 so they could celebrate their respective birthdays.

On that occasion we discovered the Paradisos Taverna. It has always been there but we just didn't find it before, a hidden gem with a beautiful view over the bay. This time we spent longer in Spinalonga Tavern enjoying the view across to Spinalonga. From there we got a cab up to Beeraki to meet our friends John, Dave and his family. The view from Beeraki is absolutely stunning and we had a wonderful afternoon.

It was a real lazy week, mainly walking round to Elounda Island Villas, enjoying some green tea, Jim reading a book and me working. I am looking forward to going back for a real holiday and not having to do any work.

Anna and I in Chania

Athens

I was offered an educational trip to Athens in December 2012. Before I went, my family and friends, even some in the travel industry were full of scepticism about austerity and riots. Our approach to Athens airport revealed a clear blue sea, the lovely coastline of the Athenian Riviera and the city itself as the light was fading into dusk.

Our hotel, NJV Athens Plaza, was situated in Syntagma Square, the home of the impressive Parliament building which occupies one side of the square. We went for a long walk around the city. After the Olympics in 2004, pedestrianised streets were created around the

Acropolis making it a pleasant city to meander through and browse round the shops, find a restaurant or bar and soak up the culture.

 The new airport, a decent metro and tram system were all created for the Olympics and made Athens a clean and pleasant city with a good infrastructure. I was surprised how little traffic there was.

Sofia, our guide, had so much knowledge and passion and spoke excellent English. We couldn't have had a more perfect guide for the weekend. After a whistle stop tour of the city which included the impressive ancient Olympic stadium seating 80,000, we had a luxury hotel to visit at Cape Sounio which is only half an hour from the airport but we took the longer scenic coast road until we could see the Temple of Poseidon getting closer.

We were blessed with unusually good weather, not too hot for our visit to Temple of Poseidon, which is impressive and well preserved. Poseidon was the God of the Sea so naturally the temple has a stunning view of the bay, the port and the beaches.

Many ruins and artefacts were discovered when the old army building was demolished to make way for the new Acropolis museum. The original foundations are visible underneath the glass floors. This museum displays what remains of the famous marbles which Lord Elgin sold to the British Museum. There are plaster casts of the ones in the British Museum to complete the jigsaw of the story that once belonged round the top of the Parthenon.

From a distance the Parthenon looks small and covered in scaffolding. Close up, it is immense and it is easier to visualise the magnificence of the palace it once was. The Parthenon suffered damage in the middle ages when the Phoenicians blew it up. Only one side of it is reasonably well preserved. The scaffolding keeps it structurally sound and prevents further erosion so future generations will be able to enjoy it. On one side of the Acropolis is the world's first theatre. The arena is still clearly visible today.

O'Dea – A Path Well Travelled
Descending the grand marble steps from the Parthenon and The Erechtheion was treacherous as it was raining heavily. We walked through the old part of the city having lunch at St George Lycabettus overlooking the Parthenon in the twilight before heading back to the airport.

Our group in Cape Sounio

Cyprus

Cyprus manages to be both Greek and British and also uniquely Cypriot. Only Cyprus has bought halloumi, lountza, Commanderia wine and Keo lager to the world. The language, religion, architecture and culture are definitely Greek. They drive on the left with easy road signs in English and Greek and they use 3-pin plugs. Familiar names like Debenhams, Next and KFC exist alongside opticians and Greek restaurants.

O'Dea – A Path Well Travelled

We enjoyed our week in Paphos and took the girls several times to the lovely, safe, sheltered beach at Coral Bay. The first time we booked the tour of the old Sodap winery. It was old and dilapidated but I really enjoyed the local wine from there. The old winery was sold off to developers and it is now the new Amavi hotel and a luxury apartment complex. The winery is now situated in Kamanterena 12 miles inland from its original location.

On Jim's 50th birthday, Cozzer and Adrian came with our family. We discovered the Piano Bar where we celebrated his big birthday and we enjoyed a few more nights there but it has long since disappeared.

We liked the Romantica Italian restaurant on Poseidonos Avenue. On that occasion it could have turned nasty. We were enjoying our dinner when a gentleman started choking. Nobody knew what to do and Jim rushed straight over and tried the Heimlich manoeuvre on him and thankfully it worked. The offending piece of steak dislodged and he started to get some colour back in his face. We ended up having our meal paid for that night.

On one occasion we were coming back from Paphos and had checked in. We were making our way to the lounge when we heard a big commotion. A couple of airport staff chased us and invited us through the baggage belt onto the runway where to my horror I saw my suitcase ripped open with my clothes and underwear strewn everywhere. I was absolutely mortified as I literally chased my knickers along the runway. Hastily stuffing everything back into the suitcase I had an instant headache as the ground handlers patched up my suitcase with gaffer tape. On arrival at Luton we disappeared into a café and waited until everyone else had already picked up their suitcases. We were too embarrassed to pick ours up in front of everybody.

At the tail end of the nineties, we thought we would try Protaras for a change, as it was cheaper than Paphos. We hoped we would still get decent weather on October half term. Indeed the weather in Protaras was glorious but unfortunately for us, the weather all over the UK was horrendous, so bad in fact, our plane couldn't take off from London so we were initially delayed by 6 hours.

The crew were out of hours, so we waited for a new crew. Finally we took off then we hit 100 mph crosswinds on our approach to Gatwick. We were just yards from the runway but we couldn't land. Sharply and suddenly we went back up into the air. It was horrendous. The toilets were out of use as so many passengers were sick. We arrived into Manchester. Snow was on the ground. They left us on the ground for 4 hours with no food or luggage, so we were tired, hungry and freezing. Most of us were just wrapped in the lime green jmc blankets from the aircraft. Eventually, they decided to take us back by coach.

We stopped in Birmingham where I found a telephone, and called Sue to tell her why I couldn't get to work. The coach was taking us back to Gatwick but we went round the M25 to get there so that took us to the Hounslow area. We asked if we could get off there along with a family of 12 that literally lived in Uxbridge but the driver wouldn't offload our luggage so we had to sit on that coach for another 2 hours. We finally arrived into Gatwick 27 hours late.

In spring 2011 after a wet winter, Cyprus was unusually green. Blossoms were everywhere. It was already very warm. We were invited by Thanos hotels, staying at the Anassa which is absolutely stunning and overlooks the beautiful Akamas Peninsula. The food was outstanding and beautifully presented. Latchi was a small fishing village, now it is a yacht harbour so consequently prices are higher in this part of Cyprus. It is very pretty with a pleasant ambience and many fish restaurants. We were able to combine this with 7 nights of accommodation I had won in Pissouri and Limassol, a couple of nights at Aphrodite Hills and an invitation to the Elysium in Paphos to make up a 2-week stay.

The city of Limassol is the second largest city and the main port, halfway between Paphos and Larnaca. The main strip of hotels is on the outskirts on a lovely strip of beach. Old Limassol has many archaeological remains. A great deal of work had been done to improve the harbour and the new promenade stretches for miles. We visited an old monastery, a winery and Curium just outside Limassol. This is a famous Roman amphitheatre, well-preserved and surrounded by beautiful mosaics.

Pissouri is almost exactly halfway between Paphos and Limassol, half an hour drive from either. The more attractive old road is still there. Pissouri is a small resort with a handful of tourist shops and restaurants. The beach is pebble and not very attractive, however, it is very peaceful with a Cypriot feel. The sky at night gives a fabulous vista of stars. We had a lovely room in the Columbia Beach hotel overlooking Pissouri Bay. The original village of Pissouri is a few kilometres up steep hills. It has a few tavernas where the prices are lower than those by the sea.

Aphrodite Hills has its own village with various shops and restaurants and its own golf course. Each night out of season they open a different restaurant or bar so we tried a couple of different ones. On St Patrick's Day, the Irish bar opened so we had a good evening despite it being almost empty.

We had lunch on the beach at the Annabelle which had recently been fully refurbished. They had Greek dancers to entertain us, then we did a site inspection at the Almyra and we sampled some delicious desserts. I hadn't visited Paphos for 11 years so I was a little apprehensive of how much it might have changed. I needn't have worried as the main road hadn't changed much and I remembered many of the restaurants there. The promenade along the front and harbour area was a vast improvement to the rocks and rubble that were there before. As well as some new builds, many of the older hotels had been thoughtfully renovated giving Paphos a smart, new feel

We gratefully accepted an invitation which my friend Gabi Birbeck had arranged with Stademos Hotels. We stayed at the Elysium which is absolutely stunning, about a half an hour stroll along the beach and walkway to the harbour.

O'Dea – A Path Well Travelled

In 2013 I went to Paphos twice, the first visit was in March, another invitation from Gabi to the Elysium and another few nights at Athena Beach which my friend Marie arranged for us.

Despite having been to Paphos many times before, there were still places I hadn't seen and the first of those was Neophytos monastery with its ancient frescoes and museum. We enjoyed a local Cypriot meal with wine in Phyti and watched the locals making lace tablecloths. After lunch, we visited the Temple of Aphrodite, which was very interesting. The sun was setting over Rock of Aphrodite, the best time to see it.

I had been to Kykkos monastery before but not for many years. The coach journey seemed to last for ever as the coach wound its way round the Troodos mountains, Kykkos's gold and silver chandeliers and its beautiful frescoes are absolutely stunning.

On the way, we stopped at the picturesque village of Omodhos and Lambouris winery near Platres. Pambos, the owner of the winery, spoke in such an expressive, passionate, entertaining and humorous way in perfect English. He can also do the same in German, so talented and unforgettable. We tasted lovely wines, both local and blended varieties, available to buy at reasonable prices.

The House of Dionysos and the ancient sites of Paphos are now deservedly a UNESCO World Heritage Site. The ancient capital of Paphos has so much to showcase in a small area. It is worth seeing the well preserved mosaics, describing stories of Greek mythology in small pebbles and tiles. Tombs of the Kings was a new experience. Somehow we had never got round to visiting it beforehand.

Theo's on Paphos harbourfront must surely be one of the best fish restaurants on earth. It seemed that every possible sea creature was served to us in an endless stream of tempting seafood dishes ranging from the smallest whitebait to melt in the mouth sea bream.

In 2015, we were invited to stay at the Mediterranean Beach in Limassol as the base for our Agents' Appreciation Weekend rather than the Elysium in Paphos and as usual we got to see some of my lovely travel friends. It was April so we had the bonus of even better weather. On that occasion, a few of us travelled together on the same British Airways flights, Gillian and Steve, Gail and Dennis, Lesley and Kevin and Karen and Graham.

Mediterranean Beach is part of the Stademos Group so we knew we would be well looked after. The excursion that was organised for us on that occasion was to Larnaca which was a pleasant surprise for all of us. The beachfront area has a nice resort feel despite being one of the largest cities.

We are always guaranteed a good stay at Athena Beach. This time we were allocated the pool suites. The bravest of us, including me, got in and had a swim. It was good for the circulation, in other words, freezing! As we were all in the same row of pool suites, it meant we could get together in one of our rooms and have pool parties on the terrace.

Using the new Blue Air flight service from Luton to Larnaca in 2016, we picked up our hire car in Larnaca. One of the benefits of the EU was being able to use free data on my phone to get to the Makronissos an area of Ayia Napa. This area was a real surprise to me as I had not expected it to be so family friendly.

We last visited Coral Bay over 30 years ago when the girls were small. It was lovely to see that the small area around the bay has hardly changed but further along, a "town" has sprung up complete with flashing lights and tacky discos but this is about a mile away from the hotels. It is nice to have a choice of entertainment by night and the quiet bay for chilling and relaxing by day. We did found a couple of decent, inexpensive bars in amongst some not so good ones.

I have been to Paphos and other parts of Cyprus many times but I had never before had the chance to join in their traditional Easter celebrations. Greek orthodox Easter or Pasxa, is nearly always on different dates than in the UK and in 2018, it happened to be the week after our own Easter. We were privileged to be invited by Constantinou Bros to join in their Easter celebrations, staying in the fabulous Asimina Suites and visiting their portfolio.

Easter is the biggest celebration of the year in Cyprus and as the weather is mild, celebrations can be outdoors as well as inside the church. In Cyprus they have many traditions so it was interesting to join in and celebrate Easter with the locals. The celebration of the risen Christ is more significant than the birth of Christ in the Greek Orthodox religion.

The streets are decorated with huge eggs and bunnies. Every hotel has decorations in their foyers, just as we do at Christmas in the UK. On Great Friday, the hotel was already preparing Tsoureki bread outside on the barbecue ready for the guests on Sunday. Traditionally the Tsoureki and the eggs are prepared on Great Friday prior to the church service at 7pm. The Great Friday evening mass is followed by the Ephitafios, a procession carrying the body of Christ through the streets.

On Saturday we visited the Greek Orthodox, Timios Stavros monastery in Omodos. Our guide told us about the monastery and the services and traditions over Easter. Great Friday is a day of sorrow, Holy Saturday is when bay leaves, laurel leaves and flower petals are spread around the church and Holy Sunday is when Christ is risen - Xristos Anesti - and the feast begins.

Saints have a much bigger significance in the Greek Orthodox religion. All baptised Greeks are named after saints. Greeks celebrate their own saint's day as well as their birthdays.

Omodos was extremely busy and already a huge bonfire was piled high, ready to light and burn an effigy of Judas Iscariot, after which there is a midnight mass when candles are lit. Immediately after midnight, everything closes down.

During Lent, Greeks don't have any meat or dairy. The feast begins immediately after midnight with Magiritsa soup made from the offal of a lamb or goat, then a traditional Easter Sunday breakfast consists of red coloured hard boiled eggs. The dyed red eggs represent the tomb being opened – they are dyed red using onion skins to represent the blood of Christ. Tsoureki is a bread containing cheese, Fanta Orange and mint, covered in toasted sesame seeds. It is a strange taste sensation, both sweet and savoury. Lunch consists of a spit roasted lamb or goat to celebrate the Lamb of God.

They play a game similar to conkers. Whoever has the last uncracked egg will have good luck for the year. We enjoyed celebrating Easter with the Cypriots. It was much more meaningful than a Cadbury's Egg and a bunch of daffodils.

In 2019, Jim and I got a brilliant deal for The Annabelle in Paphos. It was many years since we last saw the Annabelle and we liked being right in the centre. On this occasion, we discovered a bar called The Bottle Bank. We went there several times and won four or five of their t-shirts, either for dancing or singing karaoke.

Me and my friends near Larnaca

Top - Marie Rayner, Lesley Clements. Katrina Angel, Gillian Davis, me

Bottom – Zoe Herbert, Gail O'Donohue

Portugal

I was offered an educational trip to Lisbon in 2011. There were 45 of us altogether from Brazil and all over Europe. There were five Travel Counsellors, Barbara, Donna, Marina, Simone and me.

The Parque das Nações, originally a barren wasteland, was transformed for the Lisbon Expo 1998, into a conference centre, an aquarium, cable cars, many fine restaurants, landscaped gardens and a couple of hotels. The Oceanarium of Lisbon is the best I have seen anywhere in the world.

O'Dea – A Path Well Travelled

In the main square, a row of Red Tour Electric Vehicles were ready for our afternoon treat, a self-drive guided GPS fun tour of Lisbon. As we were in a group, we were guided by motor bike in a convoy. After an hour of noisy hooters being let loose round the city we got back to where we started. That was fun!

Our next ride was more sedate on one of Lisbon's classic trams. This mostly followed the scenic route 28 going through picturesque narrow streets to the Castelo de Jorge where we watched the sun set over the city and the silhouette of Christ the King over the other side of the estuary.

25 de Abril bridge looks a bit like Golden Gate Bridge in San Francisco. We passed the yacht harbour and the much photographed Monument of Discovery. Nearby is the iconic Tower of Belem and then the monastery which has been converted into two museums. The House of Braganza is where the Tombs of the Kings are situated.

Lisbon is proud of the biplane that was flown by Coutinho and Cabral across the Atlantic from Lisbon to Rio de Janeiro in 1922, however, it wasn't non-stop, so it was Lindbergh's shorter crossing from New York to Paris five years later that made it into the record books.

We drove along the sandy coast road past the beach of Carcavelos, a mecca for surfers in the autumn and winter when the Atlantic waves are at their wildest, past the busy town of Cascais, the expensive villas in Estoril and finally to the westernmost point of the whole of Europe. We were given a certificate to prove it, complete with a proper wax seal. The monument isn't particularly attractive but the lighthouse on the rocks and the beautiful green countryside surrounding it are well worth the visit.

Sintra Palace is a very interesting and impressive ancient palace with a mixture of styles including intricate Moorish details and medieval stonework. We had lunch there and afterwards we had time to visit the magnificent palace.

O'Dea – A Path Well Travelled

In the evening we had tickets for Fado which is an ancient Portuguese type of singing from the soul accompanied by a classical 12-string guitar and a Fado guitar which sounds rather like a Bouzouki but looks more like a large mandolin with extra strings. Fado is a UNESCO World Heritage experience.

Simone Taylor-Gray, Marina Simioli. Donna Puffett and Barbara O'Neil on the Lisbon Tram

The Azores

At the World Travel Market, I won a week's holiday for two people including flights on SATA the airline of the Azores with 2 nights on the coast. We booked our remaining five nights in the Talisman in the capital, Ponta Delgada.

The prize had to be taken out of season so it wasn't very warm and there wasn't much open, so it was a little too quiet. São Miguel, the main island is very green and pretty. Ponta Delgada, the capital has

114

Portuguese style mosaic-tiled narrow streets and distinctive whitewashed architecture trimmed with black volcanic stone.

We took the local bus to Villa Franca and to Ribeira. The service is limited in winter so we had to keep a careful eye on the timetables

We booked a couple of trips during our stay to see the best of the island, the tea and banana plantations and the fascinating volcanic activity, thermal lakes, bubbling mud streams and Furnas, underground cooking holes.

The hotel for the last 2 nights on the coast was lovely, but there was absolutely nothing open in resort. Colleagues of mine went later in the season and they managed to do much more than we did, including whale watching and island hopping, but I still consider myself extremely lucky to have experienced São Miguel, the remote and unique Portuguese island in the middle of the Atlantic.

The Netherlands

In 1991, our local girls club booked a trip to Amsterdam. We went by coach and ferry with Travelscene. I had just discovered that I was expecting my surprise third child and I really wasn't sure whether the North Sea and morning sickness were a good combination but the girls were looking forward to it and I didn't want to let them down. Jeanette "Jean" Joynson persuaded me to go.

We included Keukenhof Bulbfields with a rainbow of beautiful tulips and a cheese factory which came as part of the deal. Sharon has always hated cheese, everything about cheese, the smell, the texture, even just the thought of cheese, but Carol loved cheese. I guess you could say they were chalk and cheese. Sharon's face literally went green so I took her outside while Carol stayed with her cheese loving friends.

The grown-ups, myself, Vivien, Marion and Lynda explored the nightlife in the city while the girls planned a pyjama party in one of the hotel rooms. Jeanette wasn't at all happy but the girls enjoyed their pyjama party without their boring mums interfering and we had a fun night too without the girls.

Despite my family being spread over London, Cheshire and Yorkshire it was easy to organise a weekend for Martin's 21st for seven of us consisting of an age range of 20-67. Anna and Cozzer came along too. This was the last time all five of our family have travelled together.

Anna had booked assistance on arrival in Amsterdam but couldn't be bothered to wait for it as she was desperate for a smoke, but she left us bag sitting. We got on the trolley ourselves and scoured Amsterdam airport looking in every nook and cranny including the toilets. She had somehow managed to get through passport control and outside. Her passport was still in the bag we were minding. So much for security!

We booked the Botel, firstly because it was cheap and secondly we thought it would be a bit of a novelty. Botel used to be near Centraal Station but it has since moved to NDSM Wharf on the other side of the IJ river which is less convenient.

The Botel was basic, but better than many of the small B&B's in the centre of town. The sunsets across the IJ on both nights were spectacular. There was a bar boat and restaurant opposite the Botel and another bar/restaurant round the corner by the ferry so even though Botel isn't in the centre of town, it isn't totally cut off from civilisation either.

We took the ferry over on a cold, crisp, sunny day to Centraal Station. We walked along Damrak which is the main shopping street of Amsterdam, past Dam Square which had a weekend funfair.

We headed towards the flower market which had many tulips and other beautiful bulbs of every possible colour and many different varieties of cannabis seed. There were shops selling Gouda, furry clog slippers and woolly hats.

The Van Gogh Museum was temporarily inside the Hermitage museum along with "The Impressionists" exhibition. Our ticket was a double one, covering Van Gogh and Hermitage. Both museums were very interesting with original works by Van Gogh, Renoir, Gaugin and Cezanne. I love Van Gogh's paintings and the museum houses many of his lesser known works which we hadn't previously seen.

We noticed a nice pub near Dam Square called the Old Bell so we stopped for lunch and drank to our missing friend Adrian Bell who had other commitments and couldn't come with us. We strolled along Singel which has the tall, skinny houses that are characteristic of the city. We walked through parts of the Red Light District before finding a nice bar close to Centraal Station so we could time our last ferry back.

It was showery and we decided after many miles of walking around, a nice leisurely canal boat ride would be a pleasant way to spend an hour or so. We took the museum route on the Lover's cruise past the Ann Frank House which had a massive queue, past the Rijksmuseum, the Science museum and the clipper ship.

There is more to Amsterdam than canals and coffee shops. Amsterdam had plenty to suit all of us. On the way back we lost Anna again at the airport. This time we found her happily browsing in the duty free shop just as we were on the verge of abandoning her.

In November 2019, we stayed in the really pretty, less touristy area, Jordaan, still only minutes away from the centre, either walking or by tram. It's a great area to be, to enjoy the ambience and experience life with the locals.

We were lucky with the weather and although cold in November, it was dry for most of the weekend. Even if it rains there are many museums and shopping centres.

We enjoyed a long walk around the canals, avoiding the bikes along the way, finishing up in the flower market and stocking up on colourful tulips which I enjoyed in my garden last spring and they came up again this year. We were pleasantly surprised that bars have introduced a no smoking ban. Enjoying a quiet pint is a much more pleasant experience these days.

O'Dea – A Path Well Travelled

We went on the brunch boat which includes late breakfast and a couple of drinks. It was a really relaxing and a pleasant way to spend a couple of hours. The route is random and doesn't necessary cover all the tourist spots. We meandered under many of the 300-year old bridges, passing houseboats along the way.

Afterwards, we discovered the traditional and bizarre, Zwarte Piet parade, a yearly tradition of the arrival of Sinterklaas at the start of the festive season. Men with blackened faces dress in medieval clothing, abseil down from a building. Others in similar attire hand tiny biscuits out to the children in the crowd. The chef ices a cake on centre stage, Christmas floats skirt around the edge. The medieval people juggle candy striped sticks and finally the children cheer with delight as Sinterklaas arrives and waves to the crowd.

Despite having visited Amsterdam twice previously, I hadn't succeeded in booking the Ann Frank House. This time it was on my agenda. It is an audio guide tour intended to reflect in deep thought what this family and many others like them endured during the war so it is right to feel this experience without any selfies and to leave feeling humbled and speechless. Many won't visit the house as they feel it is too depressing. I thought it was very interesting and it took a good hour to get round the museum and listen to the audio tour. For the Frank family and their companions, their only crime was to be born into the Jewish faith but this young girl wanted to be a writer. She was an ordinary teenager with hopes and ambitions for her future. This really came across in the film at the end.

Our girls in Amsterdam Diana Marsh, Sharon O'Dea,
Carol O'Dea (now Ferro) and Patricia Murphy

Austria

Salzburg is a beautiful city surrounded by lakes and mountains. We ended up on "The Sound of Music" tour with a coachload of American and Japanese tourists singing all the songs from the movie. It was ever so tacky but such fun and so scenic. We had a packet of edelweiss seeds to take home, but sadly they never thrived in our window box.

I won a weekend break to Vienna with Cresta in the eighties. I had never been to Vienna so we were very excited. I loved Vienna but it was December and it was freezing. That didn't stop us going round the best flea market I've ever seen. There was also a huge fruit and veg market with fresh looking vegetables which I'd never seen before.

Sharon wanted to treat me to a European city break for my birthday in 2015. Going to Vienna gave us the added opportunity to go to Bratislava in Slovakia which neither of us had visited before.

The weather was similar to London, autumnal, not too cold with a little rain on the last afternoon. This was perfect for a city visit, and there was plenty to do, rain or shine. Since our first morning was sunny, we walked round the centre. We enjoyed our ride on the Ring Tram which took half an hour and included an audio guide, a quick but comprehensive overview of Vienna.

We ended up in a Wine Village called Grinzing. There are many restaurants and wine tasting opportunities there. We avoided the ones with the coaches outside opting for one opposite. We decided on a "Scenic" Danube Cruise. Leisurely might have been accurate but it certainly wasn't scenic. The "scenery" is very industrial and there are far better ways to spend 2-3 hours.

We took the metro to Schönbrunn Palace. There is an audio self-guide tour round the 40 staterooms. The staterooms are all very different and the history of the Austrian Royal Family is fascinating. The grounds around Schönbrunn Palace are surrounded by a huge park, the zoo, a Marionette Theatre, and the Orangery. We could have spent all day there if only we had had more time, but we were eager to get back and see more of the city.

By the time we got back it was raining heavily, although there is still plenty to do. We started with one of the famous coffee shops, Gerstner, which was established in 1847. It was more affordable than we expected for coffee and a slice of Sacher Torte. We didn't linger for too long as we had a bewildering choice of museums to choose from. We chose Albertina as it was nearby and the impressionist artwork appealed to us. There are many famous impressionists displayed, Picasso,

Cezanne, Monet, Goya, Müller, to name just a few and there was also an Edvard Munch exhibition of woodcuts which was very interesting.

Mariahilferstraße, the main pedestrianised shopping street, has the usual high street stores that are familiar in any European city. The favourable Euro rate in 2015 made things better value than in the UK.

Norway

Bergen is a beautiful city, so clean and fresh with lovely walks in the woods. I never did get to see the Northern Lights which was always on my wish list, but we did get to see the midnight sun on that trip. Even as far south as Bergen is, it only gets dark for 3-4 hours in the height of summer. It was really difficult to sleep and it was weird coming out of the pub when it was still light.

We booked "Norway in a Nutshell", which consisted of a boat round the fjords, the picturesque mountain railway up to Flåm and the coach back. This included Huldra the forest spirit from Norse mythology singing from the waterfall which is a unique experience. We stood on the beach at Gudvangen with mountains in the distance, another unusual experience. We took the funicular railway up to the top of Bergen where there were different hiking trails but we were happy just to relax and enjoy the breathtaking views below.

I was offered an Inghams educational in September 2019. There were only four of us, all from different independent agencies and our hosts from Inghams. Sasha Darling and Julie Franklin. Our home for 3 nights was the Alexandra, an historic hotel in Loen in the UNESCO World Heritage area of the Norwegian Fjords between Ålesund and Bergen. It was a long transfer and included a short stop in the pretty town of Ålesund. After the long journey, we welcomed our buffet dinner which consisted of a mountain of fresh fish and irresistible desserts.

After breakfast, our guide took us on the Troll cars. These are rather like dune buggies and each one takes six passengers. We meandered up the mountain underneath the huge and powerful waterfall to the

Briksdal Glacier in Jostedalsbreen National Park. Although Njordfjord glacier has shrunk in the last hundred years, it is still truly spectacular.

Afterwards, we went on an easy hike in Nesdal. We learned that the beautiful serene Lovatnet lake had been the scene of two terrible tsunamis in 1905 and 1936, both caused by avalanches. All the houses were devastated and a boat ended up inland a long way from the lake. It is still there today, in memory of those who died.

The brand new Loen Skylift, was a short walking distance from our hotel. The cable car is a smooth 5 minute ride up to the top of Mount Hoven at 1100m. There is a spectacular view of Lake Lovatnet below and Mount Skala. While most of the group undertook one of the hiking trails, Caroline and I enjoyed a Varmschokolade and we talked to some passengers on the Silversea cruise ship docked below. After the other four returned from the hike, we experienced the welcoming hospitality from the Hoven café and restaurant and sampled a traditional but very weird brown cheese waffle. Back at the hotel I enjoyed the outdoor thermal pool and jacuzzi which did my aching joints the world of good.

Germany

I won an eight night educational to Germany. It was my first visit there. During that trip, we covered Düsseldorf, Cologne, Hanover, Hamburg and Munster. The highlight of the trip was the Hanover Expo of 2000. It was my only visit to a World Expo. The Expo 2000 had an emphasis on new technology and innovation.

Hannover had a walking trail called the Red Thread. It looked as though it had been painted by a drunkard at 2am but it was good way of seeing the highlights of the city and I loved the tidy gardens too. I would love to revisit the quaint medieval town of Münster. We took a weekend break to Berlin on a freezing winter weekend. Central Europe can be bitterly cold in the winter. We took a Ryanair flight to Schönefeld. A temporary bus was running into the city. It took a while for us to work this out as neither of us speak German. Although the Berlin Wall had been demolished 3 years previously, there was still a definite contrast between East and West.

Most of the U-Bahn lines were in the West so getting around East Berlin was still awkward but Berlin has the advantage of being flat with wide pavements so it is easily walkable but on that occasion it was so cold and the roads were icy. We had always intended to go back to Berlin in summer. We eventually did that in 2019.

At a German Tourist Board and Eurowings event which happened to be on my birthday in 2018 we had a delicious lunch with a presentation and a quiz afterwards. I won 2 flights to Düsseldorf and one night at the Me and All Hotel, a quirky design hotel. Rather than just using the flights for a weekend break to Düsseldorf we wanted to extend our trip so we could see more of Germany using the railways. Eurowings allowed us to change the return flight to return from Berlin instead. We planned to spend 2 nights each in Düsseldorf, Leipzig, Dresden and Berlin.

It is many years since I last visited Düsseldorf and one thing that stuck in my mind from my previous trip was the Stadterhebungsmonument which I really wanted to revisit. It is amazing, smaller than I had remembered somehow, but I could spend hours studying every tiny detail of the bronze monument depicting the Battle of Worrington in 1288.

The hub of Düsseldorf is Alstadt on the riverbank which was extra busy on the weekend we were there, due to the 18th French classic car rally, an added bonus to our weekend in Düsseldorf with highly prized and polished French classic cars, Citroëns, Peugeots and Renaults, which brought back nostalgic memories of summers spent with my grandmother in Velennes, when baguettes were delivered in very battered but seemingly indestructible Citroën 2cv vans.

We took the hop on hop off bus which stops at seven points in the city. The commentary was clear and interesting. The Alstadt stop was closed for the rally so we had to do a bit of rejigging, but in doing so, we discovered things we wouldn't have noticed on the bus.

Another surprising feature of Düsseldorf is Königsallee, a tree-lined canal, with many little bridges, a haven of peace and tranquility right in the heart of the city. It isn't pedestrianised but there is hardly any traffic. That afternoon we used our KD Rhine line 1-hour Panoramic cruise which was included in our prize. The commentary was in both German and English and easy to follow.

Düsseldorf is a lively city with a great choice of bars, restaurants and fast food with prices similar to London. It is a good city for shopping with designer shops and department stores throughout the city. I had a completely different impression of Düsseldorf than I did after my last visit and we would definitely return.

In the seventies, BA had a very limited service to cover the big yearly trade fair in Leipzig, otherwise it was really difficult to get to as it was on the "wrong" side of the Berlin Wall. There are no direct flights from the UK but links by train and domestic aircraft are excellent. We reached Leipzig on a small turboprop from Düsseldorf. When we first arrived there were a few dodgy characters hanging round the station and we did feel a little uneasy but as soon as we walked into the city centre, just a few minutes away, it was fine with families happily walking and cycling around.

The thing that impressed me most about Leipzig, was the architecture, much of it carefully preserved from the turn of the 20th-century. The new university church in Augustusplatz is interesting. The original church survived World War II but it was dynamited in 1968 under communist rule. It has recently been rebuilt in the shape of the old church with a modern blue, mosaic effect facade. Leipzig has some amazing urban art on the sides of the Marriott Hotel and La Boum cocktail bar

In the main square is the impressive Frauenkirche, Nearby there are many characteristic blackened buildings, caused by a natural process of the sandstone used in the architecture blackening over the decades. Many of the buildings have ornate sculptures, some of which are decorated with gold. It is easy to walk to Zwinger Palace which is well worth seeing.

The train to Dresden is about an hour. Central Dresden can easily be explored on foot as large areas are pedestrianised. As soon as we stepped out of the station, there is a really lovely feel about Dresden. It is green and spotlessly clean.

The bus tour was in German so it wasn't my wisest decision. The few highlights were the Blue Wonder Bridge, Großen Garten, a huge park, zoo and botanical gardens on the Elbe, the 1880 dairy with its famous tiles and the brush shop next door. However, all these things are on the tram routes.

There are tourist boats on the Elbe but these are pricey and the area is very touristy with many tour groups so we decided against it. North of the river, a short walk over the bridge, is the gold horseman statue of Frid Augustus II, Elector of Saxony. The Markt Halle sells everything from fruit and veg to high quality crafts. It is much quieter there than in busy Alstadt where all the tourists are, so it is a pleasant area to enjoy a beer.

We got to the station early only to discover that our train to Berlin was delayed by over an hour. We were surprised, knowing how efficient Germany normally is. We sat patiently on the platform for nearly an hour and a half in the hot summer sunshine. The train that arrived was ancient and Czech rather than German. Luckily it wasn't full so we still managed to get seats but it wasn't very pleasant nor fragrant for that matter.

It was a long time since we were last in Berlin. In fact it was so long ago that my few grainy pictures were taken on an old film camera. East and West were still very clearly defined. Now a couple of decades later, there is no longer a definite East and West Berlin. Germany's bustling capital city is one united Berlin with a fully integrated transport system.

We stayed near Potsdamer Platz, a 15-minute walk from Checkpoint Charlie. We were surprised at how residential Berlin is, even in really central areas there are many parks and green spaces.

On a sunny Berlin morning and a forecast of rain in the afternoon, careful planning was needed, outdoors in the morning and indoors in the afternoon. We had prebooked Bundestag, which is free but must be prebooked. We forgot to bring the necessary ID for entry, but they checked us out with security questions and let us in regardless. Bundestag is close to the Brandenberg Gate and Tiergarten so a good few hours could be spent in that area of Berlin. We headed to Alexanderplatz, TV Tower and the beautiful Neptune fountain in the middle of the park. Just a short walk away is the river, museum island and the cathedral. With black clouds looming overhead it was time to discover a couple of Berlin's museums, shopping and bars. Berlin has many interesting and quirky museums, many on various aspects of its chequered history and there are some fabulous art galleries and fine examples of street art.

Montenegro

One of my most memorable trips was a 7-night trip for two to Montenegro. This was just after the end of the Yugoslav war. Montenegro was a new country. There were no direct flights and there still aren't many. We flew to Tivat via Belgrade with JAT. That was an experience I wouldn't want to repeat and never will as JAT no longer exists. We got to Belgrade which was very confusing. We couldn't get any help as nobody spoke English. We were directed to a gate for our Tivat flight but the gate indicated Thessaloniki. Eventually we found the right gate but we nearly missed our flight. We received a much warmer welcome at Tivat where I was greeted with a bunch of beautiful flowers.

We stayed on the exclusive Sveti Stefan, a favourite of many celebrities. It was no ordinary hotel, but originally a fishermen's commune with converted cottages on its own small island. The dining room in the main part of the hotel had views of the black mountains

126

(Monte Negro) which was stunning. Nowadays it is even more exclusive as it is owned by the Aman hotel group. We arrived at this posh hotel with a cheap plastic suitcase which had served us well for years. Suitcases didn't have wheels then. We warned the porter it was heavy. He ignored our warning at his peril. The handle broke and he fell over on the cobbles. He got up, brushed himself down and put the suitcase on his shoulders as though it was as light as a feather.

The first day we took a cab. The driver used to live in Acton and wanted to practice his English on us. He drove us up to a bar where he drank his weight in whisky before taking us back. We did our best to avoid him after that which was difficult as he used to wait outside for us. We wanted to see as much of Montenegro as we possibly could so after breakfast, we walked every day for half an hour along the pretty coastal path to the nearest bus stop in Milocer. We took the bus all along the coast to Petrovac, Herceg Novi and Kotor, always changing in Budva. We particularly loved Budva which had an excellent local market and some good cafés and bars. We had to use sign language as nobody had spoken English for 10 years since the war began. At that time the black market currency was Deutschmarks. They have since adopted the Euro.

We wanted to revisit Montenegro 15 years later, while we were staying in Dubrovnik. The customs clearance for day trips is time consuming so it took us about 3 hours to go the short distance across the border. We spent a pleasant couple of hours in the sun in the walled city of Kotor.

We returned to Sveti Stefan where we had stayed before. It can only be viewed from the top of the hill nowadays but it was nice to reminisce and we told the rest of the tour that we had stayed there and they were in awe. We barely recognised the old Budva. It is a pleasant enough resort, but it lacked the village charm that we fell in love with. The market had gone, to be replaced by tacky souvenir shops. Most of the welcoming little bars had disappeared making way for nightclubs and discos. Sometimes it's better to hold on to memories.

Turkey

Turkey was a new destination for the British market in the nineties. We had originally booked Side but our flight was changed. The alternative wasn't acceptable, so we rebooked and went to Kuşadası instead. The Turkish people were friendly and we got many bargains in the local market, in fact, we still own some of the clothes we bought all those years ago. We visited Ephesus on the dolmuş. The hotel however, was a nightmare.

On the last day, I drank a can of Fanta from the mini bar which I came to regret, handed in the bracelet and paid for the Fanta which was a few pence, I left all the change in the room for the cleaner, probably about a pound or two and then we checked out. We got on the coach back to the airport.

The next thing we knew, two armed policemen got on the coach, called me by name and marched me back into the hotel, where I accused of not paying for the Fanta. After one receptionist actually bothered to check with the only other receptionist on the desk, he agreed that indeed I had paid for it. I then had to get back on the coach and face an angry bunch of people who by now had waited 20 minutes for the criminal to get back on the coach. Jim thought it was hilarious and couldn't stop laughing all the way home whereas I nearly died with embarrassment and I was seething with rage all the way home.

I won a couple of nights at Istanbul Hilton in the nineties. Istanbul is such a vast and amazing city of 15 million people. It deserves more than 2 nights as there is so much to see. It was the last time I travelled with my friend Janet. We did our best to cram as much as we possibly could into our weekend. Such a short trip needs very careful planning to get the best from this vast city. The mosque is only open to the public in the morning and the Grand Bazaar closes early on a Saturday. Topkapi Palace needs much more time than we actually had and we didn't have enough time to see Dolmabahçe Palace.

I loved the atmosphere of the Old City. It was very noisy at dusk when the locals were called to prayer. We ate in the street cafés surrounded by locals sitting on the concrete floor playing dominoes on low tables and smoking shisha pipes. Two young girls wanted to interview us. They asked us to sing an English song to them. Janet chose "My Old Mans a Dustman". They looked very confused.

I've been in Wetherspoon in Manchester on a boisterous Saturday night when both Man United and Man City supporters were extremely drunk and celebrating winning at the end of the season. Multiply that by ten and that just about begins to explain Fenerbahçe fans in Istanbul. We were staying in the Taksim area and had planned an evening out enjoying the local bars. The traffic was moving albeit slowly. There were Fenerbahçe supporters actually running across the roofs of slowly moving cars waving flags, blowing whistles, chanting and screaming. We literally couldn't cross the street at any point.

Istanbul was one of those places where shopping wore me out completely. Personally I hate bartering. I would rather know I was paying a fair price instead of playing games in every shop. I got a few bargains but I would definitely have bought more if I could have browsed at leisure without being hassled even if it meant paying a little more.

One guy chased us down the street for half a mile with a faux well-known brand of perfume. Another one invited us into the shop when Janet liked the look of one of the rugs. He rolled out dozens of carpets and gave us tea. When he started rolling out the red carpets for us, we laughed. He wasn't impressed that we walked away empty-handed.

I have had the opportunity to go back to Istanbul a couple of times and I would have loved to. On the first occasion, a few years ago I won a couple of nights at the Kempinski overlooking The Bosphorus but it was too politically volatile and when I won a ticket with Pegasus at 2019 World Travel Market, actually using it in 2020 proved impossible.

O'Dea – A Path Well Travelled

I was offered a 2-night educational in Marmaris, which was cancelled. Instead, they gave us two free flights with 2 night's accommodation in a basic all-inclusive hotel in Marmaris which we gratefully accepted. We weren't keen on Marmaris. It was tacky, loud and hassly but we did like the neighbouring, more upmarket resort of İçmeler. In fairness, we only had 2 nights there so that didn't give us much time to acquaint ourselves with the area properly but we did manage to do a lovely little boat trip. Turkey is so pretty and it was a lovely break.

Malta

The girls were grown up by this time. Sharon didn't want to travel with us anymore and Carol was at university so it was just the three of us. Malta is small and buses are cheap and frequent so we got around easily. We booked a boat trip from Sliema to Gozo and Comino. We had a few hours in Gozo which looked interesting but the buses didn't run round the island in the winter season, so we could only go to Victoria, the capital. There was even less to do in Comino, which was virtually just a hotel. We didn't have long there but a couple of guys missed the boat. I don't know how they got back.

We enjoyed Valletta with its fortifications. It was just the recipe to keep a 7-year-old boy happy. We took Martin to Rinella Movie Park where they filmed "The Gladiator" and to Popeye Village. Rinella Movie Park has since closed down.

A few years ago, we were invited to our friends, Joe and Leeanne's wedding. Most of their family and friends travelled over there, around 35 of us. It was also a good opportunity to catch up with my good friends, Joe's mum, Jacqui and my old schoolfriend Shelley.

The room we had booked for ourselves was a poky little windowless hole and we couldn't stay there. The only other room available was an extra 128 euros which we paid. At least it was a suite.

Leeanne had asked for lemon roses, not an unreasonable request, but at the last minute they couldn't provide them, offering deep yellow ones instead. On the day of the wedding it was over 40 degrees. The flower bracelets had already wilted.

By the time we finished the meal, we were all feeling very hot and bothered and needed a drink but they wouldn't open the bar. We couldn't even get water. In the end after many arguments, the bar was opened early but they charged a hugely inflated amount to do so.

The cake was the wrong colour, more cream than lemon. At first the newlyweds tried to cut the cake but it was made of polystyrene. The couple had requested a Victoria Sponge but the only tier that was actually made of cake rather than polystyrene was burnt and only had jam inside and no cream.

The photographs were a disaster too and they arrived in a cheap plastic album. Luckily all of the guests found enough decent photos between them. I sent them copies of all those I had taken. The fireworks were brilliant but I chose that few minutes to go to the loo so I missed them. Despite all the disasters, Joe and Leeanne looked radiant, the guests were smiling and it didn't rain.

Croatia

We only ever went on one holiday with my dad and that was to Rabac in Croatia in 1997. He climbed hills while we sat on the beach. He swam in a freezing pool at 7am while we were still asleep but we did go on a day trip to Venice together. On that holiday, a man whose family we became friendly with, told us that he looked out of his window and there was some nutter in the pool. My dad admitted it was he.

I won 3 nights at Villa Dubrovnik at the Small Luxury Hotels event in 2013. We flew with Monarch who have now sadly disappeared. It was a gorgeous boutique hotel. They came out to the taxi and welcomed us by name. Villa Dubrovnik couldn't accommodate us on all 3 nights so the last night was spent at Hotel Adriatic in a top suite with a massive balcony overlooking the beach and the city walls. It did have the advantage of being closer to town. We enjoyed the experience in both hotels.

We were staying near Ploče Gate. Walking inside the city walls
between the two gates is a 15-minute stroll. Inside the walls is car free
so it is a pleasure to wander round, however it is best to do so late in the
afternoon when the cruise ship passengers go back for dinner. The old
walled city is really lovely on a warm summer evening and everything
is open very late

After seeing the main landmarks and medieval architecture within the
beautifully preserved city walls; the fountain, the church and the clock,
there is a labyrinth of alleyways and staircases to explore. It's easy to
get lost in colourful shops, restaurants, bars, art galleries and
interesting museums.

Dubrovnik has a very wide choice of local and international restaurants
from Pizzerias, pub grub, or one of the bakeries for a delicious
lunchtime snack to fine dining in a gourmet restaurant.

Although Dubrovnik is hilly, there is a pedestrian walkway on the Ploče
Gate side and the climb is reasonably gentle. The view from the
balcony of our hotel was picture postcard beautiful and particularly so
in the evening when the sun sets over the beach and the city walls.

On one of our walks on the Pile Gate side we found a lovely park
overlooking the sea going towards Lopud. This was a little haven away
from the tourists and there was the bonus of a free show, a group of
swordsmen practising their routine possibly for a medieval banquet
show.

We had a couple of nights in Cavtat which is a pretty little resort near
Dubrovnik. It is very hilly with a tiny market, a church and lots of
restaurants built round a picturesque little harbour and it is only a short
distance from the airport.

Bulgaria

I travelled to Sunny Beach with Sharon and Martin in 2005. One thing
that was memorable about Bulgaria was the food. I didn't think it was
possible to make a breakfast that was so uninviting and unappetising. It

largely consisted of a dried up version of the previous nights dinner, spaghetti Bolognese, dried eggs and cremated bacon with packets of cornflakes. The food was so bad, we couldn't face eating in the hotel at all. At that time Martin and I used to eat meat so we lived on chicken kebabs and pancakes. Bulgaria was extremely cheap and it was still a good value holiday even though we forfeited our half board and ate out.

The beach was gorgeous, long and sandy with a variety of watersports available. Sharon and Martin were more adventurous than I was. They went parasailing at a very reasonable price while I sat on the beach and watched them. Sunny Beach was tacky. There was everything on the walkway including dancing bears. Neighbouring Nessebar fared better with more of the real Bulgarian culture and architecture that I expected. We went on a river trip to Sozopol which we enjoyed. Sharon didn't come with us that day as she had a touch of food poisoning.

I never returned to Bulgaria. I was invited to stay at the Zornitza Estate, a gorgeous luxury country hotel very close to the Greek border in March 2020 but Covid-19 happened and it was cancelled. The hotel looked absolutely stunning and the itinerary looked amazing, definitely a missed opportunity.

Hungary

Budapest was much bigger than I expected, so it was a challenge to see everything in two days. The underground was closed for refurbishment therefore it wasn't quite as easy to get around as it should have been.

Budapest is a tale of two cities: Pest is the side where one can find embassies, museums and general business activity. Buda, on the other side is green and hilly, with more of an emphasis on spas and relaxation. Buda boasts the Fisherman's Bastion and the castle. The funicular railway makes it easy to see the views from the top overlooking the river and the Pest side of the city. Budapest reminds me of London with its Victorian bridges, the Parliament Building overlooking the river and many excellent museums.

A unique experience was the Szoborpark which translates to Statue Park, since renamed Memento Park. It was awkward to get to, but it was well worth the hassle. All the old communist statues of Lenin and others of that era which looked so fearsome looking down on the main city square are now in this museum at the edge of the city.

We revisited at the beginning of our Danube river cruise and the metro that we couldn't use on our previous visit was easy and efficient. There are many international pubs and restaurants. Budapest cashes in on its Communist past by selling Russian style fur hats, postcards and memorabilia in the market. There is also a quirky Communist bar called Red Ruin.

Poland

We flew from Luton to Gdańsk. I didn't know anything about Gdańsk but it was cheap and that was a good starting point. We mentioned our plans to the Polish barmaid in our local and she suggested taking the 20-minute train journey from Gdańsk to stay in the seaside resort of Sopot. That seemed like a good idea so we took her advice and booked a small Bed and Breakfast there. Unfortunately this resulted in our card being cloned.

We were surprised how bright and modern Sopot was. There has been a huge amount of regeneration after the Berlin Wall was demolished and the Polish people were freed from Russia. Gdańsk is an interesting town with a bustling harbour, There is a distinctive Water Tower, and interesting architecture. The tall pastel-coloured buildings on the waterfront reminded me of Amsterdam.

The most interesting thing about Gdańsk was the Solidarity museum dedicated to Lech Wałęsa, who was first a trade union leader and later became President of Poland. He risked his life for his countrymen and it was his brave actions that shaped Poland as it is today. When we visited, the museum was tiny, with a rusty hull of a ship at the entrance. Now it is housed in a modern multi-storey glass building. It was humbling to see how life has changed in Eastern Europe so quickly since the fall of the Berlin Wall.

One night we discovered a Scottish pub on the main street in Sopot. As we ordered a drink, a Glaswegian overheard our accents and asked if we minded his company. Of course we accepted. As we spoke, I mentioned my uncle Frank Skerret who was very well known in Glasgow as he had had a regular slot on Radio Clyde and a column in The Glasgow Herald. It turned out that he knew my Uncle Frank very well.

He filled me in on missing information including the news that my uncle had passed away several years earlier. My dad and his only sibling had not spoken for about 30 years. Our new friend treated us to drinks all evening and insisted that we try the local speciality, Krupnik, honey vodka. We had a bottle of it in our cupboard for years. My friend Janet swears it's a miracle cure as the cold she had had for months miraculously disappeared after she had a couple of glasses in my house one evening. She certainly left our house happy!

Estonia and Finland

In 2006, I got a great deal at The Radisson, one of the tallest buildings in Tallinn. It has a rooftop bar overlooking the whole of Tallinn. Tallinn has a really interesting hotch-potch of architecture from many different eras.

We pre-booked the fast ferry to Helsinki which takes about 2½ hours. In Tallinn it was raining heavily so we were a little worried about the crossing but in fact it was very smooth. I was surprised that Helsinki looked more Russian than Scandinavian.. The church and the buildings around the main square looks rather like pictures I have seen of St. Petersburg.

Helsinki had a lovely street market by the harbour with crafts and some very fresh-looking fruit and veg. We couldn't resist a bag of strawberries and a bag of fresh peas which we ate raw like many of the locals were doing.

There are many boat trips from Helskinki harbour but having had over 2 hours on a ferry from Tallinn that morning and facing another 2 hours back, we gave that a miss. If we ever choose Helsinki for a weekend break we will definitely try that.

That evening, back in Tallinn, we walked towards the old town. The two huge medieval towers that were the original city walls looked amazing by dusk. In front of the city walls was a row of florists with beautiful colourful bouquets from as little as £3. The Lower town is medieval with well-preserved and tastefully renovated buildings.

We made use of the 48-hour Tallinn card to get around. We took the Green route to Kadriorg, a huge park at the edge of the city, the Tsarist Russia part of the city. Kadriorg's pink palace was guarded by soldiers and beautifully preserved, a peaceful haven away from tourists. TV Tower was an ugly grey Russian concrete structure built in 1980, the highest point in northern Europe. Inside there are stained glass windows and a nice relaxing bar and restaurant with a viewing platform from which there is a clear view of the port, the airport, the beaches, Russian built tower blocks, a cluster of Scandinavian bungalows and vast areas of green forest. Even Finland is visible on a clear day.

We ended up in The Beer House, a huge bierkeller style bar and restaurant with singing, dancing, medieval serving wenches and men in lederhosen. It's touristy but fun and the beer brewed on-site is excellent. The Blue Tour going in the opposite direction covered the shopping centre, Pirita convent dedicated to St. Brigitta, the Olympic village and monument and Estonian Open Air Museum, a huge area of forest dotted with farmhouses, windmills and handicrafts from different eras and different parts of Estonia. It's a great idea, preserving and showcasing the Estonian culture to the world.

Once we got back to the Old Town we discovered the Upper Town. Toompea Castle and the beautiful Alexander Nevsky, a Russian

Orthodox cathedral, with its black tiled onion domes and its glistening white exterior with gold-leafed icons. The interior is also very beautiful, with many gold chandeliers and fabulous gold icons. Tallinn is a beautiful and incredibly diverse city, its architecture, its landscape and its people. Unfortunately it was the tourist season and it was crowded with stag parties and Baltic cruises. It plays on the medieval theme for the tourists. There are medieval theme nights, medieval restaurants, medieval shops, a museum of medieval torture instruments, medieval costumes and medieval stalls selling nuts with cinnamon.

Sweden

My first visit to Sweden was brief. I took the train across Øresund Bridge from Copenhagen to Malmö. It was midwinter so it was freezing but Malmö was still lovely with frozen lakes and green spaces.

Stockholm is a pretty city built on 14 main islands. The archipelago has around 30,000 islands so there are many places to escape to in the summer months. Stockholm is mostly flat and walkable. It was difficult to find our bearings at first as there are so many rivers and canals going in all directions. This was pre-Googlemaps so it should be easier now. Our Stockholm deal included a 48-hour Stockholm card, which is valid for over 80 museums, city transport and hop on hop off boats, plus three tickets to be used for city sightseeing, boat tours or ferries. We wanted to make use of it as much as possible.

On the afternoon we arrived, we started with a leisurely Royal Canal Tour which was an hour long and passed ABBA's old house and many of the lovely parks in the city. As we got off the boat, the city sightseeing tour was waiting. This was comprehensive and gave us a good overview of the city.

We used the hop on hop off ferry and walked to the very first open air museum called Skansen. This is over a century old and consists of recreated houses through the ages, animals, a Sami village, gardens and a funicular railway. We really enjoyed this and it would be a wonderful day out for families. There are plenty of restaurants in the park so we could have easily spent all day there. We went back to Gamla Stan, the Old Town and the original part of Stockholm. This area is full of beautiful architecture with ornamental mouldings on the doorways, cobbled streets and narrow alleyways.

Going to the Vasa Museum as soon as it opened at 10am was a good decision as there was no queue. Vasa is a 400-year old warship which sank on her maiden voyage. It was recovered in 1961 and 90% of it is perfectly preserved. By the time we finished walking round, the coaches had arrived.

The Skyride goes to the top of Globen, the world's largest spherical building and it has a great view of Southern Stockholm. This has since been renamed the Ericsson Globe. The Under the Bridges Tour was around 2 hours long and we experienced yet another part of the city. On our last day, our plans were a little ruined by the weather which took a turn for the worse, but there are so many good museums to visit.

Slovakia

While Sharon and I were in Vienna in 2015, this gave us the chance to explore two very different cities for the price of one so we got a EURegio ticket which includes the use of public transport in Bratislava. The train takes about an hour. We took our passports but they weren't required

We took the bus and walked into a lovely little square with beautiful fairy tale buildings then into a bigger and more colourful square with a church and a little market. Bratislava is a gorgeous little city with a photograph round every corner. By sheer luck, we accidentally found a route to the castle with a gentle slope which was much easier than the steep hill and staircase on the other side. At the top there is a lovely view over the city, the river and the bridge. The castle includes a museum detailing the history of Slovakia.

 St. Michael's Gate is part of the original city walls. The walls have been renovated, but sadly not blending in very well with the original. Back in the town square, we discovered The Beer House. We ordered traditional Slovakian fare with home-made bread which was ample and delicious. The Blue Church is a distinctive and unique building. By contrast across the road there is an example of badly neglected communist architecture which was strangely interesting.

Slovenia

In 2016 I applied for a tourist board fam trip. My friends, Ann and Aida were on the same trip. I stayed at Stansted with Aida and then I somehow lost her so she nearly missed the flight.

Lake Bohinj and Lake Bled were lovely even in the winter. Memories of Yugotours came flooding back with familiar hotels that have hardly changed since the seventies. Lake Bled used to be very popular in the seventies as a 2-centre holiday with Dubrovnik or Split. We had lunch at Grand Hotel Toplice which has a stunning view over Lake Bled. We sampled some local specialities of the region, which were beautifully presented as well as tasty.

After lunch we took a traditional Pletna boat over to Bled Island and rang the church bell to wish our loved ones good health. The Pilgrimage Church of the Assumption of Maria is small but interesting as there are excavations from 10th-century, frescoes from 14th-century and a beautiful 18th-century altar.

We arrived in Ljubljana in the evening in time to see the Christmas lights. Zmago Modic designed the lights for many years, always with a different theme. In 2016 the theme was Respect for Life. I am saddened to learn that he died in 2019.

Ljubljana is mostly pedestrianised so it is easy to walk around the city centre and browse the Christmas market, the river, the unusual and quirky sculptures, the unique triple bridge, the Butchers Bridge with thousands of locks and Dragon Bridge. Dragons are the symbol of Ljubljana. There is some amazing and well-preserved architecture. Ljubjana is a young city with some great bars and an outdoor culture, even in sub-zero temperatures, families can be seen outside bars and cafés by the riverside. It is a pretty city that feels safe and the locals nearly all speak perfect English.

We had an amazing meal in AS Aperitivo with Matej and Mattej our hosts from Luxury Slovenia. We had a truly wonderful evening, with good food, a few bottles of wine and some decadent strawberry cake which they recommended to us.

We did a foodie tour with the Ljubljana tourist board with an excellent guide. We walked a bit, ate a starter which was sausage for the meat-eaters and pearl barley and vegetable soup for me, walked a bit more, talked about the history of the city and then stopped for another course. The tour took around 4½ hours and covered every part of the city ending at sunset on 13th floor of what was once Slovenia's highest building.

North Cyprus

Ann and I applied for a megafam with Cyprus Premier. We met many lovely agents on that trip and have kept in touch with a few of them. I have been to Cyprus many times but never to the north. They use UK 3-pin plugs and drive on the left but there the familiarity ends.

So what makes the north different? It is much greener which surprised me, as the climate is the same. The general feel is definitely Turkish. The signs are in Turkish, the street names are Turkish, kebab shops are plentiful and the currency is Turkish Lira, but without being pestered by persistent restauranteurs constantly plying for business. The atmosphere is chilled and relaxed. It is a safe and clean destination to visit. The majority living there today are either born Turkish Cypriot or foreigners who have taken advantage of cheap property prices and living costs are lower than in the South.

Kyrenia is a walled city with a unique character. It has a very busy shopping street selling hassle free, fake designer bags and soft leather shoes. We stopped in Six Brothers Irish Pub which sells kebabs and

Turkish beer. There's not even a hint of the Emerald Isle anywhere but nevertheless, we enjoyed the harbour view and a cold Efes beer.

We stopped for an enormous buffet lunch at a hotel. We wanted to catch up on e-mails over lunch so we asked about the wi-fi. That got lost in translation and we ended up with wine. It would have been rude to refuse, wouldn't it?

Famagusta was the prime resort of Cyprus in the late sixties and early seventies but the invasion of 1974 abruptly changed everything. The famous ghost town of Varosha is a vast area with hundreds of abandoned hotels, shops, houses and other buildings on a much bigger scale than I imagined, previously having only seen it through binoculars. It is a very sad reminder of the result of political and ethnic division, stretching for many miles almost to Ayia Napa on the other side of the border.

Famagusta is a bustling town steeped in history and full of character. It is a thriving port, with ancient churches and mosques including St. Nicholas which looks very odd, like a cathedral but with a minaret stuck on the top. It has actually been a mosque since 1571 when the Ottomans invaded. The square is surrounded by walls and ancient buildings dating back to 285BC. It is a unique place to visit.

I enjoyed the visit to the 13th-century Bellapais monastery. It was originally a Catholic monastery. It became Greek Orthodox after the Ottoman invasion. As it is up in the mountains, the approach to it is hilly but well worth the climb past craft shops, inns and boutique hotels. There is an amazing view from the top and there are fantastic photo opportunities of the ruins. Unfortunately I wasn't able to bring my camera due to restrictions placed on larger electronic devices that were in place at that time originating from Turkey and the Middle East.

Luxembourg

I applied for a fam trip which was organised by Luxembourg tourist office. Apart from Ann and me, most of the others were German. They were a nice, friendly crowd and they made the effort to interact with us.

They were unanimously baffled by Brexit and were curious to know how we felt about it.

The main language spoken is Luxembourgish which is mostly a combination of German and French. Most of the people we met spoke English as well as German and French, so language isn't a problem. Luxembourg City is very walkable as there isn't a huge amount of traffic but it is hilly and cobbled. The bonus of a hilly city is the fabulous view to the valleys below.

The city caters well for tourists as the guides speak 28 languages between them. Elke, our guide was with us for 2 days to show us the sights of the city centre and Kirchberg Plateau on the outskirts. The city has the nickname "Gibraltar of the north" because it is rocky and it is fortified, but in reality it is nothing like Gibraltar. It is unique and didn't remind me of anywhere else I've been. It has much more history than I imagined with influences from bordering Belgium, Germany and France. Other Luxembourg City sights are the Royal Palace, Notre-Dame Cathedral, the Courts of Justice, some excellent museums, the fort and the usual plethora of familiar European high street shops as well as a twice-weekly market. There are some lively bars which are open until the early hours of the morning.

Kirchberg showcases the modern part of the city with some fabulous architecture including the Philharmonic arena, European Courts of Justice and European School of Luxembourg. The museum of Modern Art is built on top of the Musée Dräi Eechelen. It shows how ancient and modern can blend well. There is an open space popular with skateboarders with trees planted for all the EU Countries. The UK tree happened to be strangely and prophetically lopsided.

We visited the Moselle region and the tiny village of Schengen which was made famous by the treaties of 1985 and 1990. The Schengen agreement was signed on a river ship on the Moselle between Schengen and Germany on the other side of the river. There is a small museum with free literature in several languages. Behind Schengen are vineyards. We visited Caves St. Martin in Remich and sampled some crémant, their own version of Champagne and also their Pinot Gris, both of which were excellent. We had a wonderful buffet lunch in the restaurant which would suit even the most fussy eater.

The Marathon Coach Tour

Coach touring was something my dad did at least once a year. It was a concept that never appealed to either of us, but I won this one at World Travel Market and it included many places that we had never experienced before and wanted to see.

We took the Eurostar to Paris and booked their choice of overnight accommodation in a suburb of Paris. It wasn't included but we figured that it would be easier to join the tour from the hotel they were using.

Our group was an eclectic worldwide group and our tour was run by a Dutch/Chinese guy. He immediately referred to us as "freeloaders" to the entire coach party which wasn't the best start to our week. He made up stories as he went along mixed in with various conspiracy theories. Very little of his guiding was based on fact but and we quickly realised that most of what he said was complete bullshit but he was entertaining.

We liked the places that we saw, but it was much too rushed to enjoy it and as we were mostly staying miles from the city, we had very little time to ourselves or to see much of the places we visited. It certainly wasn't our most relaxing holiday.

It was 300 miles from Paris to the Swiss border and then a fairly short drive to Lucerne. We always enjoy going back to Lucerne. We had about an hour to browse the city which was as beautiful as I remembered, with the modern Concert Hall on one side of the lake, Chapel Bridge and the Water Tower on the other. Ibis Styles was a good hotel very close to the lake. This turned out to be the best hotel of our trip.

We had problems getting through Milan as hundreds of cyclists were racing through the city. Half the roads were closed to traffic. Finally we managed to get within walking distance of Piazza Duomo. The Duomo

143

was as magnificent as I remembered. The piazza seemed to have fewer pigeons but many more people.

Galeria Vittorio Emanuele II shopping arcade was designed in 1861 and is thought to be the world's oldest shopping mall. We browsed at windows full of Prada, Benetton and many other famous designer names. La Scala is on the other side of the shopping centre.

Verona is the city made famous by Romeo and Juliet Our coach was parked by the city walls. Casa Di Giulietta is a long walk and crowded with tourists. At the entrance is a scribbling wall to write messages to loved ones. I learned recently that the famous balcony was only added in 1937 for the tourists. What is more interesting is that the play and the house is completely fictitious and Shakespeare's play doesn't even include a balcony. We walked along the city walls, past the Colosseum, smaller than the one in Rome but still impressive. The shopping area is pedestrianised and extremely busy. We heard an alarming loud explosion but thankfully it turned out to be a battle re-enactment.

Venice, or rather, the industrial area called Mestre is convenient for the cruise port but it isn't pretty so we didn't fancy going out. Luckily the hotel had a decent restaurant and bar. As dawn broke, we went over to Venice island on the vaporetto, Most of our group went on gondolas. We didn't, preferring to stretch our legs and meander round the narrow alleyways and canals. We met up again for our short visit to a Murano glass factory. The pieces were so colourful and intricate. Beautiful craftwork inspires me more than overpriced tourist attractions.

San Marco is instantly recognisable with the iconic gateway and Doges Palace. When we arrived it was calm, with not too many people. A couple of hours later, thousands of tourists suddenly descended on the city like ants from cruise ships and other tours. I was grateful that we got there first.

We left Venice at lunchtime for a very long coach ride to Rome. We arrived at around 9pm, to a hotel miles outside the city. After a chaotic early breakfast, we were on our way to the Vatican. It was less crowded than the last time I was there, but it was raining heavily. There was a very long and wet queue to St. Peters Basilica and the Vatican museum. The opportunists were out in force selling ponchos and umbrellas. The interior was truly stunning, a must-see and surprisingly I was allowed to take photos. We made a wish in the Trevi fountain and then we chose from the huge array of pizzerias for lunch.

The Colosseum is awesome from the outside even with the scaffolding around it to preserve it from further decay. Jim didn't fancy going inside, but I persuaded him and he was glad I did.

I really liked Florence despite the crowds. We managed to beat most of them as the cruise ship tourists didn't arrive from Livorno until about midday. Our coach was parked a long way from the city so we lost a good 40 minutes walking backwards and forwards. We started off in Piazza Signores where there is a statue of David and fabulous views over the city.

The famous Ponte Vecchio is an odd and unique bridge. There are jewellery shops all along the bridge but the main industry there is leather. There are plenty of belts and bags but for every quality bag there is a cheap copy.

Pisa wasn't how I expected. There are several other magnificent buildings around the leaning tower as well a museum. Most people reckon half a day is enough and that's probably true but an hour simply wasn't long enough.

I looked forward to our day in Monte Carlo, Nice and Cannes on our wedding anniversary and these are three places I had always wanted to go to and hadn't already been. I loved Monte Carlo. There is much more to do there than I expected. Apart from the casino there is an oceanography museum and some quaint alleys with souvenir shops and the daily changing of the guard. It is clean and smart with a mixture of old houses and modern skyscrapers. The race track was just being dismantled after the Grand Prix.

O'Dea – A Path Well Travelled

We enjoyed Nice, the long Promenade des Anglais, the pebble beach and Albert 1 Park which has lots of flowers and art. It's a really pleasant walk with a cooling mist, a great idea for hot summer days.

Cannes has a sand beach. The film festival was on, so Cannes was very busy, however we were happy to sit and watch the expensive yachts in the marina from The Quays Irish bar.

We got to Lyon about midday on the last day and we felt that catching the last Eurostar back to London that evening would be a gamble so we left the group and took the RER back to Paris which took around 2 hours ensuring plenty of time to catch our train home.

After abandoning the trip in Lyon, we decided that coach touring is definitely not for us.

Our meeting point in Venice

USA AND CANADA

USA

Florida

It was 1986 and our friend Maggie kept talking about America and how fantastic it was. She had been there a few times on business as she worked for Virgin Records. Jim was always worried as all he knew of America was what he saw on the news and films and he imagined it was full of guns and violence. Eventually Maggie persuaded us that we should go. We would be perfectly safe and we would love it!

Intasun introduced holidays to Florida. A 2-centre holiday to Kissimmee and St. Pete looked really appealing so we booked. Our friends, Cozzer and Adrian added an extra week in Miami.

The seven of us, Jim and I, the two girls, Carol and Sharon and our friends, Maggie, Cozzer and Adrian travelled on my birthday on British Airways. In our excitement, we got as far as Hammersmith and accidentally handed in our little green cardboard tickets to Heathrow. We weren't used to going beyond Hammersmith. Once we realised our mistake, the station staff emptied the box with all the tickets onto the office floor. There were tickets everywhere so we all got to work sifting through hundreds of tickets until we found ours. Jim and Adrian never let us forget the "Two to Hammersmith" incident. Luckily we were early.

I got a lovely surprise as my colleagues had organised champagne on the flight. The people in front of us on the flight complained that we got champagne and they didn't and they didn't like being in front of two very excited children who had never been on a large aircraft before. We had enlisted our children onto the Skyflyers programme so they had their own passports with flight info and mileage and they got to talk to the pilot in flight. That was normal in the eighties when flying was a real pleasure and part of the holiday experience.

O'Dea – A Path Well Travelled

As we touched down in Bermuda the aerial view on the approach was amazing and Sharon was so excited.

"I can't believe my eyes!"

We had a big bulky video camera that weighed a ton. We still have the video footage of that holiday. It's so much easier with an i-phone.

Our first week was in a motel in Kissimmee. There was a Denny's opposite. On the first morning we successfully crossed the highway. and we went in to order breakfast, bacon, eggs, links and hash browns.

"What kind of eggs?" asked the waitress…

"erm, fried?"

"Is that easy over, sunny side up…." and went on to rattle off about ten different ways we could have our eggs, Carol thought she would try sunny side up because that sounded nice.

"You're a brave girl" said the waitress.

She came back with a barely cooked, very runny fried egg. Sharon usually went for bacon, pancakes and maple syrup. She still loves crispy bacon. Sharon kicked one of her flip-flops on the roof, so we had to carry her back across. We made our way back over the highway and avoided the massive muddy puddle but then a huge juggernaut came along and drowned the lot of us so after that we decided it was more sensible to drive across.

We took the girls to Disneyworld Florida, EPCOT, Seaworld and Cape Kennedy. The car parks were bigger then we could ever imagine and we had to remember where we had parked. There were thousands of cars so we had to trust at least one of the seven of us to remember Donald Duck 7 or similar. The rides and shows were nothing like Chessington Zoo. Every little detail was perfect and everything worked like clockwork. We filled our suitcases with all sorts of stuff that we would never waste our money on now: programmes, glasses, t-shirts, Mickey Mouse hats and fluffy toys.

O'Dea – A Path Well Travelled

Big Erroll was our regular taxi driver who took us to The Fox and Hounds British Pub. He kept a gun in the dash. I had never seen a real gun before. This was America! We watched him eat an entire large pizza on his own. It would easily have been big enough for all seven of us with no room to spare.

We drove the hour and half to St Pete Beach. The white talcum powder-like sand was full of huge shells and like nothing we had seen or touched before. The girls spent most of the day in the pool. They could both swim well by the end of that holiday.

Maggie had a comfortable white and green beach dress that she bought in California. We're pretty sure it was intended as a nightie but Maggie lived in it. Adrian always referred to it as "the green thing".

We were happy as we had found the perfect spot by the Swigwam bar. It was chilled with all the music that we liked. Maggie's friends Hilary and Cheryl came over from California in a Chrysler LeBaron convertible which the boys sat in for the photo.

We have had many holidays since then but that holiday was unforgettable. Maggie, Cozzer and Adrian have all passed away but all of them absolutely loved that holiday. Cozzer and Adrian went back to different parts of America year after year, with our family a few times and then on their own.

We went back to Florida in 1989 on a charter flight with Novair which had a stop in Bangor, Maine. There was snow on the ground when we touched down. This time we included Clearwater and Sunny Isles in Miami and stayed in Château-by-the-sea. It was a Swiss chalet style of motel right on the beach. On that occasion we experienced a red tide which occurs at least once a year. There is a build up of algae and loads of dead fish land up on the beach poisoned by the sea which is unpleasant but it is a completely natural phenomenon.

One year we drove to Key West. We booked a cheap motel for us and the two girls. Our room had a coin slot to operate the vibrating bed. Jim unplugged it and hid the plug behind the bed before the girls noticed it, fortunately they didn't! Key West was lovely. It had a very Caribbean feel to it. The entertainers performing at sunset is a wonderful experience and a must-see.

For Carol's 21st birthday, we booked a holiday with Virgin to Orlando and Cocoa Beach. Carol loved rollercoasters so she took Martin on all those that he was allowed to go on. Both of them loved Kennedy Space Center. We really hoped to experience a rocket launch but they were cancelled so we didn't get to see one. We tried again from the roof at Orlando airport which is still close enough and that one was cancelled too.

Carol still looked very young so we got away with two child meals and they were each given a colouring book with puzzles. It saved us a fortune but it was also a disadvantage when we tried to order a beer. Carol had to take her passport everywhere.

We were tempted by Denny's Potato soup advertised in the window. It was difficult to find vegetarian food in restaurants in 2000. Jim ordered the potato soup for a starter and I ordered a burger with guacamole. Jim's soup arrived with pink bits so he called the waiter and asked:

"Excuse me, is that ham in the soup?"

"Yes", said the waiter.

"So it's potato and ham soup then. I don't eat meat, that's why I wanted potato soup"

They called the manager and took it back. My burger arrived without the guacamole so I sent that back as well. Jim's main came up without the fries. He called the waiter over and asked where the fries were.

"I thought you didn't want potatoes" said the waiter.

"I like potatoes" said Jim, "It's ham I don't want".

On our way out there was one of those charity boxes where you put a coin in and if it lands on a platform you win a prize. The cashier called the manager who enthusiastically shouted:

"We have a win....... ner"

The 'ner' came out at least an octave lower as soon as he realised it was us, the family from hell. We won chocolate cake. We knew we were leaving town but we didn't tell him that. He must have been so relieved that we never went back to claim it.

In another restaurant we encountered Stephanie, who was absolutely delightful. We overheard her saying that she always wanted to be a waitress, how much she enjoys her job, how much she looks forward to going to work every day and how much she loves talking to people.

We said, "Thank you very much".

She said "You're welcome very much".

I've never come across anyone that deserved a tip as much as she did.

2013 proved to be our last holiday with Adrian and Cozzer. It was Anna's first visit to the USA. I had expected a few changes as it had been 24 years since we last visited this neck of the woods and there were a few more hotels along the strip. Most of the old haunts were still there but the names and ownerships had changed.

The main attraction is the gorgeous beach which stretches for many miles along the Gulf Coast. Despite hotels all the way along the beach and the watersports, the lovely beach remains unspoilt. There were hundreds of birds and a lovely warm sea abundant with fish and dolphins swimming close to the shore. We spotted manatees and pelicans on the inland waterways. The plants are protected and there are heavy fines for picking mangroves and sea oats.

We spent one morning strolling along the beach watching many bird species fishing in the sea. They all have different ways of fishing. The pelican uses its huge beak to scoop up its prey. One skims the top of the water. Another dives in from a great height. One pokes its long beak into the sand and the gulls wait for rich pickings from tourists. One gull shrieks and all his mates come from miles around to attack the hungry tourist. It was fascinating to watch them all.

O'Dea – A Path Well Travelled

Even a couple of weeks before Thanksgiving there were many bargains so we stocked up with Christmas gifts for all our family. We got the chance to sample plenty of freshly caught fish and seafood in the local restaurants. We discovered Dollar Tree, like Poundland, but even cheaper.

Florida is better known for theme parks than culture but a trolley ride to downtown St. Petersburg gave us the opportunity to visit museums, the most famous of which is the Dalí museum with original works by the Spanish artist Salvador Dalí. The Florida museum houses most of his best works. There is a City Looper and the driver told us some interesting facts along the way, an absolute bargain at just 50 cents.

The gulf coast has many inland waterways and a good way to navigate these is by pleasure boat. We found a reasonably priced one from nearby Clearwater called Calypso Queen.

Johnny "Cozzer", Maggie and Adrian 1986, all sadly missed

California

That first holiday in the USA inspired us to go back as soon as we could. We loved the relaxed way of life. We couldn't go every year, but we did manage to go a few times. In 1988, our family, along with Maggie, Cozzer and Adrian, took our friend "Old Jack" to California. He had never been on a plane since he was in a Lancaster bomber during the war. The flight was terrible as we hit an air pocket. but Old Jack loved every minute of it. He watched films and devoured the food. He even tried to eat the hot towel! He was like a kid at Christmas.

We stayed at The Kensington Motel, so it was home from home as we live in Kensington. Maggie stayed in Santa Monica with her friends and we drove up to San Francisco and back. We were in California for 3 weeks so three of us, Jim, myself and Maggie celebrated our respective birthdays.

In Pismo Beach we asked for two triple rooms so they offered us one with a Murphy. We wondered who or what Murphy was. We soon learned that it was a bed which folded out from the wall which was actually very comfortable.

We stopped at Winchester Mystery Fun House. Mrs.Winchester believed her family was cursed because of the family's association with rifles. There were many tragic deaths in the family so she built a house where nobody would find her. Number 13 can be found throughout the house from the number of windows in a room to the smallest of details. The guide had the squeakiest voice I've ever heard in my life. I still have that voice in my head. We were trapped in there for 2 hours, the house was a maze with no escape. We spent 2 nights in San Francisco. The famous tram was a novelty which the girls enjoyed and we went across to Alcatraz.

We went to Disneyland and Universal studios and also Knotts Berry Farm which was lesser known but we really enjoyed that. I found my ticket to Disneyland California recently. It was only $29 in 1988. Nowadays it is $97-$124. In Hearst Castle, featured in the film "Citizen

153

Kane", we almost had more fun watching the Japanese tourists taking pictures from every angle than we did walking round. The lengths they went to get the perfect shot were often hilarious.

We took Old Jack to the original Queen Mary in Long Beach. Old Jack had sailed on the Queen Mary during the war and he was quite happy to act as an unofficial tour guide to a fascinated bunch of tourists. We drove down to Tijuana which was one of the worst places I've ever been to. We saw Mexicans crawling through storm drains and people selling pretty well anything including carpets and chewing gum to a captive audience of cars stuck on the border control but the beer was cheap and served in buckets. San Diego was lovely. I would have liked more time there.

The boys spent most of their time in Santa Monica in the Mucky Duck and The Kings Head. One day in The Mucky Duck, Jim ended up talking to someone who turned out to be a good friend of his cousin, Kevin who lived in Ealing. On that same evening, Adrian joined in the stool dance. This involved sticking a bar stool over his head, sticking his arms through it and dancing over the tables. We had booked to go back in May 2020, at the height of the pandemic on both sides of the Atlantic so we couldn't go and probably never will now.

We usually ate dinner in The Brown Derby. It was next door and the food was good. Adrian ordered a peppered steak and sent it back, disappointed that it wasn't as peppery as the one I once cooked for him. It was only after that, I had to confess that I had dropped the entire pepper pot on the one I had cooked for him and I had to scrape it off as best I could whilst choking with my eyes watering. It has since been christened my misteak. Sharon was a fussy eater and ordered a burger. She was a very small and skinny child and her entire face literally disappeared behind the burger. She couldn't finish it!

Texas and New Orleans

In 1990 we went to Texas and New Orleans with Cozzer and Adrian. We enjoyed Dallas and Fort Worth. Dallas is a modern city full of

154

skyscrapers. Whilst visiting the memorial where President John Kennedy was shot, we noticed lampposts with wanted posters of a man that looked exactly like Cozzer!

At that time the TV series "Dallas" was on TV so we drove out to Southfork Ranch. Fort Worth is only a few miles from Dallas but it is very different. There are The Stockyards, Billy Bob's, cowboys and rodeos. The girls also loved splashing about in the Water Gardens.

In the days before Google, we literally had to look at a map and work out how many places we could go to and roughly how long the drive would be from place to place. Cozzer wanted to go to Waco.

"Why Waco"? we asked.

Cozzer loved country music and one of his favourite singers was Tanya Tucker. She sang a song about Waco so he wanted to go there. It is situated roughly half way between Dallas/ Fort Worth and Austin. As it was on the way, we agreed we would overnight in Waco. We arrived there only to discover that it was a dry town full of bible shops. We struggled to find anything to do in Waco so we asked the receptionist. With great enthusiasm she said we would love Texas Ranger Hall of Fame, a short drive away. The girls quickly got bored, they had more fun trying on cowboy hats in the shop.

We discovered one single oasis in the entire town of Waco. Two enterprising Irishmen built a pub out of two railway carriages at the edge of town on the other side of the railway tracks. We couldn't get out of Waco fast enough then Cozzer remembered the words of the song about Waco. Tanya Tucker was leaving Waco. Thanks for that…

We visited the Alamo in San Antonio, then Galveston, Corpus Christi and finally Houston. From Houston, we drove the short distance to the Johnson Space Center, and saw the very nerve centre that was in everyone's living room on a black and white TV in July 1969. We got an amazing rate at the Hyatt in Houston so we got a taste of the highlife while Cozzer and Adrian stayed in a nearby motel which was thereafter referred to as "digs". Adrian couldn't park in our car park for our pre-arranged meeting. They had cleared the area as President Reagan was visiting. We all came out on our balconies to catch a glimpse, but they had smuggled him through the back door. Cozzer and Adrian couldn't let us know because that was long before mobile phones and internet.

It was somewhere on this holiday that I got bitten by something and my leg literally swelled up like a balloon. Thankfully antihistamines did bring it down after a couple of days but it was quite scary at the time. Somewhere else on our journey, I cant remember exactly where, we ended up in a bar with peanuts on the bar. The peanut shells would then be thrown onto the floor, so we were crunching over them on the way out.

We found a lovely duplex apartment in New Orleans with a spiral staircase in a quiet, leafy area off St Charles Avenue and only a quick tram ride to Bourbon Street. We enjoyed a pleasant afternoon on the Brazos Queen paddle steamer along the Mississippi.

Florida, Georgia and The Carolinas

In 1993 we wanted to do another road trip before Martin's 2nd birthday while his airfare was still at infant rate. We travelled with Cozzer and Adrian and that proved to be the last time we travelled together as a complete family of five. We flew to Jacksonville and spent one night there before visiting St. Augustine which has a selection of America's oldest: America's oldest city with America's oldest wooden schoolhouse, the oldest masonry fort, America's first parish church, the Oldest House Museum, the oldest homestead. I'm sure I've missed a few. St. Augustine is so proud of its 400-year old history. It really made me appreciate what we have here at home.

We drove along and once we reached Jekyll Island and told them of our onward plans they told us we were heading for the Redneck Riviera. We wondered what we had let ourselves in for. Tybee Island was pleasant and charming in quite an old fashioned way. I went to the launderette and got talking to a local couple who got really excited when they realised I came from London.

"How the hell did you find Tybee Island?" they asked.

Adrian walked into a bar and mentioned the Redneck Riviera and then wondered why he had a pint thrown over him. We could see our next destination across the water in South Carolina. Hilton Head was very close as the crow flies, but we aren't crows so we had to drive all the way round. I absolutely loved Hilton Head, a really smart resort with a nice feel to it.

Savannah was interesting with its characteristic houses and green spaces, a really pretty city but at night it didn't feel very safe. Charleston was pleasant, a walkable city with a covered market and tourist horse and carts.

I was looking forward to Myrtle Beach which was a popular resort but actually it reminded me of Southend-on-Sea. We ended our trip in North Carolina and stayed in the lovely resort of Wrightsville. We visited the USS Yorktown. We had recognised this battleship from an exhibit and short film in the War Museum in Canberra so it was interesting to actually walk on it.

Seattle

In 2010 as part of our Canada and Alaska trip, we took the Amtrak Cascades train down to Seattle. That was a real surprise. We watched the sunset along the Pacific Coast. As we got on, Jim was pulled to one side and taken into a side room by immigration and in the confusion they didn't stamp my passport, That proved to be a real problem later on. It is a five hour journey from Vancouver to Seattle. It isn't very far but the border crossing is a very slow process.

We finally arrived in Seattle and our luggage was taking ages to arrive. They had completely destroyed our almost new suitcase. It took us months of form filling and emails to claim compensation from Amtrak and then there was the problem of the bank transfer from dollars to pounds so we didn't get much back after all that.

O'Dea – A Path Well Travelled

We stayed in the Fairmont Olympic which is a classic hotel. We went out early so that we had a few hours to explore Seattle before our cruise. We hoped to get a decent cup of coffee in Seattle, after all, that is what Seattle is famous for but we really struggled, there was nothing open until 10am. Eventually we did find a small bakery which was open, then we had time to visit the city. We had time for Space Needle and Pike Place Market and we walked past the world's very first Starbucks. We didn't have time for the Music Museum and the Chihuly Garden and Glass hadn't yet opened.

Las Vegas

There was a World Travel Market competition in 2015 to take a selfie on the Las Vegas stand. I've never been good at selfies, being vertically challenged with short arms, so the resulting photo was terrible but I tweeted it anyway and won! Considering how many pass through the doors over the four days, there were surprisingly few entries.

I won two BA flights to Las Vegas and $2000 to spend. I arranged the trip around the dates that Rod Stewart was playing at Caesars Palace. Unfortunately, it also coincided with Spring Break so our pool was full of college kids drinking cans of beer, shrieking and throwing stuff around.

Hotels along "The Strip", officially Las Vegas Boulevard, are immense. The MGM alone has 5,000 rooms. The hotel part of The Strip is 4½ miles long from the Stratosphere in the north to Mandalay Bay in the South.

Each hotel is an attraction or theme with no expense spared. Most of the hotels have their own casino, several restaurants and a theatre. We discovered the pub at New York, New York on the last day which was rather a shame because it had a better atmosphere than anywhere else we found, more like a proper pub. At least we discovered it during the happy hour!

O'Dea – A Path Well Travelled

Wicked Spoon buffet at Cosmopolitan was recommended to us for brunch. It was expensive at $30 each but we used to go for brunch as late as possible and that would fill us up for the day.

We wanted to be in Las Vegas for the St Patrick's Day Parade and we were able to watch it from the pool at our hotel but it barely lasted a few minutes so it was disappointing and so was O'Shea's, the Irish Bar in our hotel which was a dark and dingy saloon with a few shamrocks and a dwarf dressed up in green.

We chose the light aircraft to West Rim for our Grand Canyon trip. This included a scenic 35-minute flight to and from Boulder City, a decent lunch at Eagle Point or Guano Point and an interesting little exhibition of Native American dwellings. All in all, it was a lovely day away from the madness.

On our way back we were belted up, the propellors had started and we were ready to go until a nervous little voice from the back said:

"Excuse me, shouldn't you close the door?"

The pilot duly did so!

Hoover Dam, built in 1931, took under 5 years to build, 2 years ahead of schedule and at 700 ft high it is one of the world's greatest man-made structures even to this day. After a tour of the dam we had lunch on a paddle steamer on Lake Mead, America's largest man made lake, a reservoir which generates power to Nevada.

A couple of times we took the bus to Fremont Street, home to the famous Golden Nugget and some of the oldest casinos. It is busy but quieter and less chaotic than The Strip. It is cheaper too. We visited the Mob Museum which was small but interesting. We found a decent bar right opposite the Heart Attack Grill. For those of you who haven't heard about it, there is a larger than life picture of a mountainous 32lb burger outside, one snack almost equivalent in weight to 15kgs luggage! We also spent a little while in the container park. All the shops, bars and play equipment are built from containers. What a great idea!

The highlight of my trip was going to see Rod Stewart at Caesars. That's a memory I will always treasure. Another thing I saw while I was there was Cirque du Soleil. I only had one ticket so I went by myself. I didn't understand the weird storyline at all but it was really colourful and spectacular.

Fashion Show Mall right in the middle of The Strip was a pleasant surprise. It features Macy's, Dillard's and several other well- known department stores and shops. We managed to get many bargains in the sales. The mall at the Southern End near the airport was great for shoes and trainers.

Eight nights in Las Vegas is too long, it drove us crazy. Every day felt like Oxford Street two weeks before Christmas, and that was just getting out of the hotel.

I knew my trip to Las Vegas would be incredibly useful for work as the city was popular with my clients especially on multi-centre trips. It was useful to know the locations and suitability of the hotels and seeing them for myself helped me tremendously and I was able to offer my colleagues some good advice too.

Detroit

The USA tourist board, American Airlines and British Airways run an incentive every year so the agents with the biggest sales get a place on the trip, but they give a few extra places away as prizes. I won my place at a quiz event at Planet Hollywood. I won the tiebreak with the closest answer to how tall is Willis Tower in Chicago. I almost didn't get the place because it overlapped my trip to Valencia but two of the trips started on the day after I got back, so I applied for those and got the Lake Michigan one which was also one of the least active adventure ones. It was a great choice. I loved the area and our group.

O'Dea – A Path Well Travelled

We didn't see our tickets until we got to Heathrow and I realised to my horror that my name had been shortened, despite meticulously filling out my passport details. Since we were going to the USA I knew this would be a problem that would have to be fixed and quickly. Seema Sood, who took us on the trip, had to spend the next hour on her phone and laptop sorting it out with the two airlines, British Airways and American Airlines. Despite already being at the airport, this proved to be much easier than I expected.

Detroit is the only US city which has Canada to the south. Literally across the river is Windsor in Ontario. Ford and Motown are the two famous names that put Detroit firmly on the map. Detroit was the original Motortown, the home of Henry Ford and his friend Thomas Edison who had the original light bulb moment.

Most of our group went on a 10-mile cycle ride along the riverbank. Danielle and I went to DIA instead. There are both classic and modern paintings by famous artists and some local high school art which I found really interesting, particularly some of the posters depicting some powerful messages that we could all learn from, but the one thing that makes this museum unique and worth a visit are the incredible murals by Diego Riviera which depict the industrial revolution. There is so much tiny detail in these floor to ceiling murals.

Hitsville USA, the home of Motown, was a house with humble beginnings. Berry Gordy Junior started the Tamla and Motown labels with raw talent from the streets of Detroit, many of whom worked for Henry Ford. Diana Ross, Jackson Five, Smokey Robinson, The Temptations and many others started out from this little house which has preserved as much of its sixties interior as possible. The house is surprisingly small and the equipment remarkably simple. The echo chamber is literally a hole in the ceiling. This brought back so many memories of the music I loved so much in my youth.

Henry Ford Museum, Rouge Factory and Greenfield Village deserve at least a full day as the area is so vast and there is so much to see. Rouge Factory has a display of Ford cars from the twenties to the future. There is a thirties model with a letter from Clyde Barrow of Bonnie and Clyde thanking them for producing the V8 which was the car he most loved to steal. There was a 4-D movie about the car of the future. We walked round the Ford production plant which was fascinating to watch. There are strictly no photographs allowed.

The Henry Ford Museum of American Innovation isn't just about cars. There are so many interesting exhibits, including the car in which the JFK was shot, the bus in which Rosa Parks refused to give up her seat to a white man, the action which sparked off the civil rights movement, a Klu Klux Klan costume, the theatre chair where Abraham Lincoln sat when he was assassinated, an Oscar Meyer Wienermobile which is a hot dog shaped car, Henry Ford's private plane and so much more!

Detroit has some good restaurants and the ones we went to were great, Granite City inside the offices of General Motors and Hop Cat where many visitors have their names scratched into the tables and which had a choice of 130 beers. To sum up Detroit, it's all about cars, music, beer, food, museums and fun.

Our group at Hitsville USA where Motown began

Lake Michigan

In the shadow of Detroit is a delightful little town called Ann Arbor, the home of the University of Michigan, the learning centre for many future lawyers and doctors.

At first sight Ann Arbor is a pretty university town with lots of trees and quaint old wooden buildings but a short walk brings you to the main street, where there are lively bars and restaurants. It's easy to imagine hundreds of students enjoying a beer or two. There is also a Michigan University shop where sweatshirts and memorabilia sell like hotcakes but at rather more than student prices!

Most students start their journey staying overnight with their parents at the wonderfully quirky "The Graduate" hotel before visiting the university campus. It is a deceptively tall hotel with a boutique feel. It has a student theme which is done really well with neat little touches such as student card room keys, photos of kids on the walls, portrait

163

paintings done by local artists or possibly students, blackboards around the reception area with geometry and equations written on them in chalk, more blackboards used as notice boards and there is a comfortable outdoor area. The rooms are also student themed and have a lovely view of the city.

The main street has many independent shops, restaurants and Nickels Arcade. Michigan is proud of the 1928 cinema with its booth outside, a popcorn machine in the foyer and a beautiful original interior reminiscent of a small Victorian theatre. The developers wanted to demolish it but the locals fought to keep it intact and won.

One independent and really interesting mini chain is Zingermans Deli, which consists of the deli, the roadhouse, the creamery and the bakehouse. The Deli is quirky and fun with food and cook books from all over the world, a salad counter and dishes such as Killer Quinoa. It has a children's play area, an outdoor café, gifts for graduates and notices of local events as well as being a community meeting place.

The university has a beautiful library, the oldest building dates back to 1838. I could just imagine Hermione plotting up with Ron and Harry, not what you would expect to see in America. We walked around the campus and the town which is small but far from sleepy. Ann Arbor publishers are the main UK distributors for many USA based psychological assessments. I really loved this little town.

South Haven is a yacht harbour, very popular with local townies from Chicago and Detroit. Many of the condominia are privately owned as holiday homes, so it gets very busy in the summer.

Michigan Maritime Museum is dedicated to the aircraft which crashed into Lake Michigan. At the time it was the USA's worst air disaster and there were no survivors. After a visit, followed by a sample from the ice cream factory and shop, we watched the beautiful orange sunset by the lighthouse.

Saugatuck is a much smaller, sleepier place with wild sand dunes on Oval Beach. After a thrilling ride in a jeep up and down the sand dunes, sampling the local brew and spending the afternoon on a submarine and aircraft carrier at USS Silversides in Muskegon, we had dinner overlooking a yacht harbour and watched yet another beautiful sunset.

We spent under 36 hours in Indiana but people were so friendly and welcoming, we felt we had been there longer. Indiana National Park is the most bio-diverse in the USA. We arrived at Indiana Dunes Visitor Centre in the morning. Pinhook Bog is a preservation area of carnivorous plants floating on top of 16 metres of water. This involved walking across a floating platform with our experienced ranger. She was so knowledgeable about all the flora and fauna in the area.

After lunch, we headed to a beautiful inland beach on Lake Michigan with miles of natural sand, tidal waves and the skyline of Chicago across the lake. It is one of the most beautiful beaches I have ever seen so it is hard to believe that it isn't an oceanside beach

There were so many colourful birds and butterflies, as well as three distinct landscapes, oak trees, tall grasses and marshland and the sands of the dunes. Most of our group completed the 3-Dune Challenge successfully and bought the t-shirt.

Valparaiso, locally known as Valpo, is a lovely little American town full of small independent shops and restaurants. Elements wine bar had just opened, a brilliantly simple idea, swiping a card for wines on tap and paying at the end.

Some of our group were interviewed and we ended up on the front page of the local newspaper the following morning. A group of UK travel agents visiting is newsworthy in Valpo. We visited the biggest collegiate chapel in the US and the second biggest in the world. There are some lovely mosaics outside, seating for over 2000, an organ with 106 pipes and beautiful stained glass windows which are three storeys high.

O'Dea – A Path Well Travelled

We had a visit round Valpo Velvet ice cream factory and sampled one or two of around 50 flavours to choose from. It was unseasonably hot at over 30-degrees so we found a bar with outdoor seating to chill and relax.

Broken Wagon Bison Farm has over 100 bison of all shapes and sizes from baby ones to fully grown. These huge beasts all have their own personalities. The crafty one, Daisy follows the truck back as she knows they will always give her a little treat.

Chicago

My Kind of Town, Chicago is....

The Windy City wasn't originally so called because it is windy, it was because the politicians at the time talked a lot of hot air and the politicians elsewhere nicknamed it the Windy City and it stuck.

Chicago is surprisingly walkable and it feels quite safe. Public transport is excellent. The metro is affectionately known as the "L" because it's elevated. The "L" which opened in 1892, is one of the oldest metro systems in the world.

I could have spent an entire day just walking around Millennium Park. For music lovers, throughout the summer there are free concerts. "The Bean" is a huge installation by Indian-born British artist Anish Kapoor, officially it is called Cloud Gate but it looks like a bean. It reflects the city skyline and the people in the park in an interesting way using reflections. It isn't the only weird art installation in the park. There are frames made of shredded tyres and children splashing around in the uniquely designed fountains.

All the familiar designer names can be found in Magnificent Mile, officially North Michigan Avenue and there are plenty of outlet malls within easy reach of the city.

We took the Big Bus Tour round Chicago. I have been on quite a few of these all over the world, but this is easily the best one. Each one has a guide who is knowledgeable and entertaining. As well as Millennium

Park and Navy Pier, the bus stops at some of the city's best museums, The Art Institute, The Shedd Aquarium, Adler Planetarium and the Field Museum.

Chicago Architecture Boat Tour is more interesting than it sounds. Our guide was very informative and told us all about the buildings along the river from art deco to ultra-modern and it was interesting to hear how the river had developed. Chicago river is an oddity as it was forced to flow in reverse so that Chicago's raw sewage doesn't flow into Lake Michigan but instead into the fast flowing Mississippi river and out to sea. Most of Chicago's drinking water comes from Lake Michigan. The Riverwalk is an important feature of the city. There are different sections, street theatre and a children's playground. The newer buildings are designed to reflect the city skyline from the river.

Another place to spend a few hours is Navy Pier, to walk around, ride on the wheel, visit the shopping mall, the greenhouse, the temporary Rolling Stones exhibition, take a boat trip into Lake Michigan or sit and enjoy one of the many bars and eateries.

Chicago has its fair share of tall skyscrapers so it's possible to get a bird's eye view from Willis tower or 360 Chicago. The braver ones in our group experienced The Tilt which is a unique way of seeing the city from 1000ft up. It is the only one of its kind in the world but it's not for me.

CANADA

Alberta

Two places that were on my wish list were Canada and Alaska. In 2010 we decided to start crossing off our bucket list. After many months of precision planning of flights, hotels, coaches, tours, trains and a cruise, our dream trip had finally arrived. We got an amazing deal on the BA flights and thanks to Fairmont, we got some brilliant deals on the hotels. This was our last trip as a family of three.

O'Dea – A Path Well Travelled

We arrived in Calgary a week before the famous stampede. Many of the windows had colourful cartoons depicting cowboys, bulls and horses. We managed to find a few good Country & Western bars on the main street.

We were picked up in the morning ready for our transfer to Banff. We chose Brewster, the leading tour company of the Canadian Rockies to get from Calgary to Jasper. Brewster own and manage many of the attractions, including the Minnewanka Lake Cruise which was our first tour. Minnewanka translates to "of the water spirit". It is a pleasant, narrated motor boat cruise explaining the local legends of the lake. Banff is a young town with plenty of bars, restaurants and a couple of shopping malls. The Discover Banff tour was very enjoyable. We were lucky enough to see a few animals as well as Two Jacks Lake, Banff Gondola, Bow Falls, The Hoodoos, Tunnel Mountain and finally Surprise Corner. Banff Gondola felt very stable as it went to the top of Sulphur Mountain. That was the highlight of our morning.

At Château Lake Louise, we were lucky enough to stay in a deluxe lake view room. I have seen many pictures of Lake Louise but even on the dullest day, it is even more beautiful than the postcards. The following morning the sun shone and a perfect mirror image of the mountains reflected in the lake. I will always remember this as one of the most impressive sights I have ever seen. I had to keep pinching myself to make sure it was real.

Most of our journey was along Highway-93 otherwise known as Icefields Parkway, said to be the most scenic highway in North America. There are many miles of lakes, mountains and glaciers in Banff and Jasper national parks. We stopped at Bow Lake and the almost neon Peyto Lake but the highlight of our day was the Columbia Icefields Explorer. We had the opportunity to walk on a thousand foot thick glacier after lunch. Our final stop was the spectacular Sunwapta Falls near Jasper. Just before reaching Jasper, we spotted a black bear on the roadside.

Jasper is smaller than Banff. Most of the familiar hotels are in the same street with plenty of shops, bars and restaurants nearby. We stayed in Jasper Park Lodge a few miles out of town, Jasper Park Lodge consists of rustic lodges around a lake where deer and elk roam freely.

British Columbia and Vancouver Island

We had a very early start for our Rocky Mountaineer journey to Whistler, crossing the border from Alberta to British Columbia. Rocky Mountaineer is very expensive so we could only afford Red Leaf. We were on the train for 2 days with an overnight in Quesnel. Red Leaf only included a cold lunch box meal, so we were starving by the time we got to Whistler. Rocky Mountaineer have since scrapped Red Leaf and now only do Silver and Gold.

Whistler is purpose built as a ski and summer sports resort. Whistler village is at the base of two mountains, Blackcomb Mountain and Whistler Mountain. It is clean, modern and attractively designed with plenty of hotels, shops and restaurants. We stayed at Delta Whistler Suites which is in the heart of the village so everything was right on our doorstep. If we had had more time, we would have taken the gondola up to Blackcomb Mountain and the peak to peak cable car which goes between the two mountains. This was a new and very popular attraction in 2010. We took the Whistler Mountaineer down to Vancouver. When the Sea to Sky Highway was finally completed, this particular tourist service stopped which is rather a shame.

Our stay in Vancouver was split with a night after Whistler and a couple of nights after our cruise which began and ended in Seattle. Fairmont Vancouver is in the heart of the city near Robson and Burrard Street. Cruise ships dock right by Canada Place. It is a short walk from the most attractive parts of the city. Vancouver is clean and modern and reminds me a little of Sydney but with added bonus of Grouse Mountain, which is high enough to have snow at the top, even with temperatures in the thirties. We saw the sights of the city as well as harbour seals and a bald eagle on an enjoyable harbour cruise on a paddle steamer.

O'Dea – A Path Well Travelled

We took the ferry across to Victoria from Seattle at the end of our Alaska cruise. The Empress is a Victorian icon of the city of Victoria on Vancouver Island, dominating the Inner Harbour with its ivy covered walls.

Victoria is such a pretty city with flowers everywhere. By day there are buskers, stallholders selling arts and crafts and whale watching trips. By night the Government Buildings are lit up with fairy lights which reflect onto the Inner Harbour which is so magical.

We were lucky enough to visit Butchart Gardens on Saturday. They have a choreographed firework display which is one of the best I've seen. One of the big highlights of our trip was the seaplane back from Victoria to Vancouver. We had a beautiful aerial view of both cities and many small islands. This took us almost door to door from the Empress to the Pacific Rim.

Fairmont Pacific Rim was a brand new hotel built for the Winter Olympics in 2010, a state of the art hotel in a great location opposite the harbour. The world's greenest convention centre with its unique 6-acre grass roof and Canada Place shopping mall are virtually opposite on Vancouver harbour.

We took the 48-hour trolley tour which has two routes, red and blue. The red route goes round Stanley Park which is actually bigger than Central Park in New York. The biggest attractions inside the park are the Totem Poles, the aquarium, the Rose Garden and Prospect Point.

On one of these trolley rides, our driver was Steve Oatway. He asked where everyone came from and as soon as we said Notting Hill in London, he asked if we knew the Oatways and I said I did, I went to school with one of them. Steve Oatway had spent years tracking down the Oatways all over the world. He drove the trolley in summer and he is an actor in the winter. The trolley no longer exists but we have kept in touch with Steve.

On our last day in Vancouver the blue route took us to Granville Island, home of the Maritime Museum and Observatory, and at the other end, old warehouses that have been converted into a market and entertainment area.

THE CARIBBEAN AND BERMUDA

Bermuda

I was successful in applying for a sought after British Airways Breakaway in the mid-seventies. That was my first ever long haul trip. Our group stayed in a small hotel, away from the main tourist resorts. February in Bermuda definitely isn't sunbathing weather but it is very pleasant for lovely country walks around Harrington Sound which is a haven for indigenous fish and birds including the longtail.

Bermuda is famous for pink coral beaches which give it a distinct character. Bermuda is British but there is a great deal of American influence and the currency is tied to the US Dollar. Bermuda is well served by buses so it was really easy to get around and explore the island and visit a few hotels at our leisure. The schoolchildren had impeccable manners and stood up for any adults who boarded the bus.

The town of St. George has stocks in the main square and it has a British colonial feel about it. In Hamilton, the capital of Bermuda, policeman in shorts directed the traffic. This is a tradition that is definitely Bermudian. I loved the shops in Hamilton, lots of independent and art and craft shops with lovely, well made, unique gifts.

Cuba

I won our trip to Cuba with Cubanacan hotels in 2000. This was a 2-week trip for two of us. Prizes and educational trips are almost always out of season with lots of black out dates. We had to travel in August/September which is right in the middle of the hurricane season.

This trip was a disaster from beginning to end. We had to fly with Cubana. On the way out they sat us both in middle seats one behind the other. They didn't meet us on arrival so we had to get a taxi to the hotel.

O'Dea – A Path Well Travelled

The hotel in Havana couldn't find our reservation. We had a split stay, a night in Havana, a week in Cayo Coco and then a few nights back in Havana.

We had to get a cab to the airport in the dark. We knew this wasn't the way to the airport so we got a little scared as we went into a suburban area with bars on the windows, then the taxi stopped abruptly in the middle of the road and the driver got out. We were terrified. It turned out that he was giving another driver his spare tyre. We finally arrived at what turned out to be a little domestic airport miles from the city. We didn't have tickets to fly, just a handwritten scrap of paper, but somehow it worked.

We ended up on a Russian Tupolev which had rivets and a ladder into the tail of the aircraft. My seat was broken so I was lying down rather than sitting up. One of the bonuses of turboprops is that they don't fly very high so it stayed below the clouds. The view along the coast was stunning. That was one of the highlights of our trip despite the ancient aircraft.

We landed at Cayo Coco which was just a beach hut and they took us to our hotel. We managed a trip on a tourist train, but potholed roads are not meant for tourist trains so it was a very bumpy ride.

We went into a cave and I needed the loo after the rum and the bumpy ride. They gave me a massive candle with a huge old-fashioned wooden candlestick as the loo was pitch black and the light was broken with wires hanging out of the wall. They took us further into the cave where the guide lit his lighter to reveal thousands of bats on the ceiling which completely spooked us.

After a couple of idyllic days on the soft sand beach the weather worsened and we were told to stay indoors as a hurricane was on its way so we were stuck in our hotel room for 2 days. After the hurricane came swarms of mosquitoes. I have never had so many bites and I suffered for weeks.

Back in Havana, we organised a half day trip on our last day as our flight wasn't until the evening. We were getting later and later so we left the group and got a taxi back to the hotel to make sure we were at the airport 3 hours before our flight.

Forty of us were bumped off the flight. We were told we could pay $300 each to get home in business class. We didn't have $600 to spare. They told us we would have to fly to Paris on Air France the next day and then BA home. They did put us in a hotel overnight which was a really lovely one but they lied to us about Air France. It was a French charter called AOM that took us to Paris Orly and then just as I suspected, we were put on standby to London. We were told they did the same every week.

One couple managed to get confirmed tickets home and spent the whole day rubbing it in. I used my business card in the hope that it would help. We went back to the standby desk and got our business class tickets back to Heathrow on Air Liberté. The couple who spent all day gloating had to walk past us reading our newspaper and drinking champagne. They were in economy.

Jamaica

I did the training for Jamaica Tourist Board and I was offered a trip to Jamaica in 2000. The itinerary looked amazing, Half Moon in Montego Bay and Ciboney in Ocho Rios. We visited some stunning hotels including Round Hill and Jamaica Inn which both had wonderful views. This trip was well organised, informative and educational as we got to see a whole range of hotels from basic to de-luxe. Some of us climbed the Dunns River Falls. It looked very slippery so I stayed at the bottom and took pictures.

One girl on our trip couldn't eat anything spicy, not even pepper. In the land of Jerk Chicken and curried goat this proved to be a major issue everywhere we went. In the end it got really embarrassing. Maybe Jamaica wasn't the best choice for her.

Dunn's River Falls

Barbados

I tried my best to find something affordable over the school holidays. Virgin had a fault in their system and I booked Florida at a ridiculously low price. Virgin realised their mistake and cancelled it, but offered a discount on an alternative. The closest I could get to the half term dates was to Barbados.

It was our only visit to the Caribbean as a family. Barbados is very British so it was an easy first introduction to the Caribbean. We stayed at Time Out at the Gap which was fairly basic but it suited us well and it was just across the road from Dover Beach, a stunning long white sandy beach. The water is calmer on the west but the south is livelier and it is easier to walk out to bars and restaurants.

Our island tour included the wild east coast of Bath and Bathsheba, the sugar canes and parts of the island away from the tourists and we really enjoyed that. We also enjoyed the Atlantis submarine and seeing what wonders lie below the surface of the Caribbean Sea.

O'Dea – A Path Well Travelled
We tried to get around Barbados by bus but we soon discovered that there are two types of bus, official government buses which were blue and went from A to B and yellow buses which were a different story altogether. The yellow buses were very noisy with a ghetto blaster, animals and a crazy driver. Guess which one we ended up with? I gather the buses have changed somewhat since then.

Grenada

We were invited on a fam trip in 2003. We had some work to do, but not that much, just a few hotels to visit at a very leisurely pace. Some of the hotels were stunning especially La Luna, Secret Harbour and Spice Island but the one we all loved was True Blue Bay which is run by an English/Mexican couple Russell and Magdalena and their daughters, We visited during the day and we needed props for the Easter Bonnet Parade the next morning, so on impulse one of the group "borrowed" a tablecloth for the purpose.

We went back to True Blue Bay the following evening for our hosted dinner which was amazing and the vista of stars was incredible. Unfortunately I had totally forgotten about the tablecloth when we were showing Russell the photos of our day. He recognised his tablecloth but he did see the funny side and we all laughed about it.

We were taken to some of the loveliest spots on the island, Concorde Falls, La Sagesse and across to Carriacou on the fast ferry. Carriacou is totally different from Grenada. It looks more like a Greek island with its olive and citrus trees whereas Grenada is very green and tropical.

One night we had dinner in Patrick's in St George, the capital. At first sight it was the most unappealing restaurant you could possibly imagine, out in the open, underneath a building with peeling paint and a rough hand painted sign and just wooden benches to sit on. We ended up having the best evening ever. Patrick was a larger than life character. He kept us entertained all evening and there was an endless stream of bowls of food. Everything was home cooked and absolutely delicious.

O'Dea – A Path Well Travelled

The Grenada flight was weekly so the Monarch crew were staying in same hotel as us. We made friends with them over the week and shared many drinks at the bar. There were ten of us with eight seats available in the superior class on the return, so it was the luck of the draw. Sod's law, I ended up in a middle seat at the back in economy.

While visiting my daughter in Manchester, I went to an event with my friend Ann. At the end of the night I won the star prize, 7 nights in the Coyaba in Grenada. I had intended to go with Ann but Jim said he wanted to go. Luckily Ann had either flights or accommodation to use so in the end we all went, Jim and I and Ann with her friend Christine. We did this for our Wedding Anniversary in May 2008.

Christine knows Grenada inside out. She even thought seriously about buying property there. She hired a car and was happy to drive us around. I was keen to revisit La Sagesse which I loved last time and I wanted Jim to see it. They had since planted new palm trees so it was different but still gorgeous. In the evening she took us to Morne Rouge, a beautiful spot famous for its sunsets.

We wanted to see the best of the island. Roger, our tour guide, was excellent and took us through Gouyave, famous for its fish fry, Concord Falls, Dougaldston Spice Boucan, Belmont Plantation where lunch was included, Leaper's Hill, River's Rum Distillery and Grand Etang, the bottomless lake.

Grenada is famous for its spices, particularly nutmeg and cinnamon so it has some of the best food in the Caribbean. By this time we knew lots of people in Grenada and we wanted to revisit some hotels after the dreadful 2004 hurricane had devastated the island.

Sir Royston Hopkin, who was knighted in 2004 for his services to Grenada tourism passed away in 2020. He was a really lovely man. He treated us all to dinner at the luxury Spice Island Beach Resort which he owned. The dinner was absolutely wonderful with many courses and all our dietary needs were catered for with a smile.

As it was our Wedding Anniversary, the Coyaba hotel surprised us with flowers and champagne in our room. We dined at True Blue Bay which has a very romantic setting and the food was divine. They had done a great deal of work since I saw it last.

Sadly, the lovely craft market on Grand Anse had almost disappeared as the cruise ships lured the stallholders to the more lucrative cruiseport mall which doesn't have the same ambience as the lovely little craft market on the beach. We had drinks and lunch in The Nutmeg overlooking the harbour. This has since closed which is a real shame.

In 2009, I was delighted to win 7 nights at the lovely La Source all-inclusive hotel at Pink Gin Beach. La Source had especially high beds which proved very difficult to get into if you have short legs like mine. This was designed to look out of the window and admire the wonderful sea view. Every morning we swam in the inviting Caribbean Sea at 6.30am when it was quiet.

We really loved this beautiful, romantic setting and there was no real need to move from the resort as the all inclusive was of such high quality, but we did use the shuttle bus into St. George for a few hours. We have such fond memories of La Source which has since closed to make way for Sandals Grenada.

Saint Lucia

I was offered a megafam to Saint Lucia with the Tourist Board trip in 2003. We got to see the best of the island. We had a day in the classroom so we really learned a great deal about the island. I have sold it many times before and since. It was a busy and hectic schedule. Our trip included the helicopter from Castries to Hewanorra which was only 10 minutes but it was one of the most magical things I've ever experienced with a spectacular ariel view of the Pitons.

Our huge group was split into three, staying in different hotels and meeting up occasionally for lunch. We visited most of Saint Lucia's luxury, quirky and innovative hotels.

O'Dea – A Path Well Travelled

Ladera and Anse Chastenet were two of the most memorable hotels I have ever seen. Both hotels have rooms with three walls and they both overlook The Pitons. We visited all three Sandals hotels on that trip, Sandals Regency, Sandals Halcyon and Sandals Grande. We literally walked for miles looking at every room type.

Sandals organised dinner on the beach. We dressed up in bright clothes. I had an orange sundress which I bought in Jamaica and bundled up something else to make a headscarf. The plastic tables and chairs were dressed up in bright tablecloths but the plastic chairs had hollow legs so as we ate and the rum cocktails flowed we began to sink into the beach. The more we drank, the more we sank. We ended up on the beach with the table at a precarious angle. We were hanging onto our chicken drumsticks and our drinks for dear life. I laughed so much, I literally wet myself!

It was on that educational that we had an unforgettable evening at Bang Between the Pitons. We had a barbeque and drinks at the house and we had the privilege of meeting the owner, Lord Glenconner, who was friendly with Princess Margaret and he owned the island of Mustique. He was such an interesting and memorable character who took the time to interact with us at the table. He had his own distinctive bohemian style. He wore a floppy hat and white Indian style robes. Bang Between the Pitons is now owned by the Viceroy hotel group and is part of Sugar Beach.

At Travel Counsellors Birmingham conference in 2011, I won 7 nights at Rendezvous in Saint Lucia with Caribtours. I extended this to include 2 nights in the south of the island. This was the first time I had been on holiday instead of racing round hotels.

St Lucia has large areas of rainforest so the island is very lush and green with abundant birdlife. Rainfall is higher than most of the other islands but there is plenty of sunshine to enjoy between the showers.

Jalousie Hilton, now Sugar Beach, lies on a beautiful white sand beach on the calm turquoise Caribbean Sea in the South West overlooking the

Pitons. We had a gorgeous villa on the hillside, right in the heart of lush rainforest surrounded by natural beauty, situated close to the Diamond Botanical Gardens and Waterfall.

The next seven nights were at the busier north west of St Lucia on Malabar Beach at the edge of the capital Castries. We enjoyed Rendezvous, as we had a whole week to really wind down and relax. As it was all-inclusive we didn't have to move from the hotel except for our trip to the Skyride.

The Skyride is in an area of rainforest 20 minutes from Castries. The Aerial Tram Ride is smooth and slow, so even at 120 feet above ground, I felt relaxed despite my fear of heights. We learnt about the rainforest and the flora and fauna. The perspective coming back is totally different from a different height and facing the other way.

Antigua

By this time my friend Ann Barber was a Travel Counsellor having joined them 4 years before I did. She had won a couple of Virgin tickets with Travel Counsellors shortly before I joined them in 2006. That was my first holiday with Ann after our work trip to Israel.

We were due to leave from Gatwick. The 06.31 from Olympia was cancelled leaving us and another couple stranded and underdressed for the arctic weather on that day. We had to walk up to Kensington High Street in the snow and pick up a cab to Victoria. On our flight with Virgin, a first class passenger went berserk and slapped a stewardess so she was restrained in her seat. We were grounded until the police turned up.

Our room at Jolly Beach wasn't fancy but it overlooked a beautiful beach and one of the two wedding arbors. The booklet in our room claimed that "Our gardeners work deliquently". The staff were amazing, the food was excellent and the pool was inviting.

The entertainment left much to be desired but I do remember two things about it. The prize for the WORST karaoke singer, I can still feel the pain, it was excruciating! We left to go back to our room and polish off the rum and pineapple on our balcony. The other entertainment I remember was a fashion show and a lady, a very tall, slim Antiguan lady, had a tall ridged conical hairstyle, making her over 8ft tall. I've never seen anything like it. We tried Lydia's, the fish restaurant, one of the three a-la-carte restaurants at Jolly Beach which is on the beach in Crab Hole Village. I ordered the Red Snapper and it was delicious.

I had forgotten how much the Atlantic disagreed with me. Getting the Wadadli Cat catamaran round the entire island seemed a good idea at the time. It turned out to be literally taking the rough with the smooth. It was an idyllic trip in the Caribbean sea and it was fascinating to watch the point where the two seas met but once we hit the Atlantic, I was violently sick and went a ghastly shade of green. While I was throwing up the barbeque and rum Ann was enjoying the sailing experience immensely.

I will always remember the beautiful sunsets. Sitting on our balcony and watching the sun go down is something I will never forget. One evening we went to the famous Shirley Heights barbeque on Sunday night. It was fun but very touristy with a very long queue for the one and only toilet, however, we did enjoy the sunset and the spectacular views across English Harbour. We would have liked to see more of Antigua but the bus service is limited, taxis are very expensive and so are excursions.

One day we got the local bus into St. John's, the capital. There is a fruit and veg market, and a rather odd bust of V G Bird, a tribute to Antigua's first leader. At Heritage Quay, where the cruises dock, there are many designer shops. We found it crowded with cruise day trippers and there was a definite contrast in attitude to our happy, friendly resort of Jolly Beach which we will always remember fondly. For cruise day trippers, staying in the capital would give a different overall impression of Antigua. We found a bar called Hemingway's which had a first floor balcony outside, a lovely place to enjoy a cold beer.

Saint Lucia, Trinidad and Tobago

As a Platinum Caribbean specialist, I applied for one of the multi island educational trips organised by the Caribbean Tourist Organisation in 2010. Two of my best friends, Ann and Gillian were on the trip and Helen Rostron whom we met in Grenada. We had so much fun on that trip and it was useful from a sales point of view. We had so many wonderful, fun moments and it is a trip that I will never forget, definitely one of the highlights of my years in travel. We travelled with Lorraine Grant, Sonja Rogers, Andrew Hillier and Jackie Bookal, four lovely people who are all really knowledgeable about the Caribbean.

Although I had already been on a Saint Lucia megafam, it is a diverse island and there wasn't much duplication in the itinerary. Jade Mountain was new since my last visit and many of the hotels I had seen had since been upgraded. Lushan Country Life, a nature park, was interesting too. We went back to Sandals again for lunch and had time for a swim and a cocktails in the swim up bar.

This time we went from north to south by boat. I hadn't realised this was a possibility and it was an enjoyable journey. I enjoyed birthday drinks at Jump Up in Gros Islet where we were liming to Soca with the locals.

Andrew was in charge of the Trinidad and Tobago part of the trip. We visited the Asa Wright Bird Sanctuary, watched the Scarlet Ibises in the mangroves on the river and then did a tour of Port of Spain. Port of Spain is unlike any other city that I have seen in the Caribbean, it looks more like South America, modern with straight, wide streets and tall buildings.

On arrival, we met Michelle from the tourist office who could easily have been the headmistress I had at school. She was wearing a crimplene dress and seemed very stern.

Steely Pan, a limited edition soft toy to promote Trinidad and Tobago, was the brainchild of Andrew Hillier. It was Gillian's turn to babysit him. She was doing a great job for most of the day. She carried him round the Angostura Bitter and rum factory and made sure he didn't get drunk but in the evening he was kidnapped! Poor Gillian was distraught. The ransom note was found and given to Andrew.

Andrew was determined to get to the bottom of it. It was my job to hide Steely Pan but Andrew was searching all the bags as we got on the coach. Luckily I bought a spare pair of clean knickers with me and I pulled them out, embarrassing Andrew, so he didn't bother looking in the bottom of my bag, too scared of what else might be lurking in there. By this time, Michelle played along with it and was laughing along with the rest of us. It was time for us to go to Tobago and by this time Steely Pan had reappeared, Michelle decided we were a really fun crowd and made the time to wave us off on our last leg, Tobago.

We loved Tobago. Andrew kept the hotel visits all very short so we had more time to really enjoy the ambience. He took us to swim in Nylon Pool that would make us 10 years younger. Sadly it didn't work but, nevertheless, we enjoyed the swim in the crystal clear shallow waters. We had fun doing the conga at the barbeque with cocktails on the beach afterwards.

We stayed in Stonehaven Villas that night and had a midnight pool party in the biggest villa, which was Andrew's. It had a massive jacuzzi pool so it was time for a midnight dip with music and plenty of rum.

At the end of the trip it was time for our awards. We all sat round the swimming pool in anticipation. Ann won the cocktail making and then it was time to guess who won the David Bellamy award. We all looked at each other in bewilderment, wondering who the secret nature lover was. That's how I ended up with an official certificate proudly awarding me with the David Bellamy award….. for photography! We all fell about laughing when we realised that it should have read David Bailey. I still have that certificate, one of my few precious treasures that I didn't throw out when I retired. We've never let Andrew forget. We often reminisce about that trip which will stay in my memory forever.

Steely Pan at the Angostura Factory

Cayman Islands

In 2005 I was offered a trip to The Cayman Islands with the tourist board to Grand Cayman. We even went to Hell and back and sent the postcard, everyone does! We swam with stingrays, enjoyed the Queen Elizabeth Botanical Gardens and the Turtle Farm. I loved the Butterfly Farm which has since closed down.

We flew on a tiny aircraft and landed on a grass strip on Little Cayman. It was a step back in time, the airport shared the building with the fire station and the only school was just one classroom of children of all ages. They welcomed us into their classroom like long lost friends. That was so beautiful, a moment I will always treasure. We spent the afternoon at Booby Pond, abundant with indigenous birdlife.

183

ASIA

Hong Kong

One of the best prizes I ever won in was a competition run by British Airways and Ritz Carlton in 1994. Hong Kong was still British. Martin was only 2 and it wasn't practical to take him with us. Leaving him behind for 3 weeks was one of the hardest things I've ever done. We missed him so much.

First of all, we flew to Hong Kong, our very first trip to Asia. We got a seat upstairs in the bubble on a Boeing-747. It was economy but it was so comfortable and roomy, the best economy flight of our lives. We landed at the old Kai Tak airport which was every bit as scary as its reputation. It is said that the pilots would always include Kai Tak as part of their simulator training. If they could land at Kai Tak, they could land anywhere in the world. There were tower blocks on both sides of the runway.

The Ritz Carlton in Hong Kong was stunning. We were on a high floor with a harbour view. We watched the Star Ferries narrowly missing each other all night. That put us off using it so we used the MTR to get around. It was fast and efficient and stops were announced in English.

Jim loves his potatoes and eats them in abundance so the single new potato cut into quarters wasn't what he considered to be a portion, so we ate a lot of meals in McDonalds, his choice, not mine!

I got an invitation from the Hong Kong Tourist Board in 2006. I was keen to experience Hong Kong after the handover in 1999. Our flight was on the low cost airline Oasis. As they hadn't loaded the vegetarian meals, I ended up with just a Pot Noodle for the entire 12-hour flight. Our flight landed at the new Hong Kong airport Chek Lap Kok which opened in 1997. It was much better than the old Kai Tak.

We were a nice crowd but it was a big group so I can't remember any names apart from Alfredo whom I have met many time at events and on the Costa Brava trip. We were hosted by Marco Polo Hotels. We stayed in Kowloon which I felt had more character than Hong Kong Island with its street markets and local bars. Our group did experience Star Ferry which is the cheapest way to get to the Hong Kong Island. Disneyland Hong Kong was small but really magical. The artificial snow fell on Main Street and Mickey Mouse was looking festive.

The travel industry is very diverse with many religions and diets to consider. Many of us struggled in Hong Kong. Meat and fish are often in the same dish. We all filled out our dietary requirements but this wasn't communicated very well for one of our hosted dinners. Being unable to accommodate vegetarian, halal, kosher and various food allergies between us, we deeply offended and embarrassed the hotel. We were advised too late that it is rude to refuse a meal. It is better to accept the meal, shove it round the plate a bit, pretending that we had eaten and enjoyed it, but we were just leaving room for the next course. I doubt whether the hotel ever invited British travel agents again after that. I felt quite ashamed and I still feel embarrassed now about being the awkward non-meat eater but after that I did my best to avoid situations like these.

We visited the island of Lantau and the new Ngong Ping theme park and the Giant Buddha. Then, we had lunch at the monastery which was entirely vegetarian. It was one of the best meals I've ever eaten, certainly the best tofu without a doubt.

Our group in Hong Kong

Singapore

I won two seats in a competition run by Singapore Airlines. Jim was busy, so Sharon came instead. As soon as we arrived, we knew that Jim would have enjoyed it. I managed to get a fantastic rate at Fairmont Singapore right in the heart of the city, walking distance from Singapore River and Chinatown. Our first plan was to visit the ethnic quarters of the city. We managed two that day, starting with the furthest which is the Malay Quarter and the Peranakan houses. In the Bugis area, we were transported to the Middle East with the smell of kebabs, people in Arab dress leaving the mosque, colourful fabric shops, small cafés and handmade baskets.

The iconic Raffles hotel transported us to a bygone era. Raffles is a quiet oasis in the heart of the city. I had a quick tour of the rooms and, of course, a Singapore Sling. The Singapore Flyer is a similar concept to the London Eye. We watched the light fading to dusk and the constructions of the future in the distance, the casino, and sports stadium and remnants of Singapore's colonial past at the other end of the city.

We accidentally stumbled on the Chingay Parade, the largest street parade in Asia. This was a real treat. There were 7,000 performers in beautiful costumes from all over Asia. There were firecrackers and Chinese dragons to celebrate the beginning of spring.

We strolled past Raffles Place with its skyscrapers, past City Hall and the Fullerton Hotel towards Merlion Park and the symbol of the Lion City. Merlion has since moved. Heading towards Boat Quay, we took the bum boat on the journey past Clarke Quay, Robertson Quay and the Esplanade. This was a relaxing 45 minutes, a great way to see both the old and new facets of the city.

We took the MRT to Little India to the sights and smells of Indian spices, ornate Hindu temples, floral garlands, gold jewellery, shops selling cheap jeans and Tekka market selling colourful saris, bangles and dresses.

We experienced the hustle and bustle of colourful Chinatown, the crashing of cymbals to the Chinese dragon seeing out the end of the Chinese New Year. This is the place to buy souvenirs and there are many bargains. Laden with far too many bags including a large dragon head, we sat down for a very welcome Tiger Beer. In the evening we made our own way to Singapore Zoo and the Night Safari. We enjoyed the 45-minute tram ride seeing many nocturnal animals.

We went back to Singapore Zoo, to enjoy a huge buffet breakfast with a family of Orangutans with their 7-month old baby sitting in the trees just outside the restaurant as we ate. This was definitely one of the best things we experienced. We had time to enjoy the shows and wander round the Zoo. Singapore Zoo is a rainforest zoo where most of the animals are in a reasonably natural environment and not behind cages. A new project at Mandai is planned to replace the existing zoo and will incorporate Jurong Bird Park, which I haven't yet seen. Entry to the

Botanic Gardens is free for most of the gardens apart from the beautiful Orchid Gardens which is well worth the nominal fee.

Sentosa Island is the family fun area with the theme parks Sentosa Resort World and Universal Studios Sentosa. We walked down towards the beach station from the Sentosa Merlion through the mosaic sculpture that stretches all the way down. Free trams go to Pelawan and Siloso. The southernmost point of continental Asia is at the other end of a rope bridge in Pelawan. The beach is man-made on a major shipping lane so whilst it is a nice place to spend an afternoon, it isn't the best beach experience.

On the last day we packed to go home and to our dismay the dragon head wouldn't fit in either suitcase so we had to take a chance on checking in with the dragon head as hand luggage in the carrier bag it came in. We managed to smuggle it through check in and security but when we got on the aircraft, it wouldn't fit in the overhead bins either! Fortunately the cabin crew were really helpful and they put it in the business class cupboard for us. Sharon's husband loved the dragon head, so it was worth the effort.

In 2011, Jim and I stopped in Singapore both ways on our New Zealand trip. Jim loved Singapore. On the way back we were upgraded to a massive corner suite on a high floor covered in rose petals in the Fairmont Singapore. The suite was so big, the biggest hotel room I've ever stayed in, I could never find my way to the loo.

In 2014, Sharon moved to Singapore for a year with her job, so with the help of Emirates seat sale we planned a hectic 3-week trip to Asia, visiting Dubai, Sri Lanka, Singapore, Chiang Mai and Kuala Lumpur. At that time the Dubai to Singapore flight had a touchdown in Sri Lanka so it was an opportunity to visit for the same fare, just a little more tax and our visas.

There are some nice bars on Siloso Beach in Sentosa. An afternoon of relaxation was just what we needed after a hectic few days in Sri Lanka. We had lunch at Dempsey Hill a pretty little area with antique shops, restaurants and a koi carp pond, a pleasant place to spend an hour or two.

This time we had proper seats for Singapore's 50th Anniversary celebrations at Chingay Parade. There was a flower theme with half a million flowers made from carrier bags. It is amazing how far this city has come in 50 years. It is one of the richest countries in the world with the most efficient infrastructure, world class hotels and an ethnic mix of Chinese, Indian, Malay and European who seem to live side by side without any conflict.

Gardens by the Bay was well worth seeing and it has quickly become an icon of Singapore. There is a charge for Flower Dome and The Cloud Forest and a separate charge for the Skywalk. Flower Dome has year-round mini-exhibitions. Chinese New Year was the theme when we visited. There were flowers, cacti and baobob trees from all over the world in geographical sections all under one roof. It is both imaginative and beautifully maintained.

Cloud Forest was amazing. We accidentally caught it at spray time which added to the experience. There were some Lego exhibits of carnivorous plants in amongst the real plants. We took the lift up to the top and started the gentle walk down a tower of tropical plants and inside a display of crystals, stalagmites and stalactites. Through the glass we could see a view of the city in the changing light before dusk. We waited for the sound and light show in Gardens by the Bay and we managed to find a really good viewpoint.

We took the lift up to the bar at Marina Bay Sands, the new crazy, iconic building. On the lower floors is a posh shopping mall with all the familiar designer brand shops and in the basement there are gondolas. We took the lift up to Ku De Ta and over a cocktail, we watched the sun go down over the city. We spent our last night in Chijmes which had been closed down and rebuilt since our previous visit. It is still enjoyable but it had lost some of the charm and atmosphere it had before. We revisited an old haunt, Lot, Stock and Barrel near Raffles. It has a long Happy Hour so it's relatively cheap for Singapore.

O'Dea – A Path Well Travelled

We discovered Daiso which is a $2 shop like Poundland but with more choice and different from the stuff we get at home. It is actually Japanese but there are a few branches in Singapore. We spent most of our evenings at Robertson Quay which has some decent bars but it is more chilled than its noisier neighbours at Clarke Quay and Boat Quay. Singapore is one of my favourite cities. I have been back a few times but there are places I haven't visited yet. Singapore changes so quickly. There is always something new and innovative.

Jim and I on top of Marina Bay Sands

India

I was absolutely delighted to win a fabulous 9-night tour of the famous Golden Triangle with Indian Routes in 2013. Martin came with me. We were met by the representative from Indian Routes who took us to

O'Dea – A Path Well Travelled

Maidens where we spent our first night, but first, after a quick shower and change, a day of sightseeing.

The intense sights and sounds of Delhi take a little getting used to. Our tour began in Old Delhi at the largest mosque in Asia, Jama Masjid, which is a massive sandstone and marble construction. Our wild ride on a rickshaw round the narrow market streets was an interesting but scary experience. After lunch, we saw the palaces, war memorials, embassies and the tidy gardens of British colonial times in New Delhi. The contrast between Old and New Delhi is like seeing two completely different cities.

We ate lunch at the fairly new Waves restaurant. In the afternoon we visited Qutb Minar which, in my opinion, was the most impressive thing we saw in Delhi. This is the tallest red brick tower in the world. We should have also visited Humayun's Tomb but we were too tired to appreciate it. All we needed to do was sleep. We did have a quick photo stop at Baha'i the Sikh temple that is built like a Lotus flower.

Jaipur, the Pink City, was a long car journey from Delhi with a short stop at a café. It was a comfortable Toyota Innova on a decent road. There was more than enough amusement and interest on the roads to make our journey pass quickly. The closer we got to Jaipur, a host of animals: cows, goats, elephants, camels and buffalo joined in the general chaos of traffic creating absolute mayhem.

Our home for the next 2 nights was the Trident hotel in Jaipur which proved to be the best of the hotels we stayed at, relaxed with nice gardens and a pool which is covered by a net. This is an important feature to stop pigeons and monkeys getting into the pool. Raj Mandir claims to be the best cinema in India. We saw a comedy film in Hindi but set in London which was quite weird and, although quite long at over 2½ hours, it was enjoyable. Our guide explained the plot to us and treated us to Pepsi and popcorn at the interval.

We chose to go up to Amber Fort by jeep. We felt sorry for the poor elephants walking up and down a steep hill all day with tourists on their backs and we definitely didn't want to join them. Choosing the jeep also had the advantage of gaining another hour in the pool and a few beers at the bar back at the hotel. We also visited the magnificent Maharajah City Palace inlaid with tiny mirrors.

We were then taken to a carpet and textile factory. It was interesting to see how these were made. We got a little fed up with various different showrooms by the end of the week as there was always an expectation to buy and we felt uncomfortable declining. Jantar Mantar is the astronomical museum with futuristic sundials accurate to 2 seconds. Although this is centuries old it still looks like a seventies futuristic movie set.

We had a busy and very full day with a lunch stop at The Bagh, a boutique hotel with a bird sanctuary in peaceful Bharatpur, before visiting the abandoned multi-ethnic city of Fatephur Sikri. The sandstone buildings are beautifully preserved with lovely carvings and frescoes and finally the ultimate wonder of India, the magnificent Taj Mahal. This immense white marble structure which took 22 years to build is a perfectly symmetrical mausoleum. I'timad-ud-Daulah or Baby Taj was the original inspiration for the Taj Mahal. It is inlaid with different coloured marbles.

After getting the train from Agra to Jhansi we stopped at Orchha for lunch. Orchha Palace was incredible. We walked round the market, enjoying the colours and fragrant spices, before going to Khajuraho. In the evening was saw a Sound and Light Show explaining the history of the Western temples. In the morning we saw the Western, Eastern and Jain temples in Khajuraho. The carvings were absolutely incredible, such intricate and detailed individual characters mostly in compromising positions. Khajuraho was absolutely fascinating but it was time for our flight to Varanasi.

Varanasi, the city of learning and burning is the Indian heart of spirituality for Hindus and Buddhists, where sick people bathe in the healing waters of the Ganges. Hindus believe that if you die in Varanasi you will go straight to heaven. Many old and sick people end their days there, consequently cremations take place day and night. We participated in an open air Aarti ceremony on the banks of Ganges which consists of chants, flowers and fire. It is a beautiful and very spiritual experience.

In the morning at sunrise we had a boat ride along the Ganges passing holy men, launderers and cremation pyres on the riverbank. Varanasi is an incredibly busy city of three million people, absolute chaos with traffic and animals. It is so vibrant, colourful and thought provoking. It is difficult to describe Varanasi, chaotic and busy and yet so peaceful and spiritual. Later we went to Sarnath where Buddha preached his first sermon. Krishna, our guide, told us the story of Buddha which was absolutely fascinating.

We flew from Varanasi back to Delhi for our overnight stay before heading back to London with our heads spinning from all the sights we had seen, ancient forts and palaces, magnificent artwork and the different influences of a multi-cultural society. The sounds and smells of everyday life were just as interesting as the magnificent temples, little people carrying half the world on their heads, delicate women wearing saris, sitting side saddle on the back of mopeds with babies and animals, the relentless traffic, animals in the road, hand painted lorries and shops, colourful markets. Most of all, the warmth, politeness and friendliness of the Indian people are unforgettable.

Malaysia

Our original plan was to get the coach from Singapore to Malacca, stay a night there and then get a taxi to Kuala Lumpur. After 3 weeks of travelling we didn't fancy travelling by road. We wanted to get to Kuala Lumpur and home.

As this was the first anniversary of the missing plane, fares were even cheaper than it would have been on our original plan of going by bus. We got a great deal at the Intercontinental which is well located. The buffet dinner was excellent and inexpensive so we had this on all 3 nights. There was an amazing choice of Asian and Western food so we were both happy. We used the free bus tour to get around the city. Petronas Towers is an amazing piece of architecture. We liked the covered market and we picked up a few bargains.

Overall, I do prefer the feel of Singapore and Bangkok but in fairness I don't think we got the best from Kuala Lumpur as we were tired of travelling and sightseeing after 3 weeks in UAE, Sri Lanka, Singapore and Thailand. There was also a great deal of building works which made it difficult to get to some of the parts of the city that I wanted to see. On reflection we should have booked a proper city tour.

Thailand

Singapore to Chiang Mai was our first experience on Air Asia. The change at Bangkok Don Meung airport was straightforward. The only thing I was confused about was whether our arrival in Chiang Mai would be international or domestic so we ended up in a different place from our driver and it took us a while to find him.

We stayed in a hotel called D2, a design subsidiary of Dusit. It had many quirky design features as part of the concept but the strangest was the cube. The cube was in our room, about a foot square made from orange see through Perspex and every day it would contain a small mystery item. The problem was we couldn't always identify what the mystery item was supposed to do and a couple of times we wondered; do we drink it, wash our clothes or bathe in it? It remains a mystery!

Once we got our bearings in Chiang Mai it was easy to find our way around on foot but some of the main roads are very difficult to cross. Zebra crossings are barely visible and drivers ignore them anyway. We followed locals across the busy roads. Buddhist monks were particularly useful for this purpose.

Chiang Mai was originally a walled city. Even new maps indicate the walls. Very little of the actual wall remains. Some of it was rebuilt to get an idea of what the original wall would have looked like. There isn't

194

much distinction between inside and outside the city walls, there are a couple of beautiful and fascinating temples in the centre. Thai wats, nearly all Buddhist, are very distinctive, encrusted with gold, in a uniquely Thai style.

I was surprised how many Europeans are living in Chiang Mai and how many tourists venture so far inland. Bars and restaurants cater for Western tastes as well as Thai. The night market is absolutely massive with many bargains. It is surprisingly hassle free, leaving us free to browse at leisure.

We booked two tours from Chiang Mai, the City and Temples tour and the Doi Inthonan National Park tour. We had a driver and a guide all to ourselves. Doi Inthonan, the highest mountain in Thailand included the King and Queen's Chedis, We enjoyed the beautiful gardens with wonderful views for miles around. We had lunch and declined the Jade Factory visit.

In June 2019, Sharon and I combined her British Airways Rewards flights and my hotel discounts to create a very affordable luxury holiday experience. We travelled in business class and stayed in de-luxe hotels. I have sold so many holidays to Bangkok. This was definitely a destination that would prove useful for work. Sharon was already very familiar with the city. I had no idea that this would prove to be my last long haul trip and that just over a year later I would no longer be in the travel industry.

We loved the Anantara in Hua Hin. It was a little way from town but there is a shuttle bus and taxis are cheap. After browsing the night market we discovered the Railway Tavern. I assume this used to be a station as trains rattle past every now and again. This had a nice ambience, the music was good and they served food so this became our local.

We got back to our hotel and I heard my name called. My friend and colleague Sophie Sheth and her family were staying in the same hotel but they were leaving the next morning. It was really nice to be introduced to her husband and daughters and to share a final drink with them before they left.

Cicada is a weekend only market which is a combination of theatre, craft market and food. It had a strange cashless system. This involved having to buy tickets at a booth and then spend them on the food and drink stalls, There was always a bit left over which either got wasted or had to be topped up. It rained for a while but that didn't stop us enjoying our evening. There was a decent band playing so we stopped to watch them for a while before heading back.

I got up early the next morning and tried to sit on the balcony. I immediately regretted it as I got eaten alive within minutes by mosquitoes. On the last evening we walked along the beach and were nearly cut off by the tide. It comes in pretty fast. We got back in time to watch the sun setting over cocktails at the bar.

Our 3 days of relaxation seemed to pass so quickly. We were picked up in the morning, our next stop being Shangri-La in Bangkok. We were upgraded so we got the chance to use the Club floor but we had so much to do in Bangkok, we didn't have time to use it.

Chao Phraya River is a cheap and easy transport route with many options, ferries, tourist boats and free boats to the shopping malls. This is often the quickest way to cross the city and it is much cheaper than a taxi.

Bangkok has over 1000 wats with intricate mosaics made from colourful pottery and shells. The most famous of these is Wat Pho with the reclining Buddha, which we visited, but we made time for Wat Arun too.

We decided to book a dinner cruise. We should have done this in advance but we assumed, wrongly, that it was easy enough to do locally. We were unable to book the Shangri-La dinner cruise so we settled for Grand Chao Phraya, recommended by the hotel. This included a buffet dinner. It was a very strange set up. We soon discovered that upstairs was a Thai buffet while downstairs had its own

Indian buffet and party. Our table was in the front near the stage in the middle of a puddle. It was still pouring with rain. The rain was dripping off the stage into the loudspeakers and all the equipment. This was going to be a disaster! In the end the waiter moved us to a drier table which was an improvement. The food was disappointing and cold but the band was good and it stopped raining so in the end we enjoyed the evening.

The Tuk Tuk tour organised by Urban Adventures was great value. The downside was getting to Nuovo City hotel at the other end of Bangkok to pick up the tour at 8.30am. We were welcomed in the corner of the lobby by Miss Pam and Mr A along with an older couple and a large family with teenage kids, a good mix of people to share our tour with. Our driver took us in one of a convoy of six tuk-tuks first of all to Phra Sumeru Fortress, one of only two remaining of the original 14 and then we had time for a leisurely stroll through the gardens overlooking Chao Phraya river. Picking up the tuk-tuk again we headed for Golden Mount where the very daunting sounding 344 steps actually wasn't too bad, and the view over Bangkok was well worth the effort.

Our guide explained the significance of the beckoning lady, the hermit and the Buddha at Amulet Market. This was followed by a tour of the Market in the Little India district. A real treat to the senses was the aroma of the local vegetables and spices used in both Thai and Indian Cuisine and all the brightly coloured fabrics. This was followed by a visit to the Flower Market, where we were each given a lotus flower and taught how to fold the petals to reveal the centre, then to respect the local custom of offering our lotus flowers to the reclining Buddha at Wat Pho. We ended the tour at Grand Palace which was truly amazing. The morning tour was an excellent and well organised overview of Bangkok.

Our last evening was spent visiting the famous Moon Bar, the original rooftop bar on the 61st floor of the Banyan Tree, then we made use of the metro service to the Sukhumvit area of Bangkok, a long street lined with bars, hotels and shopping malls. We tried a couple of bars, including a German one which had a band playing. I went to the loo, passing the band on the way back. I asked if they sang Rod Stewart. They asked for suggestions, so I went through a few and they asked how one of them went, so I sang one bar of it, then they dragged me up on the stage to sing with them. Sharon can't take her mum anywhere! During our brief stay in Bangkok we managed to cover most of the main tourist sites and sample some authentic Thai cuisine.

Vietnam

Vietnam airlines were celebrating their 60th Anniversary in 2016. They had a very small window for agents to fly free with up to three companions from April to June, We had to pay the taxes, but it was a very cheap holiday and my only experience on a Dreamliner aircraft. Carol, Martin and his girlfriend, Eve came too. It was out of season so the accommodation was stupidly cheap, even without using any agents' discounts.

I was looking forward to the experience on the Dreamliner and looked forward to a reasonable sleep but you can't choose the neighbours you sit next to on an aircraft and I certainly wouldn't have chosen mine. I ended up next to a chatterbox with a bladder problem so I didn't get any sleep at all.

We arrived in Vietnam at 4am. It was a short drive to the centre of the crazy city of Hanoi. After a quick nap we had an early lunch in the café virtually opposite our hotel, the first of many delicious meals we experienced. We assumed the dishes which cost literally pennies would be very small but they weren't! We literally had a table full of food and four pints of beer for about ten pounds between us.

Our half-day tour began at 2 pm. We were all tired by then as jet lag had caught up with us but we didn't want to waste a single moment and we wanted to experience as much as we could in our limited time frame. Our guide took us to a temple, the history museum and the bridge by the lake and from there the tour included an electric cart round the highlights of the city and a water puppet theatre. I believe water puppets are unique to Vietnam. The puppeteers stand in a pool of water up to their waists and they manage the puppets on sticks from behind a curtain. It is difficult to follow but based on legends and stories of ancient Hanoi with musicians playing at the sides of the stage and it is spectacular so it's worth seeing even without actually understanding it. We were so tired by then, we kept falling asleep. Only Carol managed to stay awake throughout and being a professional storyteller, she treated herself to a couple of puppets.

Hanoi is nerve-wracking as traffic lights are few and far between and are arbitrary anyway. Hanoi even made Chiang Mai look tame. The secret is to step off the kerb and carry on walking while mopeds drive round you. Pavements are for parking mopeds and dumping rubbish, not for pedestrians. Cars are very expensive and way beyond the reach of most Vietnamese people so most of them ride mopeds. Despite this complete and utter chaos the traffic moves albeit slowly so we didn't see any traffic jams during our stay at all. Somehow it all works.

We had an early start the next morning as we were going to Hạ Long Bay for our overnight cruise. We were keeping our fingers crossed for good weather as we knew it was the rainy season but as it turned out the sun shone brightly, so we endured the high humidity to enjoy a lovely and well equipped cabin which even had a small balcony. We had four endless meals of absolutely delicious and well-presented food.

Carol, Martin and Eve went kayaking through some caves, while the older ones like me went on a boat then we all got some free time on the beach, Back on the cruise, we made spring rolls and had time to relax on deck and watch the sun go down over the beautiful UNESCO World Heritage Site of Hạ Long Bay. We had a couple of drinks on deck and watched the stars. Carol was up extra early for Tai Chi while the rest of us were still asleep. We had a quick breakfast and an early morning walk inside the limestone caves before a really substantial brunch. We arrived back just in time as the heavens opened to torrential rain as we got off the boat. What brilliant timing!

O'Dea – A Path Well Travelled

Our flight to The Imperial City of Hue was delayed by 2 hours, which was a shame as it didn't leave us long enough in Hue. We had a look around the Museum of History and the Citadel before taking an hour long cruise down the Perfume River on a Dragon Boat.

Our 2½ hour scenic drive along Hai Van pass took us to the pretty old town of Hoi An. We stayed at Ancient House Village which was between the town and An Bang Beach. The hotel had a shuttle bus to both and if that didn't work out, taxis were very cheap. The hotel was absolutely lovely, the rooms were enormous and had tropical gardens with a swing and a shower outside.

At night Hoi An was lit up with lanterns and by day it was lovely to walk round the pretty streets full of tailors and shops. We got most of our shopping in Hoi An. We had a morning on An Bang beach which was a lovely beach with some beach bar restaurants.

Hoi An is full of wonderful restaurants and the food was delicious. Many of them arrange cookery classes but we were happy just to enjoy the food and a few beers. Hoi An is really magical at night when it is all lit up.

Dragon boat in Hue

Front - Martin O'Dea and Carol Ferro

Back - Me and Eve Warren

The Philippines

At a PATA evening at the Brick Lane brewery, I won two flights to the Philippines and 2 nights in the Belmont at Manila airport. This time I travelled with my daughter, Carol. Although it was March 2018, it was below freezing. Cebu was definitely going to be warmer.

Carol has always been a minimalist packer. Her entire luggage is always substantially smaller than just my hand luggage. I don't know how she does it. We weren't able to check in the night before so we had to check in at the airport. The reason we couldn't do so was because they changed the aircraft and we were upgraded to business class. This meant we could use the lounge at Heathrow. Carol was so excited by the business class experience and the champagne she promptly dropped the glass and it shattered into a thousand pieces. At 1.30am, we were greeted with a smiley Filipino welcome and a refreshing drink. Our hotel Cebu White Sands had a huge room with a balcony.

The Philippines were named after King Philip of Spain and the Spanish influence can be seen in the language and the fact that it is over 90% Catholic, unlike most of the rest of Asia so that gives it a unique feel. Much of Cebu was destroyed during World War II. There is large percentage of reclaimed land so Cebu is much bigger now than it was 100 years ago. There is also a huge American influence so there are many signs in English. Modern Cebu includes many shopping Malls including the largest in Asia which resembles a cruise ship.

Lapu-Lapu is revered everywhere, because of his resistance to the Spanish colonisation. This reverence is seen in the form of colourful masks on the roadside to match the hoardings and concrete planters which are painted in bright colours. The quickest way to get around Cebu is by Jeepney which takes up to 16 people. These are old Suzuki jeeps left over from the war, often personalised in bright colours with quotes from the bible.

After an ample breakfast buffet consisting of Asian and Western food, we set off on the Cebu Heritage tour. We visited Casa Gorordo which is a museum of the history of Cebu City from its humble beginnings, when it was just a few settlements and houses to the large modern city it is now. Our next stop was the famous Magellan Cross and Basílica Menor del Santo Niño de Cebú which is an impressive Catholic Cathedral. Filpino Catholics worship Jesus as a child dressed in red robes as well as praying to The Virgin Mary.

After lunch, we visited the impressive Taoist Temple in the district of Beverly Hills which has a large Chinese population. I enjoyed Cebu which reminded me of Sri Lanka: the vegetation, the style of the hotels and the roads.

Bohol was 2 hours by fast ferry. Immediately we sensed a quieter island with less traffic and lush vegetation. We stayed in a small family run B&B in the Alona Beach area. In Bohol, the main mode of transportation is the tricycle, a cross between a motorbike with a sidecar and a tuk-tuk with enough room for three passengers and luggage on the top.

We booked a tour of Bohol. The Tarsier sanctuary looks after the world's smallest primates, about the size of a guinea pig. They have huge eyes which don't shut and they can turn their heads 180 degrees. These animals are normally nocturnal. The experienced guides can spot where they are clinging onto trees and branches. They look so fragile and vulnerable. Although it is a sanctuary it is open and conservation is the priority.

The journey to Chocolate Hills was on a winding road full of lush tropical vegetation. Chocolate Hills are believed to have been formed by the ancient underwater volcanoes that created the island. The round topped hills and mountains are an unusual feature. There are only a few in the world that are a natural phenomenon. In this area of Bohol, there are nearly 2000 of them as far as the eye can see. In the summer the grass on the hills turn brown, hence the name, Chocolate Hills. At the time of visiting, some had already turned brown.

Butterfly Garden was small but they have some of the world's largest moths and butterflies, a hybrid male and female butterfly and beautiful flowers. Our guide, Rey, took lots of trick shots of us having fun with butterflies.

We arrived at Loboc, past a small tourist market to see a conveyor belt of tourists queuing to get on all the boats lined up. We feared it would be a tourist trap. It was nicer than it looked as the boats are not too big and set out at intervals so it didn't feel too much like a convoy on the hour and a half river cruise. The ample buffet lunch with iced tea or beer, was full of regional cuisine with plenty of variety. The boats glide down the peaceful Loboc River to a cluster of waterfalls before turning back via a short display of local singers and dancers along the way so although it is touristy it is still lovely.

O'Dea – A Path Well Travelled

Our last stop was at Baclayon church museum which dates back to 1727 and made from Coral, lime, mortar and egg white. It was interesting to see all the ancient religious artefacts within the museum. The large effigies of Mary and Jesus are taken out along the streets when everybody lines the streets for the religious fiestas that take place. Our tour of Bohol was one of the best days of my life with so many wonderful experiences. I absolutely loved Bohol which has a Caribbean feel and it is very different from Cebu just 2 hours away.

After a short flight from Tagbilaran, we stopped overnight in Manila at The Belmont. There I had my best meal of the week which was a Kingfish steak. We had much less time than we had envisaged as the traffic and the one way system meant that it took almost an hour to get to our airport hotel, let alone having time to go shopping. It was lovely to share my experience with Carol.

Chocolate Hills, Bohol

AUSTRALASIA

Australia

We arrived in Sydney in 1993 early in the morning and went straight on the Captain Cook, before flying to Canberra. That was the last time I saw or heard from my brother, Vincent. There were some good RSL clubs in Canberra and some good museums too including the Australia War Memorial which was really interesting.

We flew back to Sydney where we stayed for a few days before going to Cairns. We visited the Great Barrier Reef and Kuranda Railway. The weather conditions weren't great in Cairns so the sea was cloudy and we didn't see the Great Barrier Reef at its best in the submersible. At that time Aborigines still lived in trees in Cairns and were considered to be outcasts. Nowadays Australia embraces and respects their heritage, their amazing artwork and the unique culture and language. We spent St. Patricks Day in a pub in Cairns, which was a really nice evening.

Lastly we visited Jim's aunt and uncle in Paradise Point in Queensland. Uncle Jim drove everywhere even if it was literally round the corner. We walked on our own along the beach, fascinated by hundreds of little crabs and finally we stopped for a meal. We rang up to tell Auntie Fran and Uncle Jim where we were and that we had walked. They didn't really believe us, but they offered to pick us up. We had walked seven miles. We chose to take the bus back round all the back streets which looked just like the set of Neighbours. It took us over an hour to get back. The next time we saw Uncle Jim was in Ireland.

We were invited to our nephew's wedding at Royal Pines hotel near Brisbane in 2007. Luckily the wedding fell on the October half term that year but our attendance depended on whether Martin's school would allow him to go. Permission was granted. Emirates had a very affordable fare with a long layover in Dubai on the way back but we didn't mind as it would give us the opportunity for a brief visit to another place we had never visited before.

Martin had a few surfing lessons which he enjoyed while we browsed the local shops and bars. We took a couple of day trips, one to Byron Bay, the easternmost point in Australia. Byron Bay is a real throwback hippy town with quaint shops and a railway station but the biggest attraction is an amazing view from the lighthouse over the bay and the beautiful beach. Our other day trip was to the Queensland Hinterland, Purlingbrook Falls, the gloworm caves, the Macadamia factory and Moolalaba on the Sunshine Coast. It was a truly memorable day.

The weather was very hit and miss. One day there was torrential rain accompanied by a really spectacular thunderstorm. Fork lightning struck the Q1, which was the world's tallest residential building when we visited but now it is only 9th in the world. Q1 has a lightning conductor on the top. Being the tallest building for miles around it gets struck by lightning fairly regularly.

Unfortunately it rained on the day of Niall and Jodie's wedding, but luckily the sun came out straight after the ceremony so the wedding photos with rainbows and dewdrops were beautiful. We enjoyed seeing our family from Ireland on the other side of the world. It was a beautiful day.

New Zealand

North Island

We began our New Zealand adventure in 2011 with a private tour of Auckland with Miles from Moa Trek whom I met at an event in London. He was so knowledgeable about the area as well as the flora and fauna. The highlights were Piha, the main wild black beach on the west coast, Kitekite Falls and Kelly Tarltons, famous for its penguins. We had lunch with Ross from Great Sights, another person I had met at the same event in London. He helped us with the buses and the Ipipiri cruise. Auckland has some lovely parks, beaches and open spaces on the outskirts and we visited Mount Eden for a wonderful view of the city. While we were in Auckland we caught up with Jim's cousin Maureen and her husband Ian on Easter Sunday. They drove us around and we had lunch. There is a rule in Auckland that you can only have a drink with a substantial meal over Easter and we already had lunch so the only place we could go on our last evening was the hotel bar.

Ipipiri was a small overnight cruise to the Bay of Islands. Sadly it no longer exists which is a real shame. We were lucky enough to have good weather for our trip and a clear night, which meant that we were able to see millions of stars, the Milky Way and Magellan galaxies and shooting stars, one of the most amazing things we had ever experienced. We had lunch in Russell, New Zealand's oldest town which was quaint and interesting and well worth a visit and we enjoyed the Russell RSA club.

Rotorua is renowned for high volcanic activity and its strong Maori culture. There are many interested things to see including: Te Puia geyser, bubbling mud pools, Maori crafts, Rainbow Springs, The Agrodome, Hells Gate, Mt. Takawera and the buried village and the steam rising from Lake Rotorua. It is a unique and fascinating place to visit. When we visited Rainbow Springs, the rain was torrential and we got absolutely drenched but it didn't stop the mud bubbling, if anything it added to it.

It was ANZAC Day when we arrived so we celebrated in the Rotorua RSA club and received a very warm welcome from the locals. The Agrodome sheep shearing was more interesting than it sounds. I hadn't realised there were so many different breeds of sheep. We enjoyed watching the Maori woodcrafters afterwards making beautiful and intricate figures.

Unfortunately, the weather wasn't kind to us for our lunch stop in Lake Taupo. There was a landslide and flooding so we were diverted to a safer road. The weather had improved by the time we reached Napier which is a pretty little seaside town full of art deco buildings. We stayed in Napier for a couple of days before going to Wellington, the tiny capital of New Zealand. Wellington has plenty to see and do: the cable car, Te Papa Museum, Carter Observatory with amazing views over the bay and Zealandia, a beautiful wildlife park. Wellington has a lovely beach. There are many bars and restaurants with a variety of cuisine.

The Hop on Hop off tour is a great way to get round hilly Wellington. We discovered The Welsh Dragon pub in Wellington. They claim to be the only Welsh pub in the Southern Hemisphere, situated in a converted public toilet, We had a great night in there. We were pleasantly surprised by Wellington. We flew direct to Dunedin from Wellington's surprisingly tiny airport.

South Island

Dunedin has many ties with Edinburgh. It is home to Cadbury's Chocolate Factory and Taeiri Gorge Railway, which runs a picturesque 4-hour round trip to Pukaweri. Dunedin Station is a beautiful example of Victorian architecture with its tiled floors and stained glass windows. We met up with friends who lived there and also some distant relatives whom we had never met.

We drove down the Southern Scenic Route to Invercargill. Invercargill is mostly industrial but there is a great pub there called Waxy O'Shea's. We had a couple of really good nights in there with a Dublin singer and entertainer, oddly named Busman's Handbag. We met and chatted with some Australians who were on holiday. There is a beautiful park and museum at the other end of town.

From Invercargill, we took a day trip with Stewart Island flights. Our trip was touch and go because of the low cloud, but luckily it went ahead. We took the speedboat to Ulva Island, which is a bird sanctuary including many endemic birds that are close to extinction. We walked through the rainforest where thousands of birds called each other noisily through the trees until we got to a wild deserted beach with just our own footprints on the sand and a few gulls at the edge of the sea.

After a lunch of delicious local green-lipped mussels we were taken on a tour by the appropriately named Stewart. Stewart Island only has 400 inhabitants, a school with 26 pupils and one supermarket. It is a really lovely little island with stunning beaches, an abundance of wildlife, including penguins and kiwis and it felt as though we had used a time machine to get there. We were pleased we took the time to visit Stewart Island.

Te Anau is a small, one-street town and a convenient place from which to visit Doubtful Sound with Real Journeys and Milford Sound with Great Sights. The journey is more convenient from Te Anau, saving about 6 hours on the journey from Queenstown. My preference was Doubtful Sound, a much smaller boat with fewer tourists, which allowed the experience to be more peaceful and leisurely. This involves a journey across Lake Manapouri, a coach ride over the mountain and a 3-hour cruise on Doubtful Sound. The route depends on the weather but we were very lucky to get out to the Tasman Sea and see two schools of dolphins, albatrosses and to Neel Island where there were hundreds of fur seals.

In Queenstown, the autumn colours were beautiful. It is a lively town with many bars and restaurants. We booked a Lord of the Rings tour with Southern Lakes Sightseeing. Richard, our guide, tailored the trip especially for our needs, and showed us some really picturesque areas and what he told us about the filming was really fascinating. We got the opportunity to handle approved replicas of swords and knives from the films. We saw Arrowtown and the original A J Hackett bungy site which is as popular and crazy as ever.

Franz Josef was really small and friendly. Our main reason for staying there was for the Air Safaris Mt Cook traverse flight. This was very scary but at the same time one of the best and most exciting things we've ever experienced. It is very weather dependent and we were very lucky that the trip went ahead. The flight is almost an hour flying over the beach, the Tasman Sea, Franz Josef and Fox Glacier, Mt. Tasman and Mt. Cook.

When we were up in the air, flying high over mountains and glaciers, we kept hearing noises so as soon as we landed, we asked what the noises were.

"Oh, that's just the engine stalling."

said the pilot casually...... eeeek!

We took the bus up to Greymouth and stopped in a little place called Hokitika which has a beach, the Jade Museum and also a sock museum which was intriguing but there wasn't enough time to visit. Once we reached Greymouth, we took the famous Tranzalpine train to Christchurch.

Christchurch was a long way to recovery following the major earthquake which destroyed the city in 2010. The Avon River and the aquarium were fully operational and the parks were mostly untouched. The CBD area was completely closed and the trams weren't operating. The buses were running on temporary schedules and there was virtually nothing open. We walked past a car showroom and the girl in there begged us to take a test drive. She hadn't seen anyone for days. The mood in the few places that were open was very sombre. We thought Christchurch would never recover but it has.

MIDDLE EAST

Israel

I was offered a rare educational to Eilat with Thomas Cook in 1996. I was paired up with Ann Barber from Thomas Cook in Bury. She looked me up and down with my huge bag. I always carried far too much luggage. She smoked and I didn't, but we were fated to share the same room. As it turned out Ann and I got on really well and we had many things in common. We enjoyed a jeep safari in the Negev Desert. By the end of the day, we were hot and sticky with dust and sand in our hair and our clothes. We looked such a mess and we cried laughing at each other. Fate bought us together again later on. We have been on many trips together since then and we are still the best of friends.

I won flights with El Al and 4 night's accommodation in 2016 at one of the many wonderful events organised by Michelle Roberts at the Israel Tourist board with 2 nights in Jerusalem and 2 nights in Tel Aviv. I extended the night in Tel Aviv and booked the taxi between Jerusalem and Tel Aviv with help from Ella Gaffen of International Travel, locally. Ella came to meet us at the hotel.

Tel Aviv airport is between Tel Aviv and Jerusalem. Both cities are easy to get to and now there is a rail service to make things easier and cheaper. We were wary of our drive towards Jerusalem passing by the high walls of the West Bank. Once we arrived in Jerusalem we felt perfectly safe and we were happy to walk around and explore on our own.

Jerusalem is an amazing city steeped in culture and history. This ancient multi-cultural walled city is so fascinating, a crossroads for Christians, Jews, Arabs and Armenians. The culmination of the melting pot of cultures, architecture and people makes it unique.

Being time-limited, we booked a walking tour. A guide is necessary to explain the complex cultures and customs and also to avoid getting hopelessly lost in the labyrinth of narrow streets. The smallest Armenian quarter is closed to visitors.

 The Golden Dome can be seen for miles shining prominently in the heart of the city. The Wailing or Western Wall is important to the Jewish community, Via Dolorosa with the Stations of the Cross and the Church of the Holy Sepulchre is important to Christians. There are churches and mosques next door to synagogues.

All the different religions shop freely in the markets whilst observing the different shopping hours to coincide with their respective beliefs. The Arab Quarter closes mostly on Friday, the Jewish quarter on Saturday and the Christian Quarter on Sunday. The citizens of Jerusalem go their own separate ways to their own places of worship but the general atmosphere is one of harmony, market buzz and cultural diversity. The markets are hassle free. It is possible to buy virtually anything from fresh fruit and vegetables, pomegranate juice, figs and dates, fresh bread, herbs and spices, rugs, jewellery, religious artefacts, ironmongery, souvenirs, you name it, it's there somewhere.

I am normally sceptical about spirituality but that day I put my hand on the Western Wall and I felt something through my whole body that I can never really explain, a sort of energy or enlightenment, I guess.

Staying in David Citadel hotel was absolutely perfect for us, being non-meat eaters. A hotel with a Kosher breakfast is such a delight. I can honestly say we have never had so much choice. We were completely bewildered with an array of fruits, yoghurt, salad, vegetables, cheeses, cereals, nuts, bread, cakes, halva and fresh fish.

We found a few decent bars including Molly Bloom's, an Irish bar near the seafront which had a great band. Most of the pubs and bars close on Friday nights for the Sabbath. We paid a little extra for the Club room which gave us access to free drinks and nibbles in the afternoon which was definitely money well spent.

Tel Aviv is on the Mediterranean Sea so we hadn't expected such massive waves. It is about an hour leisurely stroll along the promenade from the Marina to Jaffa with benches to relax on, breathe in the sea air and watch the runners and surfers along the way.

Tel Aviv is a modern city full of high rise hotels whereas Jaffa is reputed to be the world's oldest city. There are some wonderful fish restaurants by the harbour that were converted from warehouses. It is a pretty and peaceful little city, full of narrow cobbled streets, a lovely park and art galleries. There is much excavation work going on in Jaffa and also in Jerusalem, so ancient relics and more pieces of the historic jigsaw are constantly being discovered.

Dubai

It was raining when we arrived in Dubai in 2007. We thought it sensible to do the Hop on Hop off bus as we knew we didn't have much time and it is always a good way of seeing the highlights of the city. At that time Dubai was a building site. So many things were half built. There was scaffolding, hoardings and holes everywhere. Even though our stay was brief we were underwhelmed but it gave us a chance to stretch our legs between Brisbane and London and experience a different culture.

O'Dea – A Path Well Travelled
We revisited in 2014 en route to Sri Lanka and Singapore. This time we hit a dust storm. It was really windy and Jim nearly lost his hat which blew off at the airport. Things had definitely improved since our last visit, all the half built sites were finished and Dubai looked much better than it had on our previous visit.

We stayed in Sheikh Zayed Road which was very convenient for the metro and much more affordable. We planned to take a Big Bus Tour. This is good value as a few extras are included, a dhow cruise and even a sunset desert tour. There are three routes but not enough time to complete them all. We started with the beach route followed by the city tour. We had done this before but missed out on the dhow cruise which I really wanted to do. We were probably 45 minutes or so into the tour only to discover the dhow cruise had been cancelled. We decided to join the marina tour, but by that time it was so cold and windy we had to abandon that idea so we never got to see the Palm which was a real shame since I am unlikely to ever go back to Dubai.

Our hotel was a very high building of 65 floors, we were staying on 33rd floor. Burj Khalifa dwarfed our lofty home being almost three times as high! We had a power cut and I was terrified that we would have to go down 33 floors on foot to get out. Thankfully it was fixed by the morning. I couldn't use the pool because of the dust storm so although I have technically been to Dubai twice, I've not really seen much of it on either occasion.

Abu Dhabi

I won 3 nights at the Emirates Palace for the weekend courtesy of Emirates Holidays at their London event. I went with Sharon in February 2014. Emirates Palace was truly stunning. We were welcomed with a rose and upgraded to a £3k a night suite. The suite was huge and our balcony was massive!

As part of the upgrade, we were able to use the club facility which meant we could have a few glasses of wine before dinner and some snacks at lunchtime. This was a real bonus and it saved us a fortune. We had a gold doubloon as a door key. We had two massive pools to choose from and we were right on the beach. Sharon used the gym and I used the pools before breakfast. We had expected the hotel to be really expensive but actually snacks and drinks were reasonably priced. A notable feature of Emirates Palace is the gold ATM.

The Big Bus, which is great in Dubai and many other cities round the world didn't work at all in Abu Dhabi, we either couldn't find the stops or we missed the buses, although with many of the new attractions that are open now things may well have changed as the bus goes to Saadiyat and Yas Island. Everything was still being built there in 2014. I believe most of it is finished now. We got on at Emirates Towers and our first stop was the Sheikh Zayed Mosque.

The mosque was only built in 2007 but must surely rank as being one of the world's top "must do's". It is one of world's largest mosques, a huge structure built in marble with beautiful mother of pearl inlay, mosaics, glass, clever lighting, flowers made from polished natural stone and huge bejewelled chandeliers hanging from the ceiling weighing several tons.

The following day we took a cab to Heritage Village as the bus went the wrong way round. This turned out to be a tourist trap with propaganda for the much revered Sheikh Zayed throughout the complex. We left the complex only to discover we had just missed Big Bus so we took another cab to Marina Mall to use our free ticket for Sky Tower.

Sky Tower was a complete waste of time. It is free but half covered by a canopy and the top is an overpriced café. The mall is a decent place to shop and electrical goods are very cheap but we wanted to catch the bus back to Etihad Towers if only to say we had actually managed to get another ride on our 24-hour ticket.

With the bus ticket we got a half-price ticket to the "Observation Deck at 300". The Observation Deck is on the 74th floor of Jumeirah at Etihad Towers which completely dwarfs Sky Tower. There is an impressive view of all the new developments, the islands and the city.

AFRICA

Tunisia

I applied for a Panorama megafam to Tunisia in the early nineties with one of the travel papers and I was delighted to be selected. It should have been for 3 nights. We arrived at Gatwick ready for our 5pm flight. The flight was delayed but eventually we got onto the aircraft, only to be told that there was a malfunction in the equipment, so we would have to get off so they could arrange for a replacement aircraft. They sent us all back to the terminal.

We waited, first of all in the bar and after that closed, we stayed in the lounge. One guy was sent home as he was too drunk. Finally at 5am, 12 hours late, our flight was ready to leave. We arrived into Monastir at around 8am and we were expected to attend a tourist board meeting at 11am. By the time we got out of the airport and into our hotel, we were given half an hour to get ready. As we were sharing twin rooms that was literally 15 mins each to unpack, get in and out of the shower and get changed.

We tried so hard to look interested in the Minister of Tourism's speech but we were too tired. We were interested in the coffee and cakes that were passed around, at least we could have a quick caffeine and sugar hit.

In the afternoon we had three or four hotels to look at before going back to our hotel to quickly get ready for our evening excursion. The evening trip was in an arena, a typical eighties style "Taste of Tunisia". We had now been sleep deprived for around 36 hours. The dancers came out, the drums were loud and persistent, the red wine was undrinkable then Brik, a local speciality, fried egg in batter, was offered to us to eat.

The event ended around midnight and we got on the coach, tired, hungry and sober. I was so tired that I fell off the seat fast asleep and slept on the floor of the coach. I was grateful for a few hours sleep. We had to be ready at 7am to face the next day along with our luggage. It was going to be a long day but I definitely needed breakfast so we were up again at 6am.

We visited Tunis and a pretty town of Sidi Bou Said with white walls, blue doors and beautiful tiles. We browsed the souk in Sousse. Our last night was in Port el Kantaoui. In between all this we visited 16 hotels. They all merged into one. I was too tired to care. I can't remember a single person who was on that megafam. I was glad to go home for a rest and I never went to Tunisia again

Egypt

I saw a pre-Christmas cheapie just for 4 nights to Sharm-el-Sheikh with Thomas Cook. Sharm-el-Sheikh was already a popular destination and I knew that visiting would help me sell it. I went with my friend, Anna.

Being two females, we attracted attention. We were frequently told over breakfast what beautiful eyes we had. In the souk and the shops, haggling is expected and we were mercilessly hassled with prices cheaper than Argos. It was really hard work trying to buy anything. I don't enjoy haggling and being hassled, I like to browse, to admire the patterns and colours in the handicrafts, to linger and smell the spices, soak up the atmosphere and the hustle and bustle and take a few photos of street life at its best.

We tended to go to eat and drink in the Hilton Fayrouz on the beach. It had a really good pub and restaurant. Sharm-el-Sheikh is hotel based to cater for the tourists. It doesn't have a pub culture. We took a yellow submarine tour to admire the coral and the colourful Red Sea fish below the surface and sun shining up above. It was a beautiful afternoon.

St Katherines Monastery was a very long way but on the way, we admired the scenery and nature of the Sinai desert. According to the bible, the Burning Bush was on fire but Moses realised it wasn't being consumed by the flames and then the angel of the Lord spoke to Moses. I looked up at the trailing bush which the guide described to us. Anna being taller and more curious than me, managed to prick her finger on the bush and left a telling trail of blood behind leading all the way back to the bus.

I was offered a 3-night educational trip to Cairo in 2009. We were a small group and on that occasion, I shared a room with Gill Nicholls who proved to be a great companion and we have remained friends. My colleagues, Guy, Simone Adams and Rachel Varndall were also on that trip.

It was a 3-night educational and an opportunity to experience The Pyramids of Giza, The Great Sphinx and Cairo Museum, all of which were amazing. We had a few hotel visits in a very higgledy-piggledy order so we spent half of our trip stuck in traffic. Horns hoot day and night and the traffic moves inch by inch. We were late for everything as we couldn't physically get anywhere when we were supposed to.

Our guide in Cairo Museum was a diminutive ball of energy called Bim-Bam. She flew up the stairs and literally slid across the polished floor animatedly telling us about the Kings and Gods of Egypt. She was really interesting and spoke good English, one of those characters it would be impossible to forget even after all this time, but we were tired after having already looked at three hotels that morning and the museum wasn't air conditioned. We were told that a brand new museum would soon be opening in 6th October City area to replace the existing one. The hotels were purpose built for the new media and museum area. Those plans were ditched in favour of building the museum in Giza in the Summer of 2021, which actually makes more sense since anyone going to see the Pyramids would also want to see the museum and having the two in the same area would mean staying in Giza without having to go into Central Cairo at all.

The Pyramids and the Great Sphinx were even more amazing than I had imagined. They were built 7000 years ago and are still standing. I wonder how these could have been built so solidly and so accurately all those years ago. In the evening we did a riverboat cruise along the Nile, not quite a Nile cruise experience, but leisurely all the same.

Our group in GizaNamibia

I was delighted to be invited from the Namibian Tourist Board following their online training programme. We flew from Gatwick on Air Namibia on their direct service in 2008. Our flight was seven hours late and Gatwick North had nothing open after 10pm so we sat for hours waiting. At least they cancelled the seminar when we arrived so we had time to have a nap and to recharge. We had three itineraries to choose from, Etosha, the safari experience, Sossusvlei for a desert experience and the third was a cultural experience. As I am a keen amateur photographer, the distinctive red sand dunes of Sossusvlei appealed to me the most. The dunes and animals are uniquely photogenic.

I was surprised by the high standard of accommodation, and the warm hearted hosts that we met along the way. We felt so safe at all times and the diversity of the nature was amazing. We could drive for hours and not see another vehicle. One evening we went on a sundowner on

Marble Mountain. The mountain was made of white marble, I've never seen anything like it.

We stopped at Rostock Ridge for lunch. The owner introduced us to his pets, a beautiful Weimaraner dog and a zebra. We had another unique photo opportunity, the Tropic of Capricorn and then found ourselves on the roughest of dirt tracks on our way to the Cheetah Sanctuary just outside Windhoek.

Finally we reached Windhoek on our last night for a barbeque. This was a chance to meet up with the other groups and compare notes with those who had chosen Etosha or the cultural trip. It was on top of a hill overlooking Windhoek in the distance. When we needed the loo, we had to take a torch, one at a time and wander off to a 3-sided hut. It was my turn and wow!! A loo with a view, the entire universe, thousands of stars and the Milky Way, it was just incredible.

On our way back we stopped in a local restaurant where I ordered a seafood platter which cost next to nothing. It was delicious and the prawns were gigantic!

I would love to go back to Namibia. It was only a 3-day trip but it was one of the best I've ever experienced. The trip helped me immensely to answer questions about my rugby group's forthcoming trip.

Champagne breakfast in Namibia

INDIAN OCEAN

Mauritius

I was horrendously late for the Mauritius event as I went to the wrong place so I turned up very flustered and embarrassed but to my amazement ended up winning a 5-night hotel stay at the Maritim in the sheltered north west of the island in 2010. We managed to find an excellent rate on the flights with Air Mauritius so we flew direct. We were surprised at how green Mauritius is. The vegetation is very diverse and it seems that almost everything grows there from palms to pine forests.

The Maritim is a good hour from the airport. Our room was upgraded and we quickly experienced the excellent service and friendliness that was consistent throughout our stay. The food is excellent and not overly spicy, a truly international blend of flavours and plenty of fresh fish.

O'Dea – A Path Well Travelled

Vegetarians are well catered for with fresh fruit, beans, seeds, spices and vegetables in abundance.

We had prebooked a tour with White Sand Tours. We learned that the population is mostly Indian. Hindus and Muslims live happily side by side, also Tamils, Europeans and Chinese. Mauritius has been in the hands of the Dutch, Portuguese, French and British before coming independent. The influences are mostly French with the local Creole language being very close to French and the majority speak good English with a French accent. The interesting ethnic mix gives Mauritius a unique character. Hindu temples can be seen within yards of Catholic churches and shopping malls.

Caudan Waterfront is modelled on Cape Town Waterfront and does look rather like pictures I have seen of it. This has a craft market with good quality clothing at bargain prices. There are a few cafés and bars at the waterfront with prices much lower than they are in London.

Sir Seewoosagur Ramgoolam Gardens in Pamplemousse were named after the first President of Mauritius. His ashes are within the grounds. He is revered on the island with the gardens and the airport being named after him. The gardens had recently started a guided golf trolley service. This enhanced our experience and saved us walking. The gardens are famous for their giant lilies, giant tortoises and 85 varieties of palm tree.

The other tour we booked was the Scenic South with the Casela Nature Park. Michel, our guide, took us to Trou aux Cerfs, a lake at the bottom of a volcanic crater surrounded by mountain peaks, We also went to Ganga Talao, the sacred lake of Grand Bassin and the huge statue of Shiva at the only Shiva temple outside India. We stopped at the Black River Gorges National Park and the spectacular Chamarel waterfalls. Our tour included a beautifully presented 3-course lunch of local delicacies, local spicy christophine with bread, a starter of palm hearts au gratin, vegetable curry and banana mousse. Casela National Park had a stunning view from the restaurant.

Grand Baie was much nicer than we expected with a lovely beach and an old traditional, mainly Chinese bazaar. At the other end of the resort was a modern complex of designer shops and factory outlets and a couple of beachside cafés. This looked to have been recently built.

The Seychelles

I won 4 nights at Northolme on Mahe in the Seychelles in 2011. I've always been told that it's best to island hop as all the islands are different so we added Praslin. Additionally, I was offered 2 free nights at the Four Seasons on Mahe.

Mahe is the main island and the largest, housing the international airport. We stayed at the Hilton Northolme close to the main resort of Beau Vallon Bay, which was walkable during daylight hours. There are a couple of restaurants and bars in Beau Vallon Bay serving mainly local creole specialities.

The Northolme hotel consists of cottages which all look more or less the same. On one occasion, we accidentally opened the wrong door using our key and interrupted a couple in bed!

The Seychelles consist of granite islands and coraline islands. The largest ones, Mahe and Praslin are both granite islands, small but perfectly formed with stunning beaches, interesting granite rock formations and abundant rainforests. We saw many colourful birds and fruit bats. The culture in Seychelles is African Creole, which is reflected in the food and the lively music. It is a cross between reggae and country music sung in Seychelles Creole, a language that is broadly based on French.

While we were in Mahe we hired a car, which enabled us to see the beautiful bays from the hilltops. There's also the tea factory and many viewpoints along the top road. There are only a few roads, one round most of the coast and four roads across. Driving is on the left and it is a pleasant way to get round the island and petrol is cheaper than in the UK.

O'Dea – A Path Well Travelled

Victoria is the smallest capital in the world. It has historic buildings and it is home to the Botanical Gardens. There are many shops and banks, a Friday market and tourist stalls selling sarongs and gifts crafted from coconuts. Elsewhere around the island, almost everything is hotel based. Even the larger resorts like Beau Vallon Bay are small with only a few local restaurants. We were invited for lunch at the Maia hotel, a stunning hotel with butler service that overlooks two of the most beautiful bays in Mahe, Anse Louis and Anse Boileau.

We accepted the optional Hilton arrangement of a night on Silhouette Island, spending one night in the Hilton Labriz which was a short speedboat ride away. The beach is gorgeous with soft white sand and a calm turquoise sea but the crossing back was very rough! The journey to Praslin can be by catamaran or a short fifteen minute flight. We were advised that in the monsoon season the sea can be very rough and that we should fly. This proved to be good advice; flying over all the islands, which looked like little gems in the sea was a wonderful experience and well worth the extra 40 euros. There were more resort shops in Praslin than there were in Mahe. Praslin is famous for Vallée de Mai where the famous and unique Coco de Mer grows. Coco de Mer is a double coconut which looks rather like a bottom.

The Cannon Ball tree has the most beautiful flowers that open in the sun and close in the evening. More familiar are frangipani, hibiscus and bougainvillea which can be seen in abundance. We spent our last couple of nights at Four Seasons Mahe. We had a beautiful villa overlooking Petit Anse, a gorgeous white sandy bay and we had a large infinity pool all to ourselves.

When it was to time to go back, our taxi back to the airport was very late so the driver took 25 minutes to take us to the airport. This journey normally takes an hour. Fortunately, there isn't much traffic in Mahe and the airport is tiny.

Sri Lanka

On our grand Asia trip in 2014, we flew from Dubai to Sri Lanka which I was really looking forward to. There is so much history, culture and wildlife packed into the island. We had planned a packed itinerary over our four days in Sri Lanka. Our first night was in Waikkal, not far from the airport. We enjoyed our stay at Club Dolphin, with great facilities, right on the beach, excellent service, delicious food and as a bonus, we were upgraded to the best room in the hotel.

Pinnawala Elephant orphanage is on the way to Kandy, so we asked for a quote to include this. It was lovely to see so many elephants in one place but it is a tourist trap. Elephant skin dries out very quickly. They need water to moisturise their skin as well as to drink so they get taken down to the river a couple of times a day. They are chained but they enjoy playing in the river. We enjoyed watching them over lunch in the restaurant overlooking the river, a much more enjoyable experience than in the sanctuary itself. There are also some nice little handicraft and tourist shops by the river.

We used a local agency as it isn't easy to find Kandy based tours in the UK which include rail which is something we wanted to experience. We both like rail travel and we had seen this journey on television. We found Rainbow Tours which is run by an expat who organised the rail for us from Kandy at a competitive price. It was interesting to see the old rolling stock and Canadian steam engines. Our scenic rail journey rattled past tea plantations and waterfalls, stations with simple British colonial names like Hatton and stations with long and unpronounceable Singhalese and Tamil names. The Singhalese alphabet is so beautiful, it looks almost like butterflies and flowers. Signs are written in English, Singhalese and Tamil.

There are miles and miles of terraced tea plantations as far as the eye can see, and at each station we could buy virtually anything through the carriage windows. In first class, air conditioning consists of an open door and a wonky ceiling fan and the toilet waste goes straight through to the ground below. Sri Lanka Railways is the wrong place to be for a luxury trip but it was a truly unforgettable and unique experience.

Our midget driver, Tilak, met us at Nanu Oya and drove us to Mackwoods tea plantation and museum. We stopped at the Ramboda Waterfall on the way back. Jim who is a mere 5ft 3in towered above Tilak. Despite being vertically challenged, Tilak was an excellent guide. He picked us up the next day to take us to Temple of the Tooth Relic but I felt a little uncomfortable being herded past the locals waiting to pray as we were leaving. The Botanical Gardens is an oasis of peace away from the busy city. Arthur's Seat had a fabulous view over the lake and the city of Kandy. The viewpoint was named after the British author and inventor Arthur C. Clarke who wrote 2001: A Space Odyssey and lived in Colombo for many years.

In the afternoon we took the train back to Colombo Fort station. It was a rickety and uncomfortable ride but the journey through the lush rainforest in the rain was very worthwhile. When we arrived in Colombo we watched all the locals cross the tracks and followed them. We nearly met our maker as a train came thundering along. We just made it across!

We were pleased that we had organized a limo to the hotel as we were surrounded by tuk-tuk drivers wanting to take us to the Mount Lavinia hotel. I wanted to stay at this famous colonial hotel. We were lucky they weren't full as they had booked us for the wrong month but thankfully we sorted that out. It was a beautiful, historic hotel and our room overlooked the beach. Food and drink prices in the hotel were surprisingly good too.

LATIN AMERICA

Mexico

I won 7 night's accommodation at Occidental Playcar at World Travel Market in 2010. I had never been to Mexico and it was somewhere I was keen to go. It was already a popular destination with my clients and this visit would definitely help me to sell it.

Due to our 3-hour delay we didn't arrive until the evening. Our pre-arranged transfer was still waiting for us and it took another hour to get to our destination. Playacar is guarded at each end with Playa del Carmen at one end and only taxis and buses are allowed through. There is a small shopping plaza with shops and stalls and a mixture of private houses and hotels. It is roughly half an hour's walk from Playacar to Playa del Carmen.

Tulum was further than we thought. Mexico and even the Yucatan Peninsula are deceptively vast. Tulum is impressive and covers a wide area overlooking a beautiful beach. Different species of iguana roam freely among the ruins. Tulum is almost 2000 years old. Ancient Mayans, are said to have invented chocolate and chewing gum. Many modern Mexicans from the Yucatan region still have a very distinct Mayan appearance to this day.

 Coba was very impressive. We chose the bike taxi, uncomfortable but the alternative was a five kilometre walk to see the most complete Mayan ruins in existence, the Observatory and the huge pyramid which some chose to climb. We had lunch in a Mayan Village which I had expected to be a tourist trap however, it comprised genuine dwellings consisting of simple windowless huts, without furniture or possessions, just hammocks and a few pots and pans. One had a spider monkey as a pet. The village seemed to have more restaurants and tiny churches than homes or people. The experience was very humbling.

Cozumel, Mexico's largest island, was less than an hour away by catamaran. We carefully chose our day to avoid cruise ships, but Oasis of the Seas and also Norwegian EPIC, the two largest cruise ships at that time, were both docked. We were told the presence of cruise ships wouldn't affect our visit. That was true as most of our visit was to the eco park at Playasur which doesn't seem to be visited by cruise excursions.

Our visit was in a large open truck beginning with a snorkel stop including lunch and a cold beer. Our next stop was the lighthouse and museum. In this region were also pieces of coral, fossils and sponges and finally the Cozumel ruins, an ancient Mayan relic of a hurricane warning system replicating the effects of a conch shell. Directly opposite was a walkway leading to a Crocodile swamp. Even without the crocodiles, this was a very eerie place, especially under the setting sun.

The eco park is full of birds, nesting turtles and rugged bays full of vegetation and just the odd beach bar here and there. By the time we got back to the main town it was already nightfall. We were invited to sample a day room and lunch at Fairmont Mayakoba. We had a wonderful, relaxing day in our private pool suite overlooking the beautiful white sand beach.

We went to a timeshare session which involved a free visit and transport to Grand Xcaret. The guy was a real shark wearing half-moon glasses. As soon as we said we lived in Notting Hill the dollar signs were ticking over in his head. He showed us the latest Small Luxury Hotels brochure and pretended it was their portfolio, I saw through that and told him I had the same brochure at home. We managed to escape with a bottle of wine but without the timeshare.

We were surprised how much natural beauty there is in Yucatan. There are rainforests, mangroves and many indigenous animals such as the Tejon which looks a little like a raccoon and the Sereque which is rather like a hare without ears. There are also many iguanas, birds and huge butterflies.

Peru

How exciting to win trips to Taj Mahal and Machu Picchu in the same year, 2012! I won the Peru trip at World Travel Market. Our prize included flights which was a real bonus. We arrived in Lima after a long flight via Amsterdam with KLM and a long wait for our luggage in Lima. We were met on arrival by Marcelo who was our driver in Peru at the beginning and end of our fabulous trip which was well organised by Tucano Peru.

Our Peru city tour began with a tour of some of the highlights and a short walking tour which included Museo Banco Central de Reserva that had some interesting Inca artefacts and a couple of huge bank vaults.

The Cathedral is the focal point of the main square with its neat and tidy gardens. There always seems to be some sort of demonstration or festival going on in Peru. The riot police, already in the square were quite happy to pose with the tourists while getting ready for that afternoon's demonstration. We enjoyed the Monasterio San Francisco which has a fantastic ancient library full of books hundreds of years old from floor to ceiling and the catacombs in the basement.

We had a couple of hours to wander round the market in Miraflores, the first of many enticing shopping sprees. There are so many bargains to be had: jewellery, woollen and woven goods, hats, belts, rugs, wall hangings, dolls, reed crafts, all really good quality at unbelievably low prices.

Larco Museum has thousands of exhibits of Inca and Pre-Colombian clothes, pottery and jewellery which were really interesting. Afterwards, in the restaurant Café del Museo, we had an enjoyable meal that was tasty and beautifully presented followed by a taste of Pisco Sour.

It was time to leave Lima at 3.15 am for our dawn flight to Cusco and our relaxing overnight stay in the fabulous Aranwa Sacred Valley Hotel & Wellness, by far the best hotel we stayed at on our trip. This is a beautiful hotel surrounded by mountains and fresh air. We had a relaxing massage included. The reception has a stunning stained glass window of Machu Picchu which was imported from Switzerland. At certain times of the day it reflects onto the floor. While we were there, there was a wedding in the little chapel surrounded by a moat and bridge. The bride and groom had a white coach and horses in a fairy tale setting. They had a piñata at their reception. A piñata is used for celebrations in Latin America. It is a large figurine made from coloured paper and containing sweets which is smashed open when the guests arrive. The flowers throughout the grounds are familiar ones but they seem to be bigger and more vibrant than here in the UK.

We left Aranwa for our first tour of the Sacred Valley and the ancient Inca site of Pisac. We had time to visit the colourful craft market. We couldn't resist a few more bargains, then we had a typical Peruvian lunch accompanied by Pan pipers before a short visit to the village of Ollantaytambo with its narrow streets and its quaint square.

We had a couple of nights in Inkallpa near Ollantaytambo which was a lovely little hotel with pretty gardens and a beautiful view of the mountains. We ordered Piña Coladas which we drank through a straw and the next thing we knew, Jim, caught by the altitude couldn't speak and couldn't breathe. He ran into a wall to shock himself into breathing again. He has never drank Piña Colada since.

We had another tour of the Sacred Valley beginning with the agricultural terraces of Moray, the spectacular salt flats of Maras and the Inca site and museum of Chinchero where we had a substantial Peruvian lunch comprising locally grown vegetables. We watched the local women in their uncomfortable and bulky looking skirts, spinning and dyeing sheep and alpaca wools and transforming them into intricate and colourful woven and knitted jumpers, rugs and bags.

We enjoyed the train journey from Ollantaytambo to Machu Picchu past the scenic rapids of the Urubamba River. Most of the hotels including the Sumaq, deliver the luggage directly to the hotel. Saul, our guide, met us at the station and walked us through the market to the buses up to Machu Picchu. The coach journey up to Machu Picchu was a 20-minute bus ride round hairpin bends.

Machu Picchu is an even more awesome sight than we could possibly have imagined. As we turned the corner up the top of a mountain we saw the entire ancient city that had been abandoned and overgrown. This was once known only to a few local farmers until Hiram Bingham,

O'Dea – A Path Well Travelled

an Hawaiian-born, American explorer and archaeologist changed all that in 1912. He was looking for Vilcabamba, the Lost City of the Incas, which he never found, but it was discovered later and work is still ongoing, but he certainly helped to share the secret of Machu Picchu with the rest of the world.

Hotel Sumaq was lovely and the food was excellent but we were pleased to leave uninspiring Agua Calientes which had a small market, but little else. I also had a bad stomach upset so that didn't help matters.

Cusco is a lovely city but it was the only place where I had difficulty breathing, not because of the altitude but because we were staying on the main road which has a great deal of traffic, so it was pollution rather than altitude that I struggled with. Cusco cathedral is amazing with so many unique features: the wooden chapel that took one man 28 years to carve, the huge silver Virgin Mary, the Inca stone and the Jesus Christ blackened by candles over the years. In the afternoon we went to the Temple of the Sun and the incredible Inca sites of Saqsaywaman.

Cusco has a huge market and we managed to fill our suitcase for next to nothing. We discovered Paddy's Pub, the highest 100% Irish owned pub in the world. We made the classic rookie error of ordering two beers. How do you carry two bottles and two glasses? The usual solution is to put the glasses upside down on top of the bottles. The beers fizzed up spectacularly like a pair of volcanoes while the bar staff sniggered. It happens every day.

It was time to leave Cusco for the 10-hour journey on the Andean Explorer to Puno and Lake Titicaca. The Andean Explorer is one of the world's classic rail journeys with comfortable armchairs and white glove service. There is a platform at the back and a bar with music and entertainment throughout the day. There are two short stops in La Raya where there is another opportunity to shop and then at Juliaca, which is grim, but they sell absolutely everything at the sides of the railway lines.

We arrived into Puno at sunset. Our hotel was on the lakeside. We were allocated a spacious lake view room. We struggled with vegetarian meals at the hotel. On the first evening we ordered pizzas. They must have only had one pizza left as we got half a child-sized pizza each carefully pieced together in wedges like a Maltese cross, one on each plate.

Uros is made up of floating islands made from reeds. This is one of the weirdest things I have ever experienced, rather like walking across a mattress. There are many separate little islands each with two or three families living in tiny reed houses, they do have electricity though. They get around in reed boats with twin panther heads. The children go to a floating school in the middle of a cluster of islands.

Taquile was very steep. Having been told about our limitations with climbing they arranged for us to eat in a restaurant halfway up where we had a traditional meal and learnt about the quirky ways of the island including their hat hierarchy system. The chiefs wear the most colourful hats, single men and boys wear hats that are white at the top. The top of the hats store coca leaves. On the way back, we spotted many different birds amongst the reeds.

SS Yavari, on the lake at our hotel, was originally a British steamship that had been converted to a museum. It was taken in pieces by men and donkeys over the Andes and renovation work was ongoing to bring it back to its former glory. It has now been reinvented as a floating B&B.

 Sillustani is full of burial towers. It is a long way up and it was a really exhausting climb for us, but it was worth it for the fabulous view. Our flight was with TACA from Juliaca back to Lima, We spent our last night in San Ysidro, the business area of Lima.

Peru has the most stunning scenery and genuine warm, friendly and very hardworking people who are very self-sufficient. The hotels are a high standard. We had some good food made with fresh, local produce. Markets are cheap and colourful, the history is fascinating and there is culture as well as birdlife and nature. We never felt unsafe, even in

Lima. It is one of the loveliest and most interesting places we have ever visited.

CRUISES

Royal Caribbean Sovereign of the Seas

Sovereign of the Seas is retired now and so have I. It was a wrench leaving my little girls behind for a week but I had a lovely time on my very first cruise in the late eighties. It was also my first time in the Caribbean. We sailed from Miami and visited St.Thomas, Puerto Rico and a private island called Labadee off the coast of Haiti.

In St.Thomas, I left my colleagues on the beach while I got the local bus for a few cents and visited Coral World Ocean Park, one of only a handful of underwater observatories in the world, then I went back to join the rest of our group who were sunbathing on Magen's Bay.

The rain was torrential as we arrived at San Juan in Puerto Rico. It was pointless trying to do anything, so we just found the nearest bar.

On my last day I completely ran out of money. On my way back to the cabin I put 25 cents in a slot machine and won! 25 dollars was a fortune back then. The drinks were on me.

Ocean Village

I entered a competition to win a place for two on the inaugural repositioning cruise from Southampton to Barcelona in 2003. Ocean Village was the budget brand of P&O. It was the cruise "for people who don't do cruises". We were so excited and it covered our Wedding Anniversary so that was even better. It was our first cruise together. We had a lovely cruise apart from The Bay of Biscay which didn't agree with us at all. Jim was sick on that cruise and swore he would never sail over Bay of Biscay again even if it's free. We had never been to Lisbon before and it was a city that we really enjoyed. We called at Gibraltar and Malaga before sailing to Barcelona where our cruise ended. It is a pity that Ocean Village was ditched after a few years.

Sun Cruises (Airtours) Carousel

Although I had been on cruises before, we had never experienced one as a family and the girls had left home by then so we decided that we would try a Canaries cruise for Christmas for the three of us in 2001. Our fly cruise included Gran Canaria, Lanzarote, Agadir, Madeira, La Palma, and Tenerife, but I can't remember in which order.

Madeira was a lovely stop. We took the smooth cable car up to the top and watched the strange wicker toboggan ride down a steep hill. Watching it was entertaining enough. We didn't fancy the actual experience. Madeira was getting ready for their famous annual New Year firework celebrations so the harbour was all lit up and looked so pretty as we sailed away.

On our stop in Agadir, we took the day trip to Taroudant rather than stay in Agadir. On the route past the Atlas Mountains we saw goats climbing the trees. Taroudant was interesting enough but I was almost pickpocketed. Luckily Martin noticed and stopped them but that spoilt my experience of Morocco and the following year we didn't even bother getting off the ship.

I loved Christmas in the Canaries. La Palma in particular was so pretty with poinsettias trailing from the balconies and a nativity creche outdoors. The main feature of La Palma is the dormant volcano which would cause a devastating tsunami if it ever erupted.

Airtours were amazingly good value and my customers loved them too. The cabins were basic but adequate and the food and entertainment were excellent. I was very sad when Thomas Cook ditched Airtours cruises and all three ships were sold to Louis Cruises in 2004.

We booked a cruise with the same itinerary the following year on Thomson Spirit. It was nowhere near as good as the Airtours cruise. Thomson Spirit had all sorts of technical and plumbing problems, the service and food were awful and they lost our luggage in Tenerife.

Celebrity Century

An offer came up for a $299 cruise on Celebrity in 2005 which was too good to miss. We got a reasonably priced flight to Fort Lauderdale. When we got on the flight there was a group of 12 Thomas Cook agents going on an educational. I'm sure Jim wondered if it was a set up. Our flight to Philadelphia was delayed due to bad weather so we were really worried about our connection. The surly US Airlines employee wasn't much help.

We literally ran about a mile at breakneck speed only to find that the flight on our ticket was nowhere to be seen. They had rebooked us on the later flight which was also delayed so after running all that way, we had to sit at the gate for 2 hours and then on the tarmac for another 2 hours. With all the delays, it was nearly midnight by the time we got to Fort Lauderdale and then we had another hour to wait for the shuttle bus.

There were two choices, West Caribbean and East Caribbean. I particularly wanted the cruise that included Puerto Rico as I missed it last time. Unfortunately as we boarded, we learned that one of the engines had malfunctioned so we couldn't call at Puerto Rico but we got $150 compensation in on-board credit. We made friends with a Texan couple, Lin and George on our table. George ordered steak every night but one evening there was lobster on the menu, he wanted steak and he wanted lobster, he got both!

I looked forward to St. Thomas which I loved on my last visit. We docked around 3 miles from Charlotte Amalie so our transportation choices were limited. Our first stop was Mountain Top which had a fantastic view. We declined the Banana Daiquiri as it was too early in the day. We had two more stops at Caret Bay and Drake's Seat and then back to the market where we got a few bargains. We were disappointed that we couldn't explore the island on our own terms as I had done last time. St Thomas has become a duty free haven full of designer shops for US Citizens to buy jewellery and handbags. Designer shops at cruise ports are of no interest to us so we went back to the ship.

O'Dea – A Path Well Travelled

I really looked forward to Sint Maarten/St Martin. I had hoped for an island with a distinct character as it is uniquely half Dutch and half French. It is the only time I have visited either a French or a Dutch Caribbean island. We arrived on a bright and sunny morning along with six other cruise ships. The dual island has a population of approximately 10,000. The population of the seven cruise ships exceeds that. I'm sure St Maarten appreciates all the revenue from the cruise ships but it did spoil the Caribbean atmosphere that I had hoped for. Philipsburg has a strip of shops selling electrical goods at "duty free prices". We walked away from shopping hell and tried to find a side to St Maarten that we actually liked. There is an old courthouse and a market but otherwise it could have been anywhere.

The airport is on the Dutch side which is famous for being one of the world's most dangerous airports. Famously, people hang on to the fence and wait for the aircraft to take off whilst still hanging on to the fence for dear life, exhilarating for some, but extremely dangerous.

We booked a tour so that we could see the French side and experience a little more of the island. Passing through one of four border crossings, there are no soldiers, no formalities, just a simple sign saying "Welcome to the French Side", however, the two sides of the island are totally different. The smaller Dutch side has 110 voltage and the French side has 220v. The official currency in the south is Netherlands Antilles Guilder and Euro in the north, however both sides prefer US Dollars. The language in the south is Dutch and in the north, French. Both sides speak English but the French side don't speak Dutch, the Dutch side don't speak French. The north has a nudist beach at L'Orient. This is illegal in the south. The south has casinos which are illegal in the north. The south is predominantly Protestant and the north, Catholic. Phone calls from one side of the island to the other are international and very expensive. The two sides have different number plates, taxes and health and education policies.

Our drive climbed up the hill past Great Salt Pond and the gourmet town of Grand Case. Marigot Bay, the French capital, has a lovely yacht harbour, a market with plenty of handicrafts as well as the usual array of hats and t-shirts. The main street looks a little like New Orleans with wrought iron balconies. The north is a little more expensive but hassle free. A quirky little touch is Santa's House decorated with fairy lights and reindeer. This is set up every year from late November onwards.

I really needed a break, but I didn't get the break I bargained for. I was walking along the boardwalk on the beach on the French side and I tripped breaking a couple of ribs in the process. I was in agony for weeks. We went back along a different route stopping at the international viewpoint overlooking both sides of the islands and also Anguilla and St.Barts, a wonderful and unforgettable view.

On our approach to Nassau, Atlantis can be seen from miles away, a huge pink palace towers over the turquoise ocean and the white sand of Paradise Island. Our ship was late arriving so we only had 2 hours in Nassau but they didn't cancel the trip, they just rushed it. The Friday night traffic jam didn't help. We stopped at the Steps and The Water Tower. We were lucky to be allowed into the fort. They were closing but who would refuse a coachload of potential tips?

Cunard Queen Mary II

As one of the top cruise sellers in the region, I was offered a cruise on the new Queen Mary II, by far the best trip I was offered by Thomas Cook right at the end of my 21 years of working for them.

I loved the whole experience but knowing my relationship with the Atlantic, I happily paid the $47 for the sea sickness jab which proved to be money well spent. We had an upgrade to a lovely balcony cabin which was a waste on the choppy and featureless Atlantic from Southampton to New York.

I got involved in everything on that trip, ballroom dancing, art classes, lectures and the planetarium. After all, there were 6 days at sea. They arranged a visit to the bridge for our group which was really interesting.

Arriving into New York at dawn was amazing, well worth getting up at 4am. Queen Mary II was built especially to narrowly scrape under the Verrazzano Bridge by just a few feet. We sailed past the iconic sights as the sun was rising over The Statue of Liberty, the Chrysler Building and a redundant Concorde aircraft. The experience was unforgettable.

We had a few hours to spare before flying home so we had a very entertaining tour of New York before having lunch in the Pier 17 warehouse complex overlooking Brooklyn Bridge and the Hudson River.

I won a competition in a trade paper in 2007, so I got to sail on Queen Mary II from New York to the Caribbean. I didn't enjoy that as much as I had enjoyed the transatlantic journey. Queen Mary II is designed for transatlantic sailings so there is always plenty to do on board. I was very seasick and I got Norovirus so I had to stay in my cabin and couldn't go ashore for a few days.

I did go ashore at St.Kitts and Tortola. As I got off. I looked back to see Queen Mary II dwarfing Ocean Village in the next berth. Ocean Village was so big and so exciting when we did our cruise many years before and yet it looked so tiny in St Kitts. As we walked up the main street, I spotted a chemist shop which caught my eye as it was called Skerritt which is a derivation of my maiden name, a very uncommon English name. I went to a St. Kitts promotion years later and discovered that the minister of tourism was Rick Skerritt. I got the opportunity to speak to him and it turned out to be his uncle's shop.

I really enjoyed the Sugar Train which takes tourists round the island through fields of sugar cane. There was plenty of rum and food going round as we enjoyed the views and listened to the commentary. It was a wonderful afternoon.

Fred Olsen Balmoral

I won a 3-night cruise on Fred Olsen in 2009. We had a lovely cruise on Balmoral, a combination of ocean and river cruising. Fred Olsen ships are small so they can get into nooks and crannies that bigger cruise ships can't. This mini cruise appealed as it went from Dover, across the English Channel to the Seine estuary and then on to Rouen.

The cabins are basic on Fred Olsen as the ships are old and the entertainment is wartime so it really appeals to the over eighties but there were many younger than us on board, including my colleague, Trevor Smith. We had a few hours in Rouen which we enjoyed before sailing back.

It probably wouldn't have been a weekend we would have booked ourselves but we were so pleased that the opportunity fell into our laps.

NCL Norwegian Pearl

Checking in for our cruise was a complete shambles. Somehow they had Jim's name twice on the passenger list and not mine. There was no record of me having entered the USA as the Canadian authorities had forgotten to stamp my passport. It was really lucky that I had a printed copy of my ESTA which they eventually accepted.

Our journey to Alaska was on Norwegian Pearl in 2010. I loved Norwegian on my inaugural cruise ship visit a few months earlier, but it was a bad choice for the Alaska experience as the style is definitely Caribbean and for a younger clientele. After passing whales and dolphins and hundreds of small islands and little icebergs which looked like sapphires in the Pacific, we arrived at the capital Juneau on Day 3.

We had booked a tour which included Juneau and Mendenhall Glacier. It was raining heavily in Juneau, which didn't spoil our enjoyment of the glacier. If it is overcast, the glaciers look blue so it was an amazing sight and a totally different experience from the Columbia Icefields in Alberta.

Juneau is small and looks like a studio set of a cowboy town. The main road is "The Road" and the bridge is "The Bridge". We spotted many American Bald Eagles and Golden Eagles. The house of the governor of Alaska was pointed out to us. We booked Mendenhall Glacier and

238

Juneau but this was cancelled and we were all put onto the alternative tour Mendenhall Glacier and the Salmon Hatchery which none of us were happy about.

Vegetarian food proved to be a real issue on NCL. The first night we ate in the Italian restaurant but they kept leaving the door open so it was draughty. Another night we had to book the vegetarian meal 24 hours in advance but our tour was late back so the impatient waiter gave us our vegetable consommé and vegetable pancakes at the same time and we felt really rushed so after that, it was easier to use the buffet where a very large and loud family with matching t-shirts ran riot.

Skagway is the furthest point west that I have been in my lifetime. Skagway is a gold rush town. There are some good clothes and souvenir bargains in Skagway as well as the usual cruise port shops. New shops have blended in with the old in gold rush style with a mountain backdrop. We booked the White Pass and Yukon Railway. This goes from Skagway, across old wooden bridges, up the mountain and across the Canadian border. Most of the scenery is on the left on the way up, but for those sitting on the right there is a replay on the way down.

Glacier Bay is the largest area of wilderness after Antarctica. It has some of the most incredible scenery I have ever experienced. We sailed slowly in and out of bays and saw hundreds of little islands, mountains, glaciers and even a couple of beaches as well as birds, whales and a large colony of seals. We were blessed with good weather in the morning so we were able to see mountains that are rarely visible as the weather in Alaska is often dull and cloudy.

It was on this cruise that we joined in a general knowledge quiz. One of the questions was easy.

"In which country is Y-gan?"

"Could you spell that please?"

"W-I-G-A-N" aha… Wigan.

England is of course the correct answer, but the acceptable answers were Great Britain or Manchester so according to the quiz master, England was wrong and Manchester is a country.

As Alaska is 9 hours behind the UK, we saw some very strange phenomena. The evening brightened up again and we not only watched the sun going down, but also the moon at around 10.30pm when it went completely dark, but we never saw any stars. The sun rose again at around 4am.

Ketchikan is a fishing harbour with a boardwalk. We took the only Duck tour in Alaska, which was entertaining and reasonably priced. This is a half land, half water 90-minute tour. We saw the main highlights of Ketchikan and were also lucky enough to see a couple of bald eagles.

RIVER CRUISES

Shearings MPS Rotterdam

I wanted to do something different for my big birthday in 2014. After looking at many costly options, I went for the MPS Rotterdam with Shearings. I would say the average age was around 70, some more mobile than others, but we didn't feel out of place.

From the moment we got on board, Melanie, our cruise director, was welcoming and the crew were friendly, attentive and efficient. The format is generally leaving the moorings at around 6am, sailing along until just after lunch around 2pm and then staying until early the following morning. Each morning, Melanie pointed out the landmarks, the history and the legends.

We chose "Colours of Autumn" which included sections of the Rhine and the Mosel. Each day we sailed past pretty chocolate box villages, timbered houses, churches, railway tunnels and hillside vineyards. Our first stop was at Andernach and Ahr Valley. We had to get on a coach for this to see the vineyards. We stopped at Bad Neuenahr-Ahrweiler, a pretty walled town.

We loved Rüdesheim, unanimously our favourite, very pretty with some lovely independent shops, the magical year round Christmas shop and some great bars which weren't overly expensive and some had live music. We ventured out again in the evening with our new friends. There are a couple of quirky museums, Siegfried's music cabinet and the Torture museum. We have been a couple of times since then but never got the opportunity to stay overnight as we did on that cruise. We added on an extra night in Cologne and took some time to explore the city on foot.

Avalon Tapestry II

Tapestry II was the newest ship on Avalon's River Cruise fleet and we were lucky enough to be invited to sample the Paris to Rouen section of the itinerary in September 2015. Many of the clients were American. For most of them, the purpose was to see the Normandy Landings Beach of Omaha during their cruise.

My friends, Ann, Barbara and Pauline were also chosen. Our trip began in Paris so I chose the optional tour to Eiffel Tower. Our small group tour bypassed the long queue. We were soon in the lift to the 2nd floor on a beautiful clear, sunny day. We could see all over Paris as far as Sacre Coeur, Montmartre and beyond.

We were greeted with a friendly smile and a welcome drink. Our cabins were compact but well designed with plenty of wardrobe space and a Juliet balcony to enjoy the views as we sailed along. We were soon able to sample the wonderful cuisine, beautifully presented and perfect for all our tastes and dietary requirements.

Even though this was an educational trip for independent agents, we were free to choose which excursions we wanted to do and how we wanted to spend our free time. We liked this idea.

241

O'Dea – A Path Well Travelled

Most of us chose Monet's house and garden in Giverny for our first trip which was just a short distance from Vernon. This was one the loveliest trips I have ever experienced, just like being inside Monet's paintings. It was early in the morning. There were no crowds and there were dewdrops on the flowers.

In the afternoon we sailed along to the small town of Les Andelys, flanked by its distinctive white cliffs and overlooked by Château Gallard. The more energetic ones amongst us including Barbara walked up to the castle. The rest of us walked around town then relaxed on the sundeck.

We sailed in the evening to Caudebec-en-Caux where were based for 2 days. I wouldn't have gone out of my way to visit this town, but it was a good base for all the wonderful excursions there were to choose from.

From the excursions on offer, we chose "Route-des-Chaumieres". We saw the beautiful thatched and timbered cottages followed by a visit to the interesting little market town of Pont- Audemer. It was a decent market and we found a few bargains.

 In the afternoon we walked around Caudebec-en-Caux and explored Notre Dame which was badly damaged during the war. It has some very impressive restoration work at the entrance and beautiful stained glass windows. Ann and I got some food shopping in Carrefour. I was soon to regret my decision to buy cheese for my mum, although it seemed a good idea at the time.

I put my selection of French cheeses including the very best camembert, goat's cheese and Roquefort in the fridge. Later that evening we went back to the cabin and Pauline shrieked;

"What on earth is that smell! Oh my god, it's that cheese. It stinks!"

Luckily it was warm and sunny and we were able to leave the window open but it was still really strong.

Most of us chose Taste of Normandy rather than Normandy Landings, a decision influenced by the forecast of torrential rain. I was also tempted by the visit to Bayeux to see the famous tapestry. Bayeux has an impressive Cathedral of Notre Dame as well as Crêperies and little tourist shops. We had a simple, traditional lunch in Beuvron-en-Auge, a chocolate box village with timbered houses. The quiche was just like the one my mum used to make to my French grandmother's traditional recipe so I really enjoyed that. We finished off our day with a visit to a Calvados distillery and a chance to sample some Calvados with apple tart.

It was our last chance to sample the wonderful cuisine, say goodbye to our new American and Canadian friends and our friendly crew and dance along to low key entertainment. Barbara was the last one up, still dancing the night away and still bright and breezy the next morning.

The smell of cheese followed us all the way home on the Eurostar. Instead of going straight home, I got off at Paddington and took the offending cheese straight round my mum's. She appreciated it but next time I will go for a more fragrant gift!

Our group on Tapestry II

Titan Filia Rehni II

We got a special deal on a river cruise along the stretch of the Danube from Budapest to Passau covering four countries: Hungary, Slovakia, Austria and Germany in September 2016. It was interesting to see the contrasts and different cultures of each place.

My friend Barbara booked onto the same cruise. That cruise attracted a much older clientele but it was hilarious in many ways and definitely the winner for the entertainment, most of it unintentional. There were usually three cruise directors each with different responsibilities. The lady of the trio broke her leg and couldn't sail. I got the impression that the missing lady normally does all the organising as the poor men couldn't cope on their own. For instance, one announcement would say 9am on the sun deck and the other would say 9.15am on the middle deck, sometimes they would argue with each other over the tannoy, leading to both confusion and hilarity.

The DJ, Stewart, did an Elvis impression but his belt kept falling down so he asked me to come over and hitch it up for him. There were some very elderly people on board and one lady asked me to check her rear end for stains before we went to dinner. I spent the rest of the week trying to avoid her!

Budapest has some great bars including the famous Buddha Bar. Budapest cashes in on its reputation as a former communist capital and has a Communist themed bar and lots of memorabilia so there are some unusual souvenirs. A Danube cruise isn't ideal for the disabled and Budapest proved a huge challenge for our wheelchair passenger on board.

After passing the picturesque Danube Bend we reached Esztergom. Esztergom is small, but it does have some interesting sights including a couple of museums and art galleries and its crowning glory is the massive Catholic cathedral, the largest and most impressive in Hungary. At first sight this looks impossible to reach but eventually I found a gentler road leading to it and a lift to get to the cathedral itself. It was worth the hike. Some parts of the cathedral, the Cupola and the treasury are at an extra charge but there is enough to see without having to pay and there is a fabulous panoramic view from the top.

I had already been to Bratislava so this time we went to the shopping arcade which was closed on my last visit. The mall has all the well-known brand names, cheaper than neighbouring Austria but still more expensive than we expected. Linz in Austria has a cathedral which looks small on the outside but is like a tardis, huge and impressive on the inside.

We liked Passau, very walkable and set on two rivers, it is a really pretty town with character and plenty to see. It was lovely to walk around and sit by the river as we had a few hours there. The shopping is good and there is a large shopping mall. There is a more traditional high street leading to the ancient fortress and cathedral.

Melk Abbey and Gardens are bigger than the actual town. I would have liked to spend longer at the Abbey and I didn't have enough time to see the gardens but it was definitely worth the hike up to the viewpoint. Most of our group went onto Dürnstein by bus which gave them longer at the abbey, but I took the electric bus down and cruised along to Dürnstein. This was a good decision as this was by far the prettiest and most leisurely stretch of river on the entire trip and I would have been gutted to have missed this. There were only 15 of us left on board. Dürnstein was very pretty but also expensive and touristy but the walk up to the top was well worth the view over the picturesque Wachau Valley.

Uniworld River Empress

Uniworld introduced some fantastic offers which we were tempted to book and my friends Ann and Anna booked as well. Our cruise was from Amsterdam to Basel. Our arrival was touch and go due to our delayed flight. Amsterdam airport is very close to the city so we just about made it with less than half an hour to spare. Check-in on board was seamless and we were soon enjoying afternoon tea in the lounge on the sun deck enjoying the Amsterdam heatwave over a welcome blue champagne cocktail.

I've been to Cologne several times before but this time we did a walking tour and learnt there is far more to Cologne than chocolate, 4711 and beer. Colonia was originally a Roman city. Most of it has been rebuilt. The cathedral was surrounded by scaffolding during our previous visit, now the new restoration work is very impressive. There are many museums in Cologne and good shopping to suit all budgets.

O'Dea – A Path Well Travelled

We had already been to Koblenz but we had never experienced the cable car up to the Ehrenbreitstein Fortress. The excursion included both of these. The cable car was very smooth and the view on the way back down was awesome as it crosses the point at which the Rhine and Mosel meet.

We departed in the afternoon for Boppard where we stayed overnight. We enjoyed going back to Rüdesheim. Ann had already been to Rüdesheim several times so she took us down streets we hadn't seen before.

Speyer is a really interesting and historic town with an 11th-century UNESCO world heritage cathedral. It is very simple inside, but with some unusual features outside including the earliest example of a colonnaded dwarf gallery.

Because of its history and location, Alsace has been both German and French. Since the end of the war it has been French but as it is on the German border. The German influence is still very apparent and that makes the region unique. The Alsatian language is a German dialect but most are both French and German speaking. The food and wine from the Alsace region is unique with a combination of French and German influences.

Strasbourg is the capital of the Alsace and the biggest city in the region. The best way to explore Strasbourg is a combination of canal boat and walking. Seeing Strasbourg by canal showcases the different facets of the city, new and old. It is the perfect place for the ultra-modern European Parliament building, which is situated on the German border and also not far from the Swiss border but further along the canal are the distinct colourful, timbered buildings of the Alsace region and flowers cascading from balconies and bridges.

Strasbourg is also blessed with a beautiful cathedral surrounded by cafés, souvenir shops and an old fashioned carousel in the main square. The surrounding streets are mostly pedestrianised. There are opportunities for shopping for familiar brands, market stalls and local delicacies. Strasbourg, unfortunately, does have a problem with beggars and pickpockets.

Colmar is a smaller version of Strasbourg with similar architecture and canals. It caters for tourists with two Irish pubs both in keeping with the surroundings. There are many shops selling similar tourist souvenirs to Strasbourg but a little more expensive. There is a covered food market, perfect for French and German delicacies and local Alsatian produce. Many of the shops and restaurants are full of character with all sorts of things hanging from the balconies giving it a fairy tale feel.

AMA Dante

We chose AMA for Jim's big birthday. Medieval Treasures was an interesting looking itinerary on the Rhine and Main which was a new experience. It began in Basel, officially in Switzerland, but also on the borders of France and Germany. Basel is a compact city. There are trams to get around and it is easy to walk around the central area around the Rhine. It is worth walking across Middle Bridge for views along the Rhine and the city.

The only problem with river cruises is that there are only a few fully navigable rivers in Europe so duplication of a few destinations is likely. AMA have enough alternative excursions to choose from, so although we had already visited three of the destinations before, we managed to avoid duplicating what we had seen previously.

It was nice to go back to Strasbourg. This time we did a walking tour of the city. We learned that Notre Dame cathedral is unusual as it only has one spire. The reason for this is that Strasbourg has changed hands between the French and the Germans and they did so while the cathedral was being built. German churches only have one spire and French cathedrals have two so they compromised with one spire but on the left hand side rather than in the middle.

I was sitting by the cathedral when Kirsty Reid, a contact I have met many times, called my name. By coincidence, she happened to be running an educational on Fred Olsen Brabant with some agents.

248

O'Dea – A Path Well Travelled

By Day 3, we arrived in our third country in 3 days, Germany. We had visited the UNESCO World Heritage Site of Speyer the previous year. This time we chose the Schwetzingen Gardens excursion. We enjoyed a lovely walk around the palace, the cottage gardens, the orderly symmetrical gardens and statues of ancient gods. We had to wear ridiculously large felt slippers round the small museum house to protect the floor. 5

I had totally forgotten about the technical museum in Speyer, a collection of old aircraft, diesel engines, steam trains and other transport. I will certainly visit this if I go to Speyer again as it is walking distance from the dock.

We had been to Rüdesheim twice before but due to my fear of heights, I had never attempted the tiny cable cars going up to the top of the hill. Having already sampled Rüdesheimer coffee and Siegfrieds Mechanical Museum there was only one thing left to do, the dreaded cable car. I was full of apprehension, but actually it isn't that high and seeing the vineyards and autumn colours and the magnificent statue close up, as well as views along the Rhine made it a really worthwhile trip and I am so pleased I finally did it.

Going into the Main river was unknown territory for us. It turned out to be a lovely surprise, a pretty river with beautiful shades of autumn, lots of birdlife and pretty half-timbered houses with fewer tourists than the usual Rhine hotspots. I'm surprised it isn't featured on more itineraries. Our first introduction to the Main was the city of Frankfurt, which could be any financial centre in the world with its central park and tall glass buildings. What Frankfurt does have is a very attractive town square with medieval bars and restaurants and a few souvenir shops. We visited the newly restored houses recently remodelled to recreate the Frankfurt of old.

Miltenberg was gorgeous and very close to the dock so we could wander off and explore the pretty medieval town for ourselves. All the buildings were built around 1600 and almost all of them are really well preserved. There weren't too many tourists either.

Wurzburg was a big surprise. From what I had read, it was mostly industrial with an historical centre and the palace which is a UNESCO World Heritage Site. We didn't have high expectations. It turned out to be a really lovely town, walkable, easy to navigate, with an absolutely fascinating history. St Kilian, an Irish monk is the patron saint of Wurzburg. It is pretty without being overrun with tourists and there is good shopping there too.

Bamberg, on the other hand, was slightly disappointing. I had read that the entire town was UNESCO world heritage so I was eager to see it. Apart from the town hall with its impressive frescoes overlooking the river, it was full of tourists and didn't feel as pleasant as Wurzburg nor as relaxed as Miltenberg.

Our week soon came to an end after a total of 53 locks that we had gone through on the way. It is a tricky stretch which needs the skills of an expert captain and we certainly had that in the diminutive Andreas.

Our cruise finished in Nuremburg, a city I was keen to see. It is a well preserved walled city with some interesting architecture, a few decent looking pubs and plenty of shops. It also has a recreated medieval craft centre. The thing I liked about Nuremburg is that there are plenty of benches to sit on and green spaces to relax.

We were surprised how young some the guests on board were. The oldest we believe was a 94-year old lady and a couple that had been married for 62 years, but there were several couples in their thirties, maybe even late twenties which shows how the image of river cruising is changing.

Part Five: The Learning Path

World Travel Market

I went to my first World Travel Market at Olympia when I worked in Thomas Cook Hammersmith in 1985. Originally it was a 5-day event which included a public day on Saturday. I took my girls to a few of them, but the public day was scrapped quite early on. I went almost every year until 2019. Even when Martin was a year old they let me walk round with him in the buggy.

It was always a great opportunity to meet many new contacts and friends I had met from all over the world. I entered as many competitions as I could and I won a few holidays, including our fabulous 2-week tour of Peru, a week in the Azores, a few nights in Crete, a week in Cancun, the marathon coach tour and our trip to Las Vegas. I also won a spa day at The Sanctuary, many goody bags and numerous bottles of rum.

There was always food, drink, shows and parties, firstly at Olympia and Earls Court which were much more convenient for me in West London but the show outgrew Earls Court and moved to Excel which was more awkward to get to. However, I have to admit it is bigger and has a better layout all on one level.

I always looked forward to this annual event which was the highlight of the travel calendar but it was very exhausting as we walked miles from side to side and end to end to keep all the appointments.

Ann Barber, me and Kathy Hudspith at the Greek stand

World Travel Market

Events and Roadshows

I live in London so I got the opportunity to go to many events and roadshows over the years, mostly invitations from hoteliers, hotel reps, tourist boards and occasionally tour operators. Before the lockdown in March 2020, I went to an average of two events a week. As an independent agent, destination knowledge and good contacts were vital so I went to as many as I could. I especially liked the themed events from tourist boards, most notably: Israel, Hawaii, Fiji, South Africa, Vietnam, Chile and Sarawak and a very unusual event from Costa Brava Tourism.

As well as being useful to update myself on an ever changing industry, these events gave me the opportunity to meet up with my Travel Counsellor colleagues and my other travel friends including Sharon Frame, Anna Davies, Stephen Worswick, Jenny Jackson and Peter

Foster and to visit some interesting venues in London: top hotels, private members clubs, The Tower of London, The Shard, The Gherkin, The Science Museum, The Magic Circle, The Ivy and The Roof Gardens to name just a few. Sometimes we did cookery classes, wine tasting or chocolate making. Most of these were in the evening but occasionally we were invited to afternoon tea at The Ritz, The Langham, Ascot racecourse and The Mandeville. Sometimes we had breakfast trainings at The Cadogan, The In and Out Club and the Mandarin Oriental in Knightsbridge. There were sporting events such as football or polo matches. A few times I have been invited to speciality restaurants and I have also been invited to a few Thames dinner cruises.

We were invited for lunch on Lady Sandals when she was moored on the Thames. We met the owner, Gordon 'Butch' Stewart on that occasion. He was a successful Jamaican hotel owner and businessman of Irish descent. He founded Sandals Resorts. I was sorry to hear that he sadly passed away recently in January 2021.

One event I remember fondly was a Kenya Roadshow in which Virginia McKenna from The Born Free Foundation spoke. I remember the film well and she moved us all to tears telling us about her life and the foundation.

A few of the events were all day. Aspire, specialising in different aspects of luxury travel, was always very useful. PATA was usually held in the Guoman in St Katherine's dock. CTO invited us to several all-day training events and one of the most memorable was overnight at a lovely manor house with my friends Ann, Carol and Elaine. Sometimes we were invited to "behind the scenes" at Cox & Kings, Kirker and Disneyland Paris.

Occasionally I have been invited to private cinema showings or the theatre, all of which I very much enjoyed and will definitely miss. Disneyland Paris had an all-day training fairly recently with lots of surprises, then they treated us to pizzas and the Mary Poppins play which was one of the best I have ever seen. We also went, fairly recently, to see private showings of "Finding Your Feet" and "Invictus", both excellent films.

In 2019, there was an invitation from the Seattle Tourist board to see a sneak preview of the Chihuly Glass Exhibition and a tour of Kew Gardens before it opened officially. Kew Gardens and the Seattle Tourist board were so generous with some beautiful gifts for each of us at the end of the night.

I was invited to a couple of award evenings at The Lyceum. One which was particularly memorable was the year Travel Counsellors won "Homeworking Travel Agent of the Year". We all got a chance to hold the trophy and get our photos taken. It was one of my proudest Travel Counsellors moments.

On another occasion I was invited to the Caribbean Ball, a black tie event where I spent the evening with the late Maureen Hill, a travel agent who had a column in Travel Weekly for many years. She was such a lovely lady with a great sense of humour, who literally collapsed at her desk and died doing the job she loved and she is sadly missed by everyone in the industry.

One event we looked forward to was the yearly Travel Counsellors conference, especially the Malaga conference in 2008. My last conference was Glasgow 2018. We saw and listened to many star names, entrepreneurs and sports personalities over the years which we enjoyed very much.

One of my proudest moments as a Travel Counsellor at The Lyceum

Ship Visits

Most ship visits were for inspection and lunch. Some of these visits were overnight, usually for pre-launch, so we could sample the entertainment and the spa facilities as well as exploring the cabins. These included P&O. Cunard, Carnival, Celebrity, Royal Caribbean, Costa, MSC, CMV, NCL. Fred Olsen, Hebridean Island and Oceania. Most of the ship visits were in Southampton, some were in Dover and Tilbury. Very occasionally we got the opportunity to see small luxury ships in London such as Silversea and Regent. My very last ship visit was at Dover inspecting MS Fridtjof Nansen the Hurtigruten exploration ship just before lockdown in March 2020. She was a lovely, cosy little ship.

Part Six: The Final Path

King Street Hammersmith, a typical high street in its heyday of the eighties and nineties, once had eight travel agencies. They all disappeared one by one leaving just one, Thomas Cook. The rent doubled shortly before the Hammersmith branch finally closed its doors in February 2018. That was the end of an era.

When the high street shops started dwindling, customers were still looking for a specialist like me to book their holidays, an expert they could trust. I was a highly valued go-to expert in my field. At first, I could easily pick up business all across West London and many of those customers were loyal. Fast forward twelve years or so, travel homeworking had grown from being very niche to being easily accessible with many different options to choose from. Over time, we were competing with hundreds of new agents and also the internet instead of just a small handful of select travel experts.

The government tightened up package regulations to clean up the "bucket shops" and cowboys in the travel industry. These regulations were set up to protect the consumer financially and that was obviously a good thing but it meant there had to be a small premium to cover the insurance needed to refund clients when things went wrong, Many things did go wrong, storms, strikes, supplier failures, Brexit and finally Covid-19 and the protection fee had to be used more regularly in order to refund the clients when necessary. However, many consumers still didn't see beyond the price and didn't understand why there was sometimes an extra cost on a package as opposed to booking a flight and hotel separately. This wasn't always the case of course, but once I couldn't compete, clients had already gone elsewhere, never to return.

As more airlines and tour operators became web based, it became easier for customers to do their own research and bookings instead of contacting agents like me, so I found that I was losing even my regular clients. I specialised in bespoke multi-centre travel which was what I did best. The more complicated and challenging the travel arrangements were, the better I liked it. I could use my skills as a travel expert, tweaking, rerouting, researching, planning, making suggestions and finding out what worked best but all too often after weeks of unpaid research, I realised that I was simply giving my customers the information to shop around.

Brexit uncertainty made customers hold off booking and this affected the finances of a few tour operators including Monarch and Thomas Cook who both went into liquidation. Airlines and cruise lines shut down their UK offices saving on costs but this made it much more difficult to communicate with them. During the height of the pandemic it was proving impossible. Some set up premium rate numbers for agents making it very expensive for us to call them to sort out any issues.

I've always been happy to sort out of hours emergencies but it also meant that I could never really relax, as I was either checking emails or answering my mobile. Finally, as there were even more communication channels, it took over my life completely as I was also being contacted by text, Facebook Messenger, Skype, and Whatsapp.

From my point of view, it was becoming increasingly difficult to earn any reward for all the work I did. I was doing twice as much work with higher overall costs. In the end, I was even making some of my bookings at a loss, therefore effectively working for nothing, so no matter how passionate I was about the travel industry and how much I genuinely wanted to help my clients, there came a point at which I questioned my own sanity.

During the pandemic, the travel industry has been very much the forgotten sector and the worst affected. Most of us, particularly in the leisure travel sector, have always relied on the more profitable summer season to balance out the leaner winter season. In 2020 there was no summer season. We earned nothing for over a year and we watched our existing earnings disappear into a black hole of refunds.

Now I've reached the end of my path in the travel industry. I hope I get the chance to travel again and I hope you, the reader does too. Grab every opportunity you are given with both hands. Follow your dreams and enjoy them just as I have.

I hope that the travel industry recovers from the effects of Brexit and Covid-19 combined, but in order for that to happen, I believe the quickest road back is with full co-operation from the government, airlines, cruise lines and tour operators working together with agents again to restore customer confidence and for consumers and suppliers to understand and appreciate the added value and protection that travel agents bring.

Epilogue/Conclusion

Thank you for taking the time to read "A Path Well Travelled". I do hope you have enjoyed sharing the thoughts and memories of my travel journey.

Please leave a review and recommend this book to your friends and family. I would also appreciate any feedback regarding any inaccuracies, also anecdotes, anything or anyone that I may have overlooked which can be updated in the next edition. I would also be happy to offer general advice or tips on any of the destinations in the book.

Printed in Great Britain
by Amazon

17860374R00149